# The *Sams Teach Yourself in 24 Hours* Series

Sams Teach Yourself in 24 Hours books provide quick and easy answers in a proven step-by-step approach that works for you. In just 24 sessions of one hour or less, you will tackle every task you need to get the results you want. Let our experienced authors present the most accurate information to get you reliable answers—fast!

## Converting Decimal IP Addresses to Binary

It usually isn't too bad converting from binary IP addresses to decimal form; just follow the instructions in Chapter 4, "The Internet Layer." However, it can be quite the pain to convert decimal IP addresses into binary format (also covered in Chapter 4). Follow the steps below and you'll be sure to have success!

1. Write in the IP number you want to convert:

2. If the number in line 1 is >= 128 enter a 1 here; if not enter a 0:

3. If you entered a 0 in line 2 enter the number from line 1; if not subtract 128 from line 1 and enter the result:

4. If the number in line 3 is >= 64 enter a 1 here; if not enter a 0:

5. If you entered a 0 in line 4 enter the number from line 3; if not subtract 64 from line 3 and enter the result:

6. If the number in line 5 is >= 32 enter a 1 here; if not enter a 0:

7. If you entered a 0 in line 6 enter the number from line 5; if not subtract 32 from line 5 and enter the result:

8. If the number in line 7 is >= 16 enter a 1 here; if not enter a 0:

9. If you entered a 0 in line 8 enter the number from line 7; if not subtract 16 from line 7 and enter the result:

SAMS

Teach Yourself

TCP/IP

in 24 Hours

D1303444

10. If the number in line 9 is >= 8 enter a 1 here; if not enter a 0:

11. If you entered a 0 in line 8 enter the number from line 9; if not subtract 8 from line 9 and enter the result:

12. If the number in line 11 is >= 4 enter a 1 here; if not enter a 0:

13. If you entered a 0 in line 12 enter the number from line 11; if not subtract 4 from line 11 and enter the result:

14. If the number in line 13 is >= 2 enter a 1 here; if not enter a 0

15. If you entered a 0 in line 14 enter the number from line 13; if not subtract 2 from line 13 and enter the result:

16. If the number in line 15 = 1 enter a 1 here; if not enter a 0

Now, one last step – take the zeros and ones from the heavily-outlined boxes above and line them up in the table below. The number in the top row corresponds to the line number above.

| 2 | 4 | 6 | 8 | 10 | 12 | 14 | 16 |
|---|---|---|---|----|----|----|----|
|   |   |   |   |    |    |    |    |

That's it, your decimal IP address converted to binary. Don't worry, if you do this a few times you probably won't need to follow these steps anymore!

# How to Use This Book

The books in the *Sams Teach Yourself* series are designed to help you learn a topic in a few easy and accessible sessions. *Sams Teach Yourself TCP/IP in 24 Hours* is divided into six parts. Each part brings you a step closer to mastering the goal of proficiency in TCP/IP.

For the most part, this book is independent of any operating system, but several of the examples in this book use Windows NT 4.0 for a couple of reasons. First, most TCP/IP books use UNIX, and we wanted to try something different. (Windows NT is, in fact, a TCP/IP operating system. TCP/IP is the default network protocol, and you'll find a rich collection of TCP/IP features in NT.) Second, Windows NT is very common, and many readers who don't have access to a full-featured UNIX system might have access to NT. The concepts in this book, however, like TCP/IP itself, are system independent and descend from the standards defined in Internet Requests for Comments (RFCs).

Joe Casad
Bob Willsey

# SAMS
# Teach Yourself
# TCP/IP
# in 24 Hours

**SAMS**

*201 West 103rd St., Indianapolis, Indiana, 46290*

# Sams Teach Yourself TCP/IP in 24 Hours

## Copyright © 1998 by Sams Publishing

International Standard Book Number: 0-672-31248-4

Library of Congress Catalog Card Number: 98-84475

Printed in the United States of America

First Printing: November, 1998

00  99  98        4  3  2  1

## Trademarks

## Warning and Disclaimer

**EXECUTIVE EDITOR**
Jeff Koch

**ACQUISITIONS EDITOR**
Jane Brownlow

**DEVELOPMENT EDITOR**
Sudha Putnam

**PROJECT EDITOR**
Kevin Laseau

**COPY EDITOR**
Pamela Woolf

**INDEXER**
Erika Millen

**PROOFREADER**
Benjamin Berg

**TECHNICAL EDITORS**
David Kurtiak
Rodney Fournier
Art Hammond
Walter J. Glenn
Gene Steinberg

**INTERIOR DESIGN**
Gary Adair

**COVER DESIGN**
Aren Howell

**LAYOUT TECHNICIANS**
Tim Osborn
Staci Somers
Mark Walchle

# Contents at a Glance

# Contents

# About the Authors

**Joe Casad** is an engineer who has written widely on computer networking and system administration. He is an author of *MCSE Windows NT Server and Workstation Study Guide*, *MCSE Networking Essentials Training Guide*, *Windows NT Server 4.0 Professional Reference*, and *Windows 98 Professional Reference*. He is the former managing editor of *Network Administrator* magazine.

**Bob Willsey**, MCSE, MCSD, MCT, has 19 years experience in the computer field. He is a Microsoft Certified trainer who currently teaches and consults for QuickStart Technologies, Inc. His experience includes Windows NT, Windows 95, TCP/IP, SMS, and Visual Basic, as well as supporting Novell and proprietary mainframe systems. He is a contributing author of *Windows 98 Professional Reference* and *Networking with TCP/IP, Third Edition*.

## Contributing Authors

**Art Hammond** was raised by wolves in the wilds of southeastern Pennsylvania, an upbringing that helped him to easily adapt to the day to day problems encountered by a systems administrator. Art is the senior messaging analyst for King County Information and Telecommunications Services. He has a B.A. in professional writing and is also a Microsoft Certified Systems Engineer. He now lives in Seattle, WA, and has never met Bill Gates.

**Walter J. Glenn** is a freelance networking consultant and writer. He holds several certifications, including MCSE, MCP +Internet, and MCT. He specializes in Microsoft-based Internet and networking technologies, including Windows NT Server 4.0, Internet Information Server, Exchange Server, and TCP/IP. He holds degrees in literature and biology. He is the author of several books including *Sams Teach Yourself MCSE NT Server in 14 Days*, *Sams Teach Yourself MCSE Networking Essentials in 14 Days*, and *Sams Teach Yourself MCSE TCP/IP in 14 Days*.

**Gene Steinberg** has worked at several occupations. He first studied broadcasting and then worked for a number of years as a disc jockey and newscaster. Gene is now a columnist for the *Arizona Republic*'s Arizona Central Computing page, a contributing editor for MacCentral (a popular Mac-oriented Web site), a full-time writer (fact and science fiction), and a computer software/systems consultant. His books for Macmillan Computing Publishing include *Using America Online 4* and *Sams Teach Yourself AOL in 10 Minutes*. He has also written feature articles and product reviews for such magazines as *MacHome Journal*, *MacAddict*, *MacUser* and *MacWorld*.

# Dedication

*To the eternal Maurice, who hastens and chastens.*

*—Joe Casad*

# Acknowledgments

Thanks to all those at Macmillan who labored to make this book a success. Thanks to Sudha Putnam for her excellent development work, and thanks to ace acquisitions editor Jane Brownlow for keeping all the wheels turning and insisting on success. Thanks to Bob Willsey and the other authors and tech editors who worked on this book: Walter Glenn, Art Hammond, Dave Kurtiak, Gene Steinberg, and Rodney Fournier.

And thanks to those in Indianapolis who saw this book after it left my hands, including Kevin Laseau, Pamela Woolf, Erika Millen, Benjamin Berg, and the Illustration department.

—Joe Casad

I first want to extend my appreciation to Jane Brownlow and Macmillan Computer Publishing for giving me the opportunity to participate in this book. Jane made sure the book kept progressing toward its completion. I also want to thank Sudha Putnam for her excellent editing abilities and calm voice. Sudha's skills have certainly helped to make this book very readable and understandable to the reader who is new to networking with TCP/IP. Many thanks go to Joe Casad, my coauthor, for his assistance and years of technical writing experience. I'd also like to thank three very knowledgeable technical editors: Walter Glenn, Art Hammond, and David Kurtiak for their expertise in the field of networking. Their technical review comments were always accurate and on-target. They collectively made sure that the book was not focused on a single operating system but included examples from a number of operating systems.

Last but not least I would like to acknowledge my family, Kathy, Lisa, and Tony, for coping so well with my isolation and absence from family life during the development of this book. Everything always seems to take longer than expected, and this book is no exception. Now that it's finished, I think it's time to go out to dinner and to see a movie with my family.

—Bob Willsey

# Tell Us What You Think!

As the reader of this book, *you* are our most important critic and commentator. We value your opinion and want to know what we're doing right, what we could do better, what areas you'd like to see us publish in, and any other words of wisdom you're willing to pass our way.

As the executive editor for the Operating Systems team at Macmillan Computer Publishing, I welcome your comments. You can fax, email, or write me directly to let me know what you did or didn't like about this book—as well as what we can do to make our books stronger.

*Please note that I cannot help you with technical problems related to the topic of this book, and that due to the high volume of mail I receive, I might not be able to reply to every message.*

When you write, please be sure to include this book's title and author as well as your name and phone or fax number. I will carefully review your comments and share them with the authors and editors who worked on the book.

Fax:       317-817-7070
Email:     opsys@mcp.com
Mail:      Executive Editor
           Operating Systems
           Macmillan Computer Publishing
           201 West 103rd Street
           Indianapolis, IN 46290 USA

# Introduction

Welcome to *Sams Teach Yourself TCP/IP in 24 Hours*. This book provides a clear and concise introduction to TCP/IP for newcomers and also for users who have worked with TCP/IP but would like a little more of the inside story.

## Does Each Chapter Take an Hour?

You can learn the concepts in each of the 24 chapters within one hour. If you want to experiment with what you learn in each hour, it might take longer than an hour. However, the chapters are designed to be short enough to read all at once. In fact, you should be able to read a chapter in less than one hour and still have time to take notes and reread more complex sections in your one-hour study session.

## How to Use this Book

The books in the *Sams Teach Yourself* series are designed to help you learn a topic in a few easy and accessible sessions. *Sams Teach Yourself TCP/IP in 24 Hours* is divided into six parts. Each part brings you a step closer to mastering the goal of proficiency in TCP/IP.

- Part I, "TCP/IP Basics," introduces you to TCP/IP and the TCP/IP protocol stack.

- Part II, "The TCP/IP Protocol System," takes a close look at each of TCP/IP's protocol layers: the Network Access, Internet, Transport, and Application layers. You'll learn about IP addressing and subnetting, as well as physical networks and application services. You'll also learn about the protocols that operate at each of TCP/IP's layers.

- Part III, "TCP/IP Utilities," introduces you to some of the common utilities used to configure, manage, and troubleshoot TCP/IP networks. You'll learn about Ping, Netstat, FTP, Telnet, and other network utilities.

- Part IV, "Name Resolution," describes the services and protocols providing name resolution on TCP/IP networks. You'll learn about Hosts files and DNS. You'll also learn about NetBIOS name resolution using LMHOSTS, WINS, and broadcast name resolution methods.

- Part V, "TCP/IP in Network Environments," shows how to configure and operate TCP/IP in several common operating systems and network operating systems, including Windows, Macintosh, NetWare, and UNIX.

- Part VI, "Advanced Topics," describes dynamic IP address assignment and introduces TCP/IP network management protocols RMON and SNMP. You'll also learn about advanced topics such as IP version 6 and Point to Point Tunneling Protocol (PPTP). Part VI ends with a case study showing how the components of TCP/IP interact in a real working environment.

For the most part, this book is independent of any operating system, but several of the examples in this book use Windows NT 4.0. There are several reasons for this. First, most TCP/IP books use UNIX and we wanted to try something different. (Windows NT is, in fact, a TCP/IP operating system. TCP/IP is the default network protocol, and you'll find a rich collection of TCP/IP features in NT.) Second, Windows NT is very common, and many readers who don't have access to a full-featured UNIX system might have access to NT. The concepts in this book, however, like TCP/IP itself, are independent of a system and descend from the standards defined in Internet Requests for Comment (RFCs).

# How This Book Is Organized

Each hour in *Sams Teach Yourself TCP/IP in 24 Hours* begins with a quick introduction and a list of goals for the hour. You'll also find the following elements.

## Main Section

Each hour contains a main section that provides a clear and accessible discussion of the chapter's topic. You'll find figures and tables helping to explain the concepts described in the text. Interspersed with the text are special elements called Just a Minutes, New Terms, and Time Savers. These elements come with definitions, descriptions, tips, or warnings that will help you build a better understanding of the material.

> These boxes clarify a concept that is being discussed in the text. A Just a Minute might add some additional information or provide an example, but Just a Minutes typically aren't essential for a basic understanding of the subject. If you're in a hurry, or if you only want to know the bare essentials, you can bypass these sidebars.

**NEW TERM**  *New Terms* are definitions. You might see a New Term element with an important word or concept that can't be easily described in the main text—or isn't directly related to the main text.

A Time Saver is a special tip: a shortcut designed to save you time.

## Q&A

Each hour ends with some questions designed to help you explore and test your understanding of the concepts described in the hour. Complete answers to the questions are also provided.

## Workshops

Some of the chapters that are oriented around real-life configuration topics include workshops—exercises designed to help you through the details or give you practice with a particular task. Not all chapters have workshops. You'll only find them in chapters where a little real-world exploration will help build a better understanding of the material. Even if you don't have the necessary software and hardware to undertake some of the exercises in the workshop, you might benefit from reading through the exercises to see how to proceed in a real network implementation.

## Key Terms

Each hour includes a summary of important new terms that are introduced in the chapter. The key terms are compiled into an alphabetized list at the end of each hour.

# PART I
# TCP/IP Basics

## Hour

# HOUR 1

# What Is TCP/IP?

*By Joe Casad*

TCP/IP is a protocol system—a collection of protocols that support network communications. And the answer to the question *What is a protocol?* must begin with the question *What is a network?*

This chapter describes what a network is and shows why networks need protocols. You'll also learn what TCP/IP is, what it does, and where it began.

## Goals for this Hour

At the completion of this hour, you'll be able to

- Define network
- Explain what a network protocol suite is
- Explain what TCP/IP is
- Discuss the history of TCP/IP
- List some important features of TCP/IP

- Identify the organizations that oversee TCP/IP and the Internet
- Explain what RFCs are and where to find them

# Networks and Protocols

A *network* is a collection of computers or computer-like devices that can communicate across a common transmission medium, as shown in Figure 1.1.

**FIGURE 1.1**

*A typical local network.*

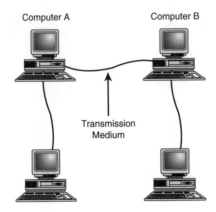

In a network, requests and data from one computer pass across the transmission medium (which might be a network cable or a phone line) to another computer. In Figure 1.1, Computer A must be capable of sending a message or request to Computer B. Computer B must be capable of *understanding* Computer A's message and respond to it by sending a message back to Computer A.

A computer interacts with the world through one or more applications that perform specific tasks and manage input and output. If that computer is part of a network, some of those applications must be capable of communicating with applications on other network computers. A *network protocol suite* is a system of common rules that helps to define the complex process of transferring data. The data travels from an application on one computer, through the computer's network hardware, across the transmission medium to the correct destination, and up through the destination computer's network hardware to a receiving application (see Figure 1.2).

**FIGURE 1.2**

*The role of a network protocol suite.*

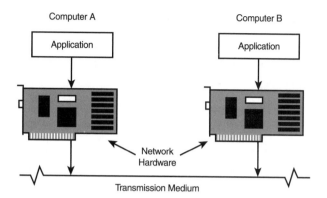

The protocols of TCP/IP define the network communication process and, more importantly, define how a unit of data should look and what information it should contain so that a receiving computer can interpret the message correctly. TCP/IP and its related protocols form a complete system defining how data should be processed, transmitted, and received on a TCP/IP network. A system of related protocols, such as the TCP/IP protocols, is called a protocol suite.

The actual act of formatting and processing TCP/IP transmissions is performed by a software component that is known as the vendor's *implementation* of TCP/IP. For instance Microsoft TCP/IP is a software component that enables Windows NT to process TCP/IP-formatted data and thus to participate in a TCP/IP network. As you read this book, be aware of the following distinction:

- A *TCP/IP standard* is a system of rules defining communication on TCP/IP networks.

- A *TCP/IP implementation* is a software component that performs the functions that enable a computer to participate in a TCP/IP network.

The purpose of the TCP/IP standards is to ensure the compatibility of all TCP/IP implementations regardless of version or vendor.

The important distinction between the TCP/IP standards and a TCP/IP implementation is often blurred in popular discussions of TCP/IP, and this is sometimes confusing for readers. For instance authors often talk about the layers of the TCP/IP model providing services for other layers. In fact it is not the TCP/IP model that provides services. The TCP/IP model *defines the services that should be provided*. The vendor software implementations of TCP/IP actually provide these services.

# The Development of TCP/IP

Present-day TCP/IP networking represents the synthesis of two developments that began in the 1970s and have subsequently revolutionized the world of computing:

- The Internet
- The local area network

## The Internet

TCP/IP's design is a result of its historical role as the protocol system for what was to become the Internet. The Internet, like so many other high-tech developments, grew from research originally performed by the United States Department of Defense. In the late 1960s, Defense Department officials began to notice that the military was accumulating a large and diverse collection of computers, some of which weren't networked and others that were grouped in smaller, closed networks with incompatible *proprietary* protocols.

**NEW TERM**  *Proprietary*, in this case, means that the technology is controlled by a private entity, such as a corporation. That entity might not have any interest in divulging enough information about the protocol for users to use it to connect to other (rival) network protocols.

Defense officials began to wonder if it would be possible for these disparate computers to share information. Accustomed as they were to considerations of security, the Defense Department reasoned that if such a network were possible it would likely become a target for military attack. One of the primary requirements of this new network, therefore, was that it must be decentralized. Critical services must not be concentrated in a few, vulnerable failure points. Because every failure point is vulnerable in the age of the missile, they wanted a network with no failure points at all—where a bomb could land on any part of the infrastructure without bringing down the whole network. These visionary soldiers created a network that became known as ARPAnet, named for the Defense Department's Advanced Research Projects Agency (ARPA). The protocol system that supported this interconnectable, decentralized network was the beginning of what we now know as TCP/IP.

A few years later, when the National Science Foundation wanted to build a network to interconnect research institutions, it adopted ARPAnet's protocol system and began to build what we know as the Internet. As you'll learn later in this book, the original decentralized vision of ARPAnet survives to this day in the design of the TCP/IP protocol system and is a big part of the success of TCP/IP and the Internet.

Two important features of TCP/IP that provide for this decentralized environment are listed here:

- End node verification—The two computers that are actually communicating— called the end nodes because they are at each end of the chain passing the message—are responsible for acknowledging and verifying the transmission. All computers basically operate as equals, and there is no central scheme for overseeing communications.

- Dynamic routing—Nodes are connected through multiple paths, and the routers choose a path for the data based on present conditions. You'll learn more about routing and router paths in later hours.

## The Local Area Network (LAN)

As the Internet began to emerge around universities and research institutions, another network concept, the *local area network (LAN)* was also taking form. LANs developed along with the computer industry and were a response to the need for offices to share computer resources.

Early LAN protocols did not provide Internet access and were designed around proprietary protocol systems. Many did not support routing of any kind. Eventually, some companies began to want a protocol that would connect their incompatible, discontiguous LANs, and they looked to TCP/IP. As the Internet became more popular, LAN users began to clamor for Internet access, and a variety of solutions began to emerge for getting LAN users connected. Specialized *gateways* provided the protocol translation necessary for these local networks to reach the Internet. Gradually LAN software vendors began to provide more complete support for TCP/IP. Recent versions of NetWare, MacOS, and Windows have continued to expand the role of TCP/IP on the local network.

 The term *gateway* is used inconsistently in discussions of TCP/IP. A *gateway* is sometimes just an ordinary router (see the discussion of routers later in this hour), and sometimes the term is used to refer to a routing device that performs some form of protocol translation.

As you'll learn in Hour 3, "The Network Access Layer," the need to accommodate local area networks has caused considerable innovation in the implementation of the hardware-conscious protocols that underlie TCP/IP.

# TCP/IP Features

TCP/IP includes many important features that you'll learn about as you study this book. In particular, pay close attention to the way the TCP/IP protocol suite addresses the following problems:

- Logical addressing
- Routing
- Name service
- error checking and flow control
- Application support

These issues are at the heart of TCP/IP. The following sections introduce these important features. You'll learn more about these features later in this book as well.

## Logical Addressing

A network adapter has a unique and permanent physical address. The physical address is a number that was given to the card at the factory. On a local area network, low-lying, hardware-conscious protocols deliver data across the physical network using the adapter's physical address. There are many network types and each has a different way of delivering data. On an Ethernet network, for example, a computer sends messages directly onto the transmission medium. The network adapter of each computer listens to every transmission on the local network to determine if a message is addressed to its own address.

On large networks, of course, every network adapter can't listen to every message. (Imagine your computer listening to *every* piece of data sent over the Internet.) As the transmission medium becomes more populated with computers, this type of scheme cannot function efficiently.

Network administrators often segment networks using devices such as routers in order to reduce network traffic. On routed networks, administrators need a way to subdivide the network into smaller *subnetworks* (called *subnets*) and impose a hierarchical design so that a message can travel efficiently to its destination. TCP/IP provides this subnetting capability through *logical addressing*. A logical address is an address configured through the network software. In TCP/IP a computer's logical address is called an *IP address*. As you'll learn in Hour 4, "The Internet Layer," and Hour 5, "Internet Layer: Subnetting," an IP address can include:

- A network ID number, identifying a network.
- A subnet ID number, identifying a subnet on the network.
- A host ID number, identifying the computer on the subnet.

The IP addressing system also lets the network administrator impose a sensible numbering scheme on the network so that the progression of addresses reflects the internal organization of the network.

> If your network is isolated from the Internet, you are free to use any IP addresses you want (as long as your network follows the basic rules for IP addressing). If your network will be part of the Internet, however, the Internet Assigned Numbers Authority (IANA) will assign a network ID to your network, and that network ID will form the first part of the IP address.

In TCP/IP a logical address is resolved to and from the corresponding hardware-specific physical address using the ARP and RARP protocols, which are discussed in Hour 4.

## Routing

A *router* is a special device that can read logical addressing information and direct data across the network to its destination.

At the simplest level, a router divides a local subnet from the larger network (see Figure 1.3). Data addressed to the local subnet does not cross the router and therefore doesn't clutter up the transmission lines of the greater network. If data is addressed to a computer outside the subnet, the router forwards the data accordingly. As this chapter has already mentioned, very large networks, such as the Internet, include many routers and provide multiple paths from the source to the destination (see Figure 1.4).

**FIGURE 1.3**

*A router connecting a LAN to a large network.*

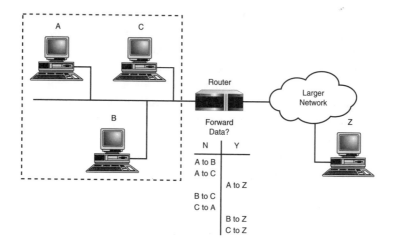

**FIGURE 1.4**

*A routed internetwork.*

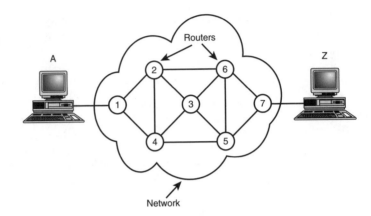

TCP/IP includes protocols that define how the routers will find a path through the net-work. You'll learn more about TCP/IP routing and routing protocols in Hour 9, "Routers, Brouters, and Bridges."

> As you'll also learn in Hour 9, a device called a *bridge* can also filter traffic and reduce network traffic. Because a bridge works with physical addresses rather than logical addresses, a bridge cannot perform the complex routing functions shown in Figure 1.4.

## Name Resolution

Although the numeric IP address is probably more user-friendly than the network adapter's prefabricated physical address, the IP address is still basically designed for the convenience of the computer rather than the convenience of the human. People might have trouble remembering whether a computer's address is 111.121.131.146 or 111.121.131.156. TCP/IP, therefore, provides for a parallel structure of human-oriented alphanumeric names, called *domain names* or *DNS* (Domain Name Service) names. This mapping of domain names to an IP address is called *name resolution*. Special computers called *name servers* store tables showing how to map these domain names to and from IP addresses.

The computer addresses commonly associated with email or the World Wide Web are expressed as DNS names (for example, `www.microsoft.com`, `falcon.ukans.edu`, `idir.net`). TCP/IP's name service system provides for a hierarchy of name servers that supply domain name/IP address mappings for DNS-registered computers on the network. This means that the everyday user rarely has to enter or decipher an actual IP address.

You'll learn more about TCP/IP name resolution in Part IV, "Name Resolution."

## Error Checking and Flow Control

The TCP/IP protocol suite provides features that ensure the reliable delivery of data across the network. These features include checking data for transmission errors (to ensure that the data that arrives is exactly what was sent) and acknowledging successful receipt of a network message. TCP/IP's Transport layer (see Hour 6, "The Transport Layer") defines many of these error checking, flow control, and acknowledgment functions for the internetwork through the TCP protocol. But lower-level protocols at TCP/IP's Network Access layer (see Hour 3) also play a part in the overall system of error checking.

## Application Support

The protocol suite must provide an interface for applications on the computer so that these applications can access the protocol software and thus gain access to the network. In TCP/IP this interface from the network to the applications running on the local computer is accomplished through a system of logical channels called *ports*. Each port has a port number that is used to identify the port. You can think of these ports as logical pipelines within the computer through which data can flow from the application to (and from) the protocol software (see Figure 1.5).

**FIGURE 1.5**

*Applications access the network through port addresses.*

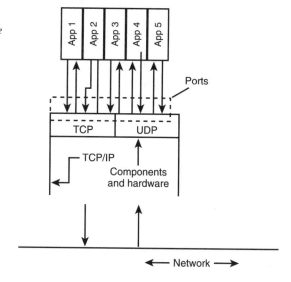

Hour 6 describes TCP and UDP ports at TCP/IP's Transport layer. You'll learn more about application support and TCP/IP's Application layer in Hour 8, "The Application Layer."

The TCP/IP suite also includes a number of ready-made applications designed to assist with various network tasks. Some typical TCP/IP utilities are shown in Table 1.1. You'll learn more about these TCP/IP utilities in Part III, "TCP/IP Utilities."

**TABLE 1.1** TYPICAL TCP/IP UTILITIES

| Utility | Purpose |
| --- | --- |
| ftp | File transfer |
| lpr | Printing |
| ping | Configuration/Troubleshooting |
| route | Configuration/Troubleshooting |
| telnet | Remote access |
| traceroute | Configuration/Troubleshooting |

# Standards Organizations and RFCs

Several organizations have been instrumental in the development of TCP/IP and the Internet. Another way in which TCP/IP reveals its military roots is in the quantity and obscurity of its acronyms. Still, a few organizations in the past and present of TCP/IP deserve mention, as follows:

- Internet Advisory Board (IAB)—The governing board that sets policy for the Internet and sees to the further development of TCP/IP standards.
- Internet Engineering Task Force (IETF)—The branch of the IAB that studies and rules on engineering issues. The IETF is divided into workgroups that study particular aspects of TCP/IP and the Internet such as Applications, Routing, Network Management, and so forth.
- Internet Research Task Force (IRTF)—The branch of the IAB that sponsors long-range research.
- Internet Assigned Numbers Authority (IANA)—The agency that assigns important Internet numbers such as Internet IP addresses and TCP and UDP port numbers.
- InterNIC—The Internet information service. You can register Internet domain names through InterNIC. Contact InterNIC through the World Wide Web at http://internic.net.

Most of the official documentation on TCP/IP is available through a series of *Requests for Comment (RFCs)*. The library of RFCs includes Internet standards and reports from workgroups. IETF official specifications are published as RFCs. Many RFCs are intended to illuminate some aspect of TCP/IP or the Internet. Anyone can submit an RFC for review. You can either send a proposed RFC to the IETF, or you can submit it directly to the RFC editor via email at rfc-editor@rfc-editor.org.

The RFCs provide an essential technical background for anyone wanting a deeper understanding of TCP/IP. The list includes several technical papers on protocols, utilities, and services, as well as a few TCP/IP-related poems and Shakespeare takeoffs that sadly do not match the clarity and economy of TCP/IP.

You can find the RFCs at several places on the Internet. Try www.rfc-editor.org. A few representative RFCs are shown in Table 1.2.

TABLE 1.2   REPRESENTATIVE EXAMPLE OF THE 2,000+ INTERNET RFCs

| Number | Title |
| --- | --- |
| 791 | Internet Protocol |
| 792 | Transmission Control Protocol |
| 793 | Simple Mail Transfer Protocol |
| 794 | File Transfer Protocol |
| 968 | Twas the night before start-up |
| 1180 | TCP/IP Tutorial |
| 1188 | Proposed Standard for transmission of datagrams over FDDI networks |
| 1597 | Address Allocation for Private Internets |
| 2000 | Internet Official Protocol Standards 2/24/97 |
| 2001 | The PPP NetBIOS Frames Control Protocol |

# Summary

This hour describes what networks are and why networks need protocols. You learned that TCP/IP began with the U.S. Defense Department's experimental ARPAnet network and that TCP/IP was designed to provide decentralized networking in a diverse environment.

This hour also covers some important features of TCP/IP, such as logical addressing, name resolution, and application support; describes some of TCP/IP's oversight organizations; and discusses RFCs—the technical papers that serve as the official documentation for TCP/IP and the Internet.

# Q&A

**Q** **What is the difference between a protocol standard and a protocol implementation?**

**A** A protocol standard is a system of rules. A protocol implementation is a software component that applies those rules in order to provide a computer with networking capability.

**Q** **Why did the designers of ARPAnet want a decentralized network?**

**A** They envisioned a network that would be used for military purposes, and they didn't want to concentrate critical services in a central location that would become the focus on an attack.

**Q** **Why was end-node verification an important feature of ARPAnet?**

**A** By design, the network was not supposed to be controlled from any central point. The sending and receiving computers therefore had to take charge of verifying their own communications.

**Q** **Why do larger networks employ name resolution?**

**A** IP addresses are difficult to remember and easy to get wrong. DNS-style domain names are easier to remember because they let you associate a word or name with the address.

# Workshop

## Key Terms

Review the following list of key terms:

- ARPAnet—An experimental network that was the birthplace of TCP/IP.
- Domain name—An alphanumeric name associated with an IP address through TCP/IP's DNS name service system.
- Gateway—A router that connects a LAN to a larger network. The term *gateway* sometimes applies specifically to a router that performs some kind of protocol conversion.
- IP address—A logical address used to locate a computer on a TCP/IP network.
- Logical address—A network address configured through the protocol software.
- Name service—A service that associates human-friendly alphanumeric names with network addresses.

**1**

- Physical address—A permanent address burned into a network adapter in the factory.
- Port—An internal address that provides an interface between an application and TCP/IP's Transport layer.
- Protocol system—A system of standards and procedures that enables computers to communicate over a network.
- RFC—Request for Comment—An official technical paper providing relevant information on TCP/IP or the Internet.
- Router—A network device that forwards data by logical address.
- TCP/IP—A network protocol system used on the Internet and also on many other networks around the world.

# HOUR 2

# How TCP/IP Works

*By Joe Casad*

TCP/IP is a system (or suite) of protocols, and a protocol is a system of
rules and procedures. For the most part the hardware and software of the
communicating computers carry out the rules of TCP/IP communications—
the user does not have to get involved with the details. Still, a working
knowledge of TCP/IP is essential if you want to navigate through the configuration and troubleshooting problems you'll face with TCP/IP networks.

This hour describes the TCP/IP protocol system and shows how the components of TCP/IP work together to send and receive data across the network.

# Goals for this Hour

At the completion of this hour, you will be able to

- Describe the layers of the TCP/IP protocol system and the purpose of each layer
- Describe the layers of the OSI protocol model and explain how the OSI layers relate to TCP/IP
- Explain TCP/IP protocol headers and how data is enclosed with header information at each layer of the protocol stack
- Name the data package at each layer of the TCP/IP stack
- Discuss the important protocols TCP, UDP, and IP and how they work together to provide TCP/IP functionality

# The TCP/IP Protocol System

Before looking at the elements of TCP/IP, it is best to begin with a brief review of the responsibilities of a protocol system.

A protocol system such as TCP/IP must be capable of the following tasks:

- Dividing messages into manageable chunks of data that will pass efficiently through the transmission medium.
- Interfacing with the network adapter hardware.
- Addressing—The sending computer must be capable of targeting data to a receiving computer. The receiving computer must be capable of recognizing a message that it is supposed to receive.
- Routing—The system must be capable of routing data to the subnet of the destination computer, even if the source subnet and the destination subnet are dissimilar physical networks.
- Performing error checking, flow control, and acknowledgment—For reliable communication, the sending and receiving computers must be capable of identifying and correcting faulty transmissions and controlling the flow of data.
- Accepting data from an application and passing it to the network.

In order to accomplish the preceding tasks, the creators of TCP/IP settled on a modular design. The TCP/IP protocol system is divided into separate components that theoretically function independently from one another. Each component is responsible for a piece of the goal of network communication.

The advantage of this modular design is that it lets vendors easily adapt the protocol software to specific hardware and operating systems. For instance, the Network Access layer (as you'll learn in Hour 3, "The Network Access Layer") includes functions relating to a specific LAN architecture such as token ring or Ethernet. Because of TCP/IP's modular design, a vendor such as Microsoft does not have to build a completely different software package for token ring TCP/IP (as opposed to Ethernet TCP/IP) networks. The upper layers are not affected, only the Network Access layer must change. TCP/IP protocol system is subdivided into layered components that each perform specific duties (see Figure 2.1). This model, or *stack*, comes from the early days of TCP/IP and it is sometimes called the TCP/IP model. The official TCP/IP protocol layers are as follows. Compare the functions in the following list with the responsibilities listed earlier in this section, and you'll see how the responsibilities of the protocol system are distributed among the layers.

**2**

The four-layer model shown in Figure 2.1 is a common model for describing TCP/IP networking, but it isn't the only model. The ARPAnet model, for instance, as described in RFC 871, describes three layers: the Network Interface layer, the Host-to-Host layer, and the Process-level/Applications layer. Other descriptions of TCP/IP call for a five-layer model, with Physical and Data link layers in place of the Network Access layer (to match OSI). Still other models may exclude either the Network Access or the Application layer, which are less uniform and harder to define than the intermediate layers.

The names of the layers also vary. The ARPAnet layer names still appear in some discussions of TCP/IP, and the Internet layer is sometimes called the Internetwork layer or the Network layer.

This book uses the four-layer model, with names as shown in Figure 2.1.

**FIGURE 2.1**

*The TCP/IP model's
protocol layers.*

| Application Layer |
| Transport Layer |
| Internet Layer |
| Network Access Layer |

- Network Access layer—Provides an interface with the physical network. Formats the data for the transmission medium and addresses data for the subnet based on physical hardware addresses. Provides error checking for data delivered on the physical network.

- Internet layer—Provides logical, hardware-independent addressing so that data can pass among subnets with differing physical architectures. Provides routing to reduce traffic and support delivery across the internetwork. The term *internetwork* refers to an interconnected greater network of LANs, for example, what you find in a large company or on the Internet. Relates physical addresses (used at the Network Access layer) to logical addresses.

- Transport layer—Provides flow control, error checking, and acknowledgment services for the internetwork. Serves as an interface for network applications.

- Application layer—Provides applications for network troubleshooting, file transfer, remote control, and Internet activities. Also supports the network Application Programming Interfaces (APIs) that enable programs written for a particular operating environment to access the network.

Hours 3–8 provide more detailed descriptions of the activities at each of these TCP/IP protocol layers.

When the TCP/IP protocol system prepares a piece of data for transmission across the network, each layer on the sending machine adds a *layer* of information to the data that will be relevant to the corresponding layer on the receiving machine. For instance, the Internet layer of the computer sending the data adds a header with some information that is significant to the Internet layer of the computer receiving the message.

The term *layer* is used throughout the computer industry for protocol component levels such as the ones shown in Figure 2.1. Header information is indeed applied in layers to the data as it passes through the components of the protocol stack. (You'll learn more about this later in this hour.) When it comes to the components themselves, however, the term *layer* is somewhat metaphorical.

Diagrams such as Figure 2.1 are meant to show that the data passes across a series of interfaces, and as long as the interfaces are maintained, the processes within one component are not affected by the processes in other components. If you turned Figure 2.1 sideways, it would look more like an assembly line, and this is also a useful analogy for the interrelation of the protocol components. The data stops at each point in the line and, as long as it arrives at each point as specified, the components can basically operate independently.

# TCP/IP and the OSI Model

The networking industry has a standard seven-layer model for network protocol architecture called the Open Systems Interconnection (OSI) model. The OSI model represents an effort by the International Standards Organization (ISO) to standardize the design of network protocol systems in order to promote interconnectivity and open access to protocol standards for software developers.

TCP/IP was already on the path of development when the OSI standard architecture appeared and, strictly speaking, TCP/IP does not conform to the OSI model. The two models did, however, have similar goals, and there was enough interaction among the designers of these standards that they emerged with a certain compatibility. The OSI model has been very influential in the growth and development of protocol implementations, and it is quite common to see the OSI terminology applied to TCP/IP. Figure 2.2 shows the relationship between the four-layer TCP/IP standard and the seven-layer OSI model. Note that the OSI model divides the duties of the Application layer into three layers: Application, Presentation, and Session. OSI splits the activities of the Network Interface layer into a Data Link layer and a Physical layer. This increased subdivision adds some complexity, but it also adds flexibility for developers by targeting the protocol layers to more specific services.

**FIGURE 2.2**

*The seven-layer OSI model.*

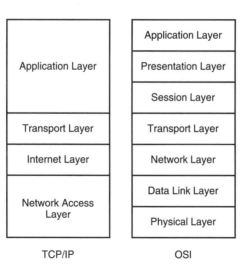

The seven layers of the OSI model are as follows:

- Physical layer—Converts the data into the stream of electric or analog pulses that will actually cross the transmission medium and oversees the transmission of the data.

- Data Link layer—Provides an interface with the network adapter; maintains logical links for the subnet.
- Network layer—Supports logical addressing and routing.
- Transport layer—Provides error checking and flow control for the internetwork.
- Session layer—Establishes sessions between communicating applications on the communicating computers.
- Presentation layer—Translates data to standard format; manages encryption and data compression.
- Application layer—Provides a network interface for applications; supports network applications for file transfer, communications, and so forth.

It is important to remember that the TCP/IP model and the OSI model are standards, not implementations. Real-world implementations do not always map cleanly to the models shown in Figures 2.1 and 2.2, and the perfect correspondence depicted in Figure 2.2 is also a matter of some discussion within the industry.

Notice that the OSI and TCP/IP models are most similar at the important Transport and Internet (called *Network* in OSI) layers. These layers include the most identifiable and distinguishing components of the protocol system, and it is no coincidence that protocol systems are sometimes named for their Transport and Network layer protocols. As you'll learn later in this book, the TCP/IP protocol suite is named for TCP, a Transport layer protocol, and IP, an Internet/Network layer protocol.

# Data Packages

The important thing to remember about the TCP/IP protocol stack is that each layer plays a role in the overall communication process. Each layer invokes services that are necessary for that layer to perform its role. As an outgoing transmission passes down through the stack, each layer includes a bundle of relevant information called a *header* along with the actual data. The little data package containing the header and the data then *becomes* the data that is repackaged at the next lower level with the next lower layer's header. This process is shown in Figure 2.3. The reverse process occurs when data is received on the destination computer. As the data moves up through the stack, each layer unpacks the corresponding header and uses the information.

As the data moves down through the stack, the effect is a little like the nested Russian wooden dolls you may have seen; the innermost doll is enclosed in another doll, which is then enclosed in another doll and so on. At the receiving end the data packages will be unpacked one by one as the data climbs back up the protocol stack. The Internet layer on the receiving machine will use the information in the Internet layer header. The Transport layer will use the information in the Transport layer header. At each layer, the package of data takes a form that will provide the necessary information to the corresponding layer on the receiving machine. Because each layer is responsible for different functions, the form of the basic data package is very different at each layer.

> The networking industry has as many analogies as it has acronyms, and the Russian doll analogy, like any of the others, illustrates a point but must not be taken too far. It is worth noting that on a physical network such as Ethernet, the data is typically broken into smaller units at the Network Access layer. A more accurate analogy would call for this lowest layer to break the concentric doll system into smaller pieces, encapsulate those pieces into tinier dolls, then grind those tiny dolls into a pattern of ones and zeros. The ones and zeros will be received, reconstituted into tiny dolls, and rebuilt into the concentric doll system. The complexity of this scenario causes many to eschew the otherwise-promising analogy of the dolls.

**FIGURE 2.3**

*At each layer the data is repackaged with that layer's header.*

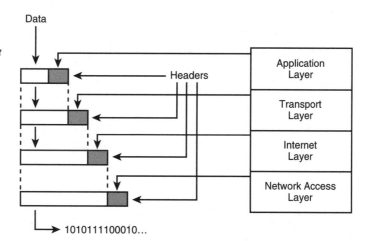

The data packet looks different at each layer, and at each layer it goes by a different name. The names for the data packages created at each layer are as follows:

- The data package created at the Application layer is called a *message.*
- The data package created at the Transport layer, which encapsulates the Application layer *message,* is called a *segment* if it comes from the Transport layer's TCP protocol. If the data package comes from the Transport layer's UDP protocol, it is called a *datagram.*

- The data package at the Internet layer, which encapsulates the Transport layer *segment*, is called a *datagram*.
- The data package at the Network Access layer, which encapsulates and may subdivide the datagram is called a *frame*. This frame is then turned into a bit-stream at the lowest sublayer of the Network Access layer.

You'll learn more about the data packages for each layer in Hours 3–8.

# A Quick Look at TCP/IP Networking

The practice of describing protocol systems in terms of their *layers* is widespread and nearly universal. The layering system does provide insights into the protocol system, and it's impossible to describe TCP/IP without first introducing its layered architecture. However, focusing solely on protocol layers also creates some limitations.

First, talking about *protocol layers* rather than *protocols* introduces an additional layer of abstraction to a subject that is already excruciatingly abstract. Second, itemizing the various protocols as subheads within the greater topic of a protocol layer can give the false impression that all protocols are of equal importance. In fact, though every protocol has a role to play, most of the functionality of the TCP/IP suite can be described in terms of only a few of its most important protocols. It is sometimes useful to view these important protocols in the foreground against the backdrop of the layering system described earlier in this hour.

Figure 2.4 describes the basic TCP/IP protocol networking system. There are, of course, additional protocols and services in the complete package, but Figure 2.4 shows you most of what is going on.

The basic scenario is as follows:

1. Data passes from a TCP/IP application or from a network application program interface through a TCP or UDP port to either of the two Transport layer protocols (TCP or UDP). Programs can access the network through either TCP or UDP, depending on the program's requirements.
   - TCP is a connection-oriented protocol. As you'll learn in Hour 6, "The Transport Layer," connection-oriented protocols provide more sophisticated flow control and error checking than connectionless protocols. TCP goes to great effort to guarantee the delivery of the data. TCP is more reliable than UDP, but the additional error checking and flow control means that TCP is slower than UDP.
   - UDP is a connectionless protocol. It is faster than TCP, but it is not as reliable. UDP offloads more of the error-checking responsibilities to the application.

**FIGURE 2.4**

*A quick look at the basic TCP/IP networking system.*

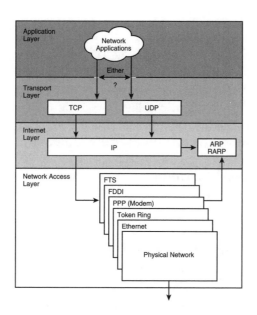

2. The data segment passes to the Internet level, where the IP protocol provides logical-addressing information and encloses the data into a datagram.

3. The IP datagram enters the Network Access layer, where it passes to software components designed to interface with the physical network. The Network Access layer creates one or more data frames designed for entry onto the physical network. In the case of a LAN system such as Ethernet, the frame may contain physical address information obtained from lookup tables maintained using the Internet-layer ARP and RARP protocols. (ARP, Address Resolution Protocol, translates IP addresses to physical addresses. RARP, Reverse Address Resolution Protocol, translates physical addresses to IP addresses.)

4. The data frame is converted to a stream of bits that is transmitted over the network medium.

Of course there are endless details describing how each protocol goes about fulfilling its assigned tasks. For instance, how does TCP provide flow control, how do ARP and RARP map physical addresses to IP addresses, and how does IP know where to send a datagram addressed to a different subnet? In later hours in this book we explore these questions.

You'll learn more about each of these protocols, and about the procedures described in this section, in later hours also.

# Summary

In this hour you learned about the layers of the TCP/IP protocol stack and how those layers interrelate. You also learned how the classic TCP/IP model relates to the seven-layer OSI networking model. At each layer in the protocol stack, data is packaged into the form that is most useful to the corresponding layer on the receiving end. This chapter discusses the process of encapsulating header information at each protocol layer and outlines the different terms used at each layer to describe the data package. Lastly, you got a quick look at how the TCP/IP protocol system operates from the viewpoint of some of its most important protocols: TCP, UDP, IP, ARP, and RARP.

# Q&A

**Q  What is the principal advantage of TCP/IP's modular design?**

**A**  Because of TCP/IP's modular design, the TCP/IP protocol stack can adapt easily to specific hardware and operating environments.

**Q  What functions are provided at the Network Access layer?**

**A**  The Network Access layer provides services related to the specific physical network.

**Q  Which OSI layer corresponds to the TCP/IP Internet layer?**

**A**  TCP/IP's Internet layer corresponds to the OSI Network layer.

**Q  Why is header information enclosed at each layer of the TCP/IP protocol stack?**

**A**  Because each protocol layer on the receiving machine needs different information to process the incoming data, each layer on the sending machine encloses header information.

# Workshop

## Key Terms

Review the following list of key terms:

- Application layer—The layer of the TCP/IP stack that supports network applications and provides an interface to the local operating environment.
- Datagram—The data package passed from the Internet layer to the Network Access layer, or a data package passed from UDP at the Transport layer to the Internet layer.

- Frame—The data package created at the Network Access layer according to the specification of the physical network.
- Header—A bundle of protocol information enclosed with the data at each layer of the protocol stack.
- Internet layer—The layer of the TCP/IP stack that provides logical addressing and routing.
- IP—The Internet layer protocol that provides logical addressing.
- Message—In TCP/IP networking a message is the data package passed from the Application layer to the Transport layer. The term is also used generically to describe a message from one entity to another on the network. The term *message* doesn't always refer to an Application layer data package.
- Modular design—A design that calls for the complete system to be built from individual components that pass information across well-defined interfaces.
- Network Access layer—The layer of the TCP/IP stack that provides an interface with the physical network.
- Segment—The data package passed from TCP at the Transport layer to the Internet layer.
- TCP—Transmission Control Protocol: a Transport layer, connection-oriented protocol.
- Transport layer—The layer of the TCP/IP stack that provides error checking and acknowledgment and serves as an interface for network applications.
- UDP—User Datagram Protocol: a Transport layer, connectionless protocol.

**2**

# PART II

# The TCP/IP Protocol System

## Hour

# HOUR 3

# The Network Access Layer

*By Joe Casad*

At the base of the TCP/IP protocol stack is the Network Access layer, the collection of services and specifications that provide and manage access to the network hardware. In this hour you'll learn about the duties of the Network Access layer and how the Network Access layer relates to the OSI model. This hour also looks at some common physical network technologies you'll find in the Network Access layer.

## Goals for this Hour

At the completion of this hour, you'll be able to

- Explain what the Network Access layer is
- Discuss how TCP/IP's Network Access layer relates to the OSI networking model

- Explain what a network architecture is
- List the contents of an Ethernet frame
- Identify the methods that Ethernet, token ring, and FDDI use for controlling access to the transmission medium

# Protocols and Hardware

The Network Access layer is the most mysterious and least uniform of TCP/IP's layers. Basically, the Network Access layer manages all the services and functions necessary to prepare the data for the physical network. These responsibilities include:

- Interfacing with the computer's network adapter.
- Coordinating the data transmission with the conventions of the appropriate access method. You'll learn more about access methods later in this hour.
- Formatting the data into a unit called a *frame* and converting that frame into the stream of electric or analog pulses that pass across the transmission medium.
- Checking for errors in incoming frames.
- Adding error-checking information to outgoing frames so that the receiving computer can check it for errors.
- Acknowledging receipt of data frames and resending frames if acknowledgment is not received.

Of course, any formatting tasks performed on an outgoing frame must occur in reverse when the frame reaches its destination and is received by the computer to which it is addressed.

The Network Access layer defines the procedures for interfacing with the network hardware and accessing the transmission medium. Below the surface of TCP/IP's Network Access layer you'll find an intricate interplay of hardware, software, and transmission-medium specifications. Unfortunately, at least for the purposes of a concise description, there are many different types of physical networks that all have their own conventions, and any one of these physical networks can form the basis for the Network Access layer. You'll learn about these physical network types later in this hour. A few examples include:

- Token ring
- Ethernet
- FDDI
- PPP (Point-to-Point Protocol; through a phone modem)

Not every networked computer is on a LAN. The network-access software may provide support for something other than a standard network adapter and a LAN cable. One of the most common alternatives is a modem connection to a remote network, such as the connection you establish when you dial in to an Internet service provider (ISP). Modem protocol standards such as Serial Line Internet Protocol (SLIP) and Point-to-Point Protocol (PPP) provide network access for the TCP/IP protocol stack through a modem connection. You'll learn more about these protocols in Hour 10, "Dial-up TCP/IP."

The good news is that the Network Access layer is almost totally invisible to the everyday user. The network adapter driver, coupled with key low-level components of the operating system and protocol software, manages most of the tasks relegated to the Network Access layer, and a few short configuration steps are usually all that are required of a user. These steps are becoming simpler with the improved plug-and-play features of desktop operating systems.

As you read through this chapter, remember that the logical IP-style addressing discussed in Hours 1, 2, 4, and 5 exists entirely in the software. The protocol system requires additional services to deliver the data across a specific LAN system and up through the network adapter of a destination computer. These services are the purview of the Network Access layer.

It is worth mentioning that the diversity, complexity, and invisibility of the Network Access layer has caused some authors to exclude it from discussions of TCP/IP completely, asserting instead that the stack rests on LAN drivers below the Internet Access layer. This viewpoint has some merit but the Network Access layer *really is* part of TCP/IP and no discussion of the network-communication process is complete without it.

## The Network Access Layer and the OSI Model

As Hour 2, "How TCP/IP Works," mentioned, TCP/IP is officially independent of the seven-layer OSI networking model, but the OSI model is often used as a general framework for understanding protocol systems. OSI terminology and concepts are particularly common in discussions of the Network Access layer because the OSI model provides additional subdivisions to the broad category of network access. These subdivisions reveal a bit more of the inner workings at this layer. The OSI model has been influential with computer networking vendors, and the recent trend toward multiprotocol standards such as NDIS and ODI (discussed later in this section) have accentuated the need for a common terminology that the OSI model provides to describe the services of the lower levels.

As Figure 3.1 shows, the TCP/IP Network Access layer roughly corresponds to the OSI Physical and Data Link layers.

The OSI Physical layer is responsible for turning the data frame into a stream of bits suitable for the transmission medium. In other words, the OSI Physical layer manages and synchronizes the electric or analog pulses that form the actual transmission. On the receiving end, the physical layer reassembles these pulses into a data frame.

**FIGURE 3.1**

*OSI and the Network Access layer.*

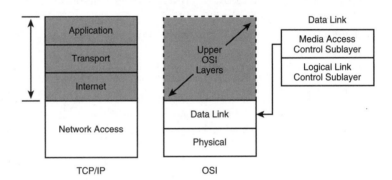

The OSI Data Link layer performs two separate functions and is accordingly subdivided into the following two sublayers:

- Media Access Control (MAC)—This sublayer provides an interface with the network adapter. The network adapter driver, in fact, is often called the MAC driver.
- Logical Link Control (LLC)—This sublayer performs error-checking functions for frames delivered over the subnet and manages links between devices communicating on the subnet.

In real network protocol implementations the distinction between the layers of TCP/IP and OSI systems has become further complicated by the development of the Network Driver Interface Specification (NDIS) and Open Data-Link Interface (ODI) specification. NDIS (developed by Microsoft and 3Com Corp.) and ODI (developed by Apple and Novell) are designed to let a single protocol stack (such as TCP/IP) use multiple network adapters and to let a single network adapter use multiple upper-layer protocols. This effectively enables the upper-layer protocols to *float* independently of the network access system, which adds great functionality to the network, but also adds complexity and makes it even more difficult to provide a systematic discussion of how the software components interrelate at the lower layers.

# Network Architecture

In practice, local area networks are not really thought of in terms of protocol layers but by what is called *LAN architecture* or *network architecture*. (Sometimes a network architecture is referred to as a LAN type or a LAN technology.) A network architecture, such as Ethernet, provides a bundle of specifications governing media access, physical addressing, and the interaction of the computers with the transmission medium. When you decide on a network architecture you are, in effect, deciding on a design for the Network Access layer.

A network architecture is a design for the physical network and a collection of specifications defining communications on that physical network. The communication details are dependent on the physical details, so the specifications usually come together as a complete package. These specifications include considerations such as the following:

- Access method—An access method is a set of rules defining how the computers will share the transmission medium. To avoid data collisions, computers must follow these rules when they transmit data.

- Data frame format—The IP-level datagram from the Internet layer is encapsulated in a data frame with a predefined format. The data enclosed in the header must supply the information necessary to deliver data on the physical network. You'll learn more on data frames later in this chapter.

- Cabling type—The type of cable used for a network has implications on certain other design parameters, such as the electrical properties of the bit-stream transmitted by the adapter.

- Cabling rules—The protocols, cable type, and electrical properties of the transmission have implications on the maximum and minimum lengths for the cable and for the cable connector specifications.

Details such as cable type and connector type are not the direct responsibility of the Network Access layer, but in order to design the software components of the Network Access layer, developers must assume a specific set of characteristics for the physical network. Thus, the network access software must come with a specific hardware design.

## Physical Addressing

As you learned in Part I, "TCP/IP Basics," the Network Access layer is necessary in order to relate the logical IP address, which is configured through the protocol software with the actual permanent physical address of the network adapter. The physical address is burned into the card at the factory. Data frames sent across the LAN must use this physical address to identify the source and destination adapters, but the lengthy physical address (48 bits in the case of Ethernet) is so unfriendly that it is impractical for people to use. Also, encoding the physical address at higher protocol levels compromises the flexible modular architecture of TCP/IP, which requires that the upper layers remain independent of physical details. TCP/IP uses the Address Resolution Protocol (ARP) and Reverse Address Resolution Protocol (RARP) to relate IP addresses to the physical addresses of the network adapters on the local network. ARP and RARP provide a link between the logical IP addresses seen by the user and the (effectively invisible) hardware addresses used on the LAN.

You'll learn about ARP and RARP in Hour 4, "The Internet Layer."

## Anatomy of a Frame

The Network Access layer software accepts a datagram from the Internet layer and converts that data to a form that is consistent with the specifications of the physical network (see Figure 3.2). Because many forms of physical networks exist, there are many formats for data at the Network Access layer and it would not be easy or useful to describe all these formats in detail.

As an example of what happens to the data at the Network Access layer consider the case of Ethernet, the most common of the LAN architectures. When the Ethernet software receives a datagram from the Internet layer, it performs the following steps:

1. Breaks IP layer data into smaller chunks, if necessary, which will be sent in the data field of the Ethernet frames. The total size of the Ethernet frame must be between 64 and 1,518 bytes (not including the preamble).

**FIGURE 3.2**

*The Network Access layer formats data for the physical network.*

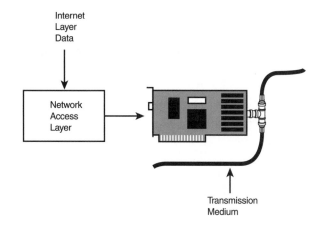

2. Packages the chunks of data into *frames*. Each frame includes data as well as other information that the network adapters on the Ethernet need in order to process the frame. An IEEE 802.3 Ethernet frame includes

> Preamble—A sequence of bits used to mark the beginning of the frame (8 bytes, the last of which is the 1-byte Start Frame Delimiter).

> Recipient address—The 6-byte (48-bit) physical address of the network adapter that is to receive the frame.

> Source address—The 6-byte (48-bit) physical address of the network adapter that is sending the frame.

> Length—A 2-byte (16-bit) field indicating the size of the data field.

> Data—The data that is transmitted with the frame.

> Cyclical Redundancy Check (CRC)—A 4-byte (32-bit) checksum value for the frame. The CRC is a common means of verifying data transmissions. The sending computer calculates a CRC value for the frame and encodes it in the frame. The receiving computer then recalculates the CRC and checks the CRC field to see if the values match. If the values don't match, some data is lost or changed during transmission.

3. Passes the data frame to lower-level components corresponding to OSI's Physical layer, which will convert the frame into a bit-stream and send it over the transmission medium.

The other network adapters on the Ethernet receive the frame and check the destination address. If the destination address matches the address of the network adapter, the adapter software processes the incoming frame and passes the data to higher layers of the protocol stack.

IEEE 802.3 is not the only Ethernet standard. The Ethernet II standard, used by some vendors, has a slightly different frame format.

# LAN Technologies

The most common network architectures are the following:

- Ethernet, including variants such as the following:
    - 10Base-2—An Ethernet standard using thin coaxial cable.
    - 10Base-5—An Ethernet standard using thick coaxial cable.
    - 10Base-T—An Ethernet standard using twisted-pair cable in a star configuration.
    - 100Base-TX—A standard similar to 10Base-T with faster transmission speed (100Mbps).
- Token ring

The following sections will examine Ethernet and token ring in greater detail, along with another emerging LAN technology: FDDI.

The Institute of Electrical and Electronic Engineers (IEEE) has produced a set of standards for LAN architectures. Although token ring and Ethernet were both created before the IEEE standards, the IEEE specifications for IEEE 802.3 (Ethernet) and IEEE 802.5 (token ring) now provide vendor-neutral standards for these important LAN technologies.

## Ethernet

Ethernet and its newer sibling Fast Ethernet are the LAN technologies most commonly used today. Ethernet has become popular because of its modest price; Ethernet cable is inexpensive and easily installed. Ethernet network adapters and Ethernet hardware components are also relatively inexpensive.

On Ethernet networks, all computers are attached to a common transmission medium. Ethernet uses an access method called Carrier Sense Multiple Access with Collision Detect (CSMA/CD) for determining when a computer is free to transmit data on to the access medium. Using CSMA/CD, all computers monitor the transmission medium and wait until the line is available before transmitting. If two computers try to transmit at the same time a collision occurs. The computers then stop, wait for a random time interval, and attempt to transmit again.

CSMA/CD can be compared to the protocol followed by a room full of polite people. Someone who wants to speak first listens to determine if anybody else is currently speaking (this is the Carrier Sense). If two people start speaking at the same moment then both people will detect this, stop speaking, and wait before speaking again (this is Collision Detect).

Ethernet works well under light to moderate usage but suffers under heavy use from high collision rates.

Ethernet is capable of using a variety of media and can operate at baseband speeds of either 10 or 100Mbps. Table 3.1 lists terms used to identify cabling media, speeds, and maximum distances.

**TABLE 3.1**  ETHERNET MEDIA TECHNOLOGY

| Technology Name | Media Type | Operating Speed | Maximum Distance |
|---|---|---|---|
| 10Base-2 | Thin coax | 10 Megabits | 185 meters |
| 10Base-5 | Thick coax | 10 Megabits | 500 meters |
| 10Base-T | CAT3 or CAT5 UTP | 10 Megabits | 100 meters |
| 10Base-F | Fiber optic | 10 Megabits | 2,000 meters |
| 100Base-TX | CAT 5 UTP or STP | 100 Megabits | 100 meters |
| 100Base-FX | Fiber optic | 100 Megabits | 2,000 meters |

# Token Ring

Token-ring technology uses a completely different concept for allowing network adapters to transmit data on the media. This access method is known as *token passing*.

Under the token passing access method, the computers on the LAN are connected so that data is passed around the network in a logical ring (see Figure 3.3). The token-ring configuration calls for the computers to be wired to a central hub. This doesn't exactly look like a ring, but the hubs are wired so that the data passes from one computer to the next in a circular motion. The computers pass a packet of data called a *token* around the network. Only the computer that holds the token can transmit a message on to the ring.

**FIGURE 3.3**

*A token ring.*

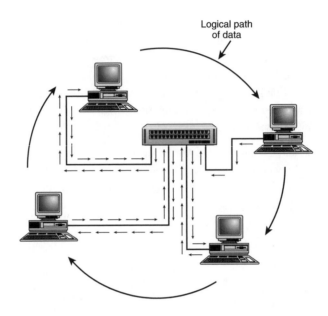

Token ring is technically more sophisticated than Ethernet, and it includes a number of built-in diagnosis and correction mechanisms that can help troubleshoot network problems. Also, because data is transmitted in a more orderly fashion, token ring does not suffer as badly under heavy data traffic. Almost everything about token ring is, by comparison, more expensive than Ethernet—the cable, the network adapters, and the other components as well.

Token ring typically operates at either 4Mbps or 16Mbps. IBM has recently announced a 100Mbps token ring.

## FDDI

Fiber Distributed Data Interface *(FDDI)* is a relatively new and expensive LAN technology that employs a pair of fiber-optic rings. One ring is considered primary and the second ring is principally there to repair the primary ring in the event of a breakdown. FDDI uses a token-passing access method similar to token ring's.

Like token ring, FDDI also has error detection and correction capabilities. In a normally operating FDDI ring the token passes by each machine every so often. If the token is not seen within the maximum amount of time that it takes to circulate the largest ring, it indicates a problem has occurred such as a broken cable.

Fiber-optic cable such as the cable used with FDDI can support very large volumes of data over large distances. FDDI operates at 100Mbps over a distance of 100 kilometers.

# Summary

In this hour you learned about the Network Access layer, the most diverse and arguably the most complex layer in the TCP/IP protocol stack. The Network Access layer defines the procedures for interfacing with the network hardware and accessing the transmission medium. There are many types of LAN architectures, and therefore many different forms that the Network Access layer can take. This chapter also describes the contents of an Ethernet frame and briefly discusses Ethernet, token ring, and FDDI.

# Q&A

**Q What types of services are defined at the Network Access layer?**

**A** The Network Access layer includes services and specifications that manage the process of accessing the physical network.

**Q Which OSI layers correspond to the TCP/IP Network Access layer?**

**A** The Network Access layer roughly corresponds with the OSI Data Link layer and Physical layer.

**Q What are the two most common LAN architectures?**

**A** The most common LAN architectures are Ethernet, with its several cabling variants, and token ring.

**Q What is CSMA/CD?**

**A** CSMA/CD is Carrier Sense Multiple Access with Collision Detect, a network-access method used by Ethernet. Under CSMA/CD, the computers on a network wait for a quiet moment to transmit, and if two computers attempt to transmit at once then they both stop, wait for a random interval, and transmit again.

**Q What is token passing?**

**A** Token passing is a network-access method used by token ring and FDDI. A packet of data called a *token* circulates around the network. Only the computer with the token can transmit data.

3

# Workshop

## Key Terms

Review the following list of key terms:

- Access method—A procedure for regulating access to the transmission medium.
- CRC—Cyclical Redundancy Check, a checksum calculation used to verify the contents of a data frame.
- CSMA/CD—The network access method used by Ethernet.
- Data frame—A package of data transmitted over an Ethernet network.
- Data Link layer—The second layer of the OSI model.
- Ethernet—A very popular LAN architecture, using the CSMA/CD network-access method.
- FDDI—A token-passing network architecture using fiber-optic cable.
- Logical Link Control sublayer—A sublayer of OSI's Data Link layer that is responsible for error checking and managing links between devices on the subnet.
- Media Access Control sublayer—A sublayer of OSI's Data Link layer that is responsible for the interface with the network adapter.
- Network architecture—A complete specification for a physical network, including specifications for access method, data frame, and network cabling.
- Physical address—A permanent network address burned into the adapter card by the manufacturer that is used to deliver data across the physical network.
- Physical layer—The first OSI layer, responsible for translating the data frame into a bit-stream suitable for the transmission medium.
- Preamble —A series of bits marking the beginning of a data frame transmission.
- Token passing—The network access method used by token ring.
- Token ring—A LAN architecture featuring a ring topology and a token-passing network access method.

# Hour 4

# The Internet Layer

*By Bob Willsey*

The Internet layer of the TCP/IP protocol stack is where three key TCP/IP protocols reside. These three protocols are IP, ARP, and ICMP, and each has a specific purpose. Two additional minor protocols at the Internet layer exist: RARP and IGMP. Of the five TCP/IP protocols that operate at the Internet layer, IP and ARP are the most heavily used.

In this hour we discuss IP, ARP, and ICMP, their purpose, and how they function. We briefly mention RARP and IGMP. We also discuss IP addressing and address classes, and explain how to convert binary numbers to decimal and decimal back to binary, as well as how to convert a 32-bit binary number into a form known as dotted-decimal notation.

# Goals for this Hour

At the completion of this hour, you will be able to

- Explain the purpose of IP, ARP, and ICMP
- Explain what a network ID and host ID are
- Explain what an octet is
- Convert a decimal number to its binary equivalent
- Convert a 32-bit binary IP address into dotted-decimal notation
- Describe the construction of an IP header
- Explain the purpose of the IP address
- List the characteristics and uses of Class A, B, C, D, and E addresses
- Identify the network ID and host ID fields for Class A, B, and C addresses

# Internet Protocol (IP)

TCP/IP operates in part because hundreds of millions if not billions of computers use a single, common addressing scheme called *IP addressing*. The IP protocol uses IP addresses capable of quickly and efficiently sending data in the form of datagrams to a specific computer anywhere in the world. For instance, if I'm in California reading Web pages from a Web site in Hong Kong, the datagrams carrying the Web content might pass through dozens of networks and routers as they travel from Hong Kong to my computer. Each datagram might be carried in any number of different Network Access layer protocols. The datagram might start on an Ethernet network then go through a router to a token-ring network then through another router to a Sonet network, and then through another router to an X.25 network, and so on. Finally the datagram arrives at the network adapter in my computer and is given to the IP protocol at its destination.

The point of this is twofold. First, the IP protocol uses a constant addressing scheme. The protocols (such as Ethernet, X.25, token ring, and Sonet) that operate at the lowest layer of the TCP/IP stack and actually carry the datagrams have incompatible addressing schemes. The addressing schemes used to carry datagrams on each network segment change as the datagram passes from network segment to network segment. However the IP addressing scheme remains constant, it is insulated from and unaffected by the unique implementation of each underlying network technology.

Second, ARP is used on every segment a datagram passes through to map IP addresses to physical addresses used by that network segment. These two protocols IP and ARP work together and with the Network Access layer to move datagrams between two endpoints.

One endpoint is the IP protocol located on the computer sending the datagram, often designated by the Source IP address. The other endpoint is the IP protocol located on the ultimate destination computer, defined by the Destination IP address.

The *Internet Protocol (IP)* is software that performs a number of functions. It is responsible for how datagrams are created and moved across a network. IP performs one set of tasks when transmitting data to a computer and a different set of tasks when receiving data from another computer. Three key 32-bit fields (areas of information) within the IP software are integral to its operation:

- IP Address field—A unique 32-bit address assigned to a computer, or more accurately, to a node. (The term node will be described later in this chapter.)
- Subnet Mask field—A 32-bit pattern of bits used to tell IP how to determine which part of the IP address is the network portion and which part is the host portion.
- Default Gateway field—An optional 32-bit address that, if present, identifies the address of a router. Datagrams destined for another network are sent to this address to be routed appropriately.

When sending data, IP on the source computer must determine whether the destination is on the same network (local), or if it is on a different network (remote). IP determines this by performing two calculations and comparing the results. If the results are identical, the destination is determined to be local; otherwise, the destination is determined to be remote. If the destination is local, IP can initiate direct communication. However, if the destination is remote then IP must communicate via a gateway (router), which in most cases is the default gateway. When the Source IP is finished preparing the datagram for transmission, it passes the datagram to the Network Access layer, which transmits the datagram on to the media to begin its journey to the destination computer.

When data arrives at the destination computer the Network Access layer receives it first. The Network Access layer checks the frame for corruption and delivery to the correct physical address. Assuming the frame arrived correctly, the Network Access layer extracts the data payload from the rest of the frame and passes it up to the protocol designated by the frame level type field. In this case we'll assume the data payload is passed to IP.

IP, upon receiving the datagram from the Network Access layer, first verifies that the datagram itself has not been corrupted in transit. Next, IP verifies that the datagram was delivered to the correct computer by comparing the Destination IP address contained within the datagram to the IP address of the computer. If these two addresses match, the datagram has been delivered to the correct destination. IP then checks fields within the datagram to see what instructions the Source IP has sent. These instructions request the Destination IP to perform some function; often the instructions are to deliver the data to either TCP or to UDP in the next higher layer of the TCP/IP stack.

4

# IP Header Fields

In networking virtually every layer or protocol needs to include information for its own use. This information is usually placed prior to the data and is generically referred to as a header. IP uses headers, as do Ethernet and token ring in the Network Access layer, and UDP and TCP in the Transport layer. A header has several distinct units of information, referred to as *fields*. A field might hold the address of where the datagram is headed or might describe what to do with the data when it arrives at its destination.

Every IP datagram contains an IP header in addition to the data payload it is carrying. *Data payload* refers to the data that any layer carries. The data payload is the entire data structure that was either passed down from the next higher layer at the sending end or passed up to the next higher layer at the receiving end.

IP on the source computer constructs the IP header. As mentioned earlier, IP at the destination examines instructions in the IP header to determine what it should do with the data payload of this datagram. A great deal of information exists in the IP header, including the IP addresses of the source host and destination host; there can even be instructions to routers. Every router through which the datagram travels on its path from the source computer to the destination computer also examines, and even updates, a portion of the IP header.

> For additional information about IP headers see RFC 791.

The minimum size for an IP header is 20 bytes. A header contains the information shown in Figure 4.1. The figure includes a scale across the top to help you identify how many bits are devoted to each field. The fields in the IP header are 4, 8, 16, or 32 bits in length.

- Version—Indicates which version of IP is being used. The current version of IP is 4. The binary pattern is 0100.
- Internet Header Length (IHL)—The length of the IP header in 32-bit words. The minimum header length is five 32-bit words. The typical binary pattern for this field is 0101.
- Type of Service—The Source IP can designate special routing information. The main choices include Low or Normal Delay, Normal or High Throughput, and Normal or High Reliability. There are seven other rarely used options.
- Total Length—Identifies the length, in octets, of the IP datagram. This length includes the IP header and the data payload.

**FIGURE 4.1**

*An IP header field.*

| 0 1 2 3 | 4 5 6 7 | 8 9 10 11 12 13 14 15 | 16 17 18 19 20 21 22 23 24 25 26 27 28 29 30 31 |
|---|---|---|---|
| Version | IHL | Type of Service | Total Length |
| Identification | | Flags | Fragment Offset |
| Time to Live | Protocol | Header Checksum | |
| Source IP address | | | |
| Destination IP address | | | |
| IP data payload (many bytes) | | | |

- Identification—An incrementing sequenced number assigned to datagrams by the Source IP.

- Flags—Flags indicate fragmentation possibilities. There are a total of three flags, the first of which is unused. A DF (Don't Fragment) flag will signify whether fragmentation is allowed, and the MF (More Fragments) flag will signify that the datagram is a fragment. When set to 0, the MF flag indicates that no more fragments exist or that it never was fragmented.

> Fragmentation occurs when the source of a TCP/IP datagram is on a network that allows large data payloads, such as token ring. For instance, a TCP/IP datagram could start with a data payload of 4,000 bytes. If the datagram is routed through an Ethernet network where the maximum IP data payload is 1,480 bytes, fragmentation must occur. If fragmentation is allowed, the router will break the large data payload into several smaller data fragments and send them through the Ethernet network as several datagrams. At the destination the fragmented datagrams are reassembled.

- Fragment offset—A numeric value assigned to each successive fragment. IP at the destination uses the fragment offset to reassemble the fragments into the proper order.

4

- Time to Live—Indicates the amount of time in seconds or *router hops* that the datagram can survive before being discarded. Every router examines and decrements this field by at least 1, or by the number of seconds the datagram is delayed inside the router. The datagram is discarded when this field reaches zero.

**NEW TERM**   A *hop* or a *router hop* correlates to a router that a datagram travels through on its way to its destination. If a datagram passes through five routers before arriving at its destination, the destination is said to be five hops, or five router hops, away.

- Protocol—This field holds the protocol address to which IP should deliver the data payload.

| Protocol Name | Protocol Address |
| --- | --- |
| ICMP | 1 |
| TCP | 6 |
| UDP | 17 |

- Header checksum—This field holds a 16-bit calculated value to verify the validity of the header only. This field is recomputed in every router as the TTL field decrements.
- Source IP address—This address is used by the Destination IP when sending a response.
- Destination IP address—This address is used by the Destination IP to verify correct delivery.
- IP data payload—This field typically contains data destined for delivery to TCP or UDP in the Transport layer, ICMP, or IGMP. The amount of data is variable but could include thousands of bytes.

# IP Addressing

IP addresses, like street addresses, ensure that items can be delivered to the correct location. A mail carrier uses both the street name and the address number to know where to deliver the mail. The IP address is also divided into two portions, the network ID and the host ID. The network ID correlates to a street name; every house on the street uses the same street name. Likewise, every computer on a network uses the same network ID. Following the same analogy, every house on a street has a different street address. Likewise, every computer on a network has a different host ID.

Some streets are short and only have a few addresses; other streets are long and have many addresses. And to make the analogy work, some streets are of medium length with a medium number of addresses. The network ID correlates to the number of streets (and the number of available networks). A large network ID correlates to many streets (that is, networks) while a small network ID correlates to a fewer number of streets. The host ID correlates to the number of addresses on a street, or addresses on a network. A large host ID allows for many addresses, while a small host ID allows a small number of addresses.

## Network ID and Host ID

Theoretically, every computer that uses TCP/IP should have a unique 32-bit address.

> In practice, the use of proxy server software bends the rule that requires every computer to have a unique 32-bit address, but this is an advanced topic that we can safely ignore right now.

The 32-bit address is broken into two distinct groupings. One group of bits is the network ID. The remaining group of bits is the host ID. The actual location where the network ID ends and host ID begins is based on the address class to which the network ID belongs. This is covered in detail in the section "Address Classes" later in this chapter.

In a network such as a LAN, every computer using TCP/IP should have the same network ID, because all the computers are part of the same network. Also, within the network (LAN), every computer must have a unique host ID. Local administrators assign addresses that contain unique host IDs when installing and configuring TCP/IP on computers. You can either lease a network ID from your ISP, or you can be assigned a network ID by the Internet Assigned Numbers Authority (IANA).

Because all IP addresses on a network share the same network ID, local administrators must assign unique host IDs, which when combined with the network ID create unique IP addresses. The word *host* is used to identify a computer that is attached to a network. Most computers are configured with only one IP address, and for these computers you can think of the IP address as the IP address for the computer. However, computers such as servers typically have multiple network adapters, hence, multiple IP addresses. It is even possible to assign multiple IP addresses to a single network adapter. In these situations you don't want to correlate a computer with a single IP address because it actually has multiple addresses. So, to be more exact we use the term *node*, where a node is a point of contact such as a NIC card, for example. To summarize, each host ID corresponds to a node, and a single computer host can have multiple host IDs and therefore, multiple nodes.

# Working with Octets

As mentioned previously, IP uses a 32-bit address, which is a pattern of 32 0s and 1s. It is difficult for people to remember 32 of anything in order, let alone a seemingly meaningless pattern of 0s and 1s. To make this pattern easier to work with, the pattern is broken into four groupings known as *octets*. Each octet contains eight binary bits that are converted into a single decimal number for easier use. With eight bits there are exactly 256 possible combinations; any octet pattern will always convert to a number from 0 to 255.

In order to work with TCP/IP you need to know how to convert a binary octet into a decimal number and also be able to perform the reverse conversion, which converts a decimal number into a binary octet. Although these conversions are easily performed with a scientific calculator, TCP/IP technicians should know how to perform the conversion using pencil and paper.

The following sections show how to perform the conversions, as well as compute a variation of the binary octet to decimal number conversion in which a 32-bit binary number is converted into what is called dotted-decimal notation.

## Converting a Binary Octet to a Decimal Number

Before we get into converting you must first learn the powers of 2 because a binary number is based on powers of 2. Figure 4.2 shows the eight different powers of 2 that you must learn. Binary numbers always start with the number 1 and double each time. The pattern goes like this 1, 2, 4, 8, 16, 32, 64, and 128. That's it! Notice that the number 1 is located to the right end of the figure while the number 128 is located at the left end of the figure. This correlates to the decimal system with 1s, 10s, 100s 1,000s and so on, which places the larger numbers to the left and the smaller numbers to the right.

**FIGURE 4.2**

*Powers of 2 and their decimal equivalents.*

| Binary (powers of 2) | $2^7$ | $2^6$ | $2^5$ | $2^4$ | $2^3$ | $2^2$ | $2^1$ | $2^0$ |
|---|---|---|---|---|---|---|---|---|
| Decimal equivalent | 128 | 64 | 32 | 16 | 8 | 4 | 2 | 1 |

If you can add then you can convert from binary to decimal.

Start by writing down the decimal equivalents for only those bit positions where one bit is present, that is you ignore the positions that have 0s. Then add the numbers you have written down. For instance, given the pattern 10000001 with one bits at either end of the pattern, the one bit at the left end of the pattern represents the number 128, and the one bit at the right end of the pattern represents the number 1. To convert, add the number 128 to the number 1; the result is 129. You could write this as an addition problem, for example 128 + 1 = 129. Therefore, the binary pattern 10000001 is equivalent to the decimal number 129.

Now lets try a little more difficult pattern. Given the pattern 10010100 the bits that are ones represent the decimal numbers 128, 16, and 8. Writing this down as an addition problem becomes 128 + 16 + 8 = 148. Therefore, the binary pattern 10010100 is equivalent to the decimal number 148.

If you feel you need more practice with converting binary to decimal you can check the Workshop section near the end of this hour, which has a number of practice problems with the correct answers.

## Converting 32-Bit Binary Number to Dotted-Decimal Notation

In the previous section you learned how to convert an 8-bit octet to its decimal number equivalent. Remember that IP uses 32 bits, not 8. To represent an entire 32-bit binary number we use what is known as *dotted-decimal notation*, which is basically four decimal numbers separated by decimal points. An example of dotted-decimal notation number appears as 192.59.66.200. In this case the four numbers are arbitrary; each individual number could have been any number between 0 and 255.

> Because the numbers in each of the four locations are variable, sometimes the letters w, x, y, and z are used to represent the four variables. You might also see dotted-decimal notation represented as w.x.y.z or even as a combination of decimal numbers and letters such as 172.10.y.z. This might be confusing at first but will make more sense as you gain experience.

To convert the binary pattern 11000000001110110100001011001000 into the much more usable dotted-decimal notation format, follow these steps:

1. Write the 32-bit binary pattern:

   11000000001110110100001011001000

2. Rewrite the pattern as four octet (8-bit) patterns:

   11000000 00111011 01000010 11001000

3. Take one octet at a time and convert it to its decimal number equivalent:

   11000000 equates to 128 + 64 = 192

   00111011 equates to 32 + 16 + 8 + 2 + 1 = 59

   01000010 equates to 64 + 2 = 66

   11001000 equates to 128 + 64 + 8 = 200

4. Write the dotted-decimal notation by combining the results from step 3:

   192.59.66.200

## Converting a Decimal Number to a Binary Octet

Converting from decimal to binary requires a number of steps, but again it is not difficult. In the following example we convert the decimal number 207 into its binary equivalent.

To convert a decimal number to a binary octet, follow these steps:

1. Write down the decimal number you want to convert:

   207

2. Compare the decimal number (in this case 207) to the number 128. If the decimal number is greater than or equal to 128, subtract 128, otherwise, subtract 0 to create a new decimal number.

   Is 207 >= 128        Answer = Yes        207 - 128 = 79

3. Take the result from step 2 (in this case 79) and compare it to the number 64. If the decimal number is greater than or equal to 64, subtract 64; otherwise, subtract 0 to create a new decimal number.

   Is 79 >= 64          Answer = Yes        79 – 64 = 15

4. Take the result from step 3 (in this case 15) and compare it to the number 32. If the decimal number is greater than or equal to 32, subtract 32; otherwise, subtract 0 to create a new decimal number.

   Is 15 >= 32          Answer = No         15 – 0 = 15

5. Compare the result from step 4 to each successively smaller power of 2 (as you have been doing so far). If the answer in the comparison is Yes, subtract the power of 2; if the answer is No, subtract 0.

   Is 15 >= 16          Answer = No         15 – 0 = 15

   Is 15 >= 8           Answer = Yes        15 – 8 = 7

   Is 7 >= 4            Answer = Yes        7 – 4 = 3

   Is 3 >= 2            Answer = Yes        3 – 2 = 1

   Is 1 >= 1            Answer = Yes        1 – 1 = 0

6. Write down Y for Yes and N for No to create a pattern of eight Ys and Ns that match the eight comparisons you performed.

   YYNNYYYY

7. Convert each Y to a 1 and each N to a 0.

   11001111

You have now converted the decimal number 207 to its binary equivalent 11001111. Over time you will be able to develop shortcuts to reduce the number of steps. But until you are comfortable converting, you should use this method. It is fairly easy to follow and it works for any decimal number between 0 and 255.

# Address Classes

When TCP/IP was in its infancy, nobody imagined the extent to which it would grow. A 32-bit binary number can represent over four billion different numbers. If the 32-bit numbers are used as addresses then theoretically they should support over four billion computers. In practice however, the number of computers capable of being supported by TCP/IP is not four billion, but it is nonetheless a very large number of computers.

This extremely large address range has been broken down into smaller groups known as classes. The three most important classes are Class A, B, and C and these are used to refer to different types of network IDs.

- Class A addresses have 8-bit network IDs and are assigned to entities (that is organizations, companies, or countries) that can demonstrate a need for a large number of IP addresses. There is a maximum of 126 possible Class A networks.

- Class B addresses have 16-bit network IDs and are assigned to entities that can demonstrate a need for a medium number of IP addresses. There are about 16,000 Class B networks.

- Class C addresses have 24-bit network IDs and are assigned to entities that can demonstrate a need for a small number of IP addresses. There are over two million Class C networks.

## Class A

A Class A network contains eight network ID bits and 24 host ID bits. This means Class A networks can support approximately $2^{24}$ or 16,777,216 computers. In practice the actual number of computers supported is actually less. In a Class A network the leftmost bit is always off and therefore is always 0, but the remaining 31 bits can contain either 0 or 1 bits.

Some combinations of 0 and 1 bits are not allowed. A technique to calculate unusable addresses is presented in Hour 5, "Subnetting."

In a Class A network the leftmost 8 bits comprise the network ID and the rightmost 24 bits comprise the host ID. In the following layout each *x* character represents a variable that could be either a 0 or a 1. The *N* characters represent the bit positions that relate to the network ID, and the *H* characters represent the bit positions that relate to the host ID.

0xxxxxxx xxxxxxxx xxxxxxxx xxxxxxxx

NNNNNNNN HHHHHHHH HHHHHHHH HHHHHHHH

IP uses a pattern of 32 bits called a subnet mask to help separate the network ID from the host ID. The default subnet mask for a Class A network follows.

11111111 00000000 00000000 00000000

Notice the 1 bits correspond to the location of the network ID and the 0 bits correspond to the location of the host ID. If you convert the Class A default subnet mask to dotted-decimal notation it appears as 255.0.0.0.

If you convert just the 8 bits that comprise the network ID into all the possible combinations, the decimal equivalents fall between 0 and 127. Table 4.1 shows a few entries from the beginning and end of the range of possible numbers.

**TABLE 4.1**  BEGINNING AND ENDING CLASS A NETWORK IDS

| Leftmost Octet | Decimal Equivalent | Purpose |
| --- | --- | --- |
| 00000000 | 0 | This Network |
| 00000001 | 1 | First Usable Class A network ID |
| 00000010 | 2 | Usable Class A network ID |
| 00000011 | 3 | Usable Class A network ID |
| 0xxxxxxx | 4–123 (all intervening) | Usable Class A network IDs |
| 01111100 | 124 | Usable Class A network ID |
| 01111101 | 125 | Usable Class A network ID |
| 01111110 | 126 | Last usable Class A network ID |
| 01111111 | 127 | Loopback or localhost |

Remember that for Class A network IDs the leftmost bit is always 0, so there are only seven network bits that can be manipulated. Notice the first usable network ID is 1 and the last usable network ID is 126.

In general throughout TCP/IP, patterns that contain all zeros or all ones have special meaning and are never assigned to nodes.

In Class A networks, the all 1s pattern (decimal 127), has the designated purpose of referring to whatever computer you are currently working on.

To summarize Class A networks

- The leftmost octet has a decimal number between 1 and 126.
- Each Class A network supports approximately 16.7 million hosts.
- Class A network IDs are assigned to entities that need to support a very large number of hosts.

## Class B

A Class B network contains 16 network ID bits and 16 host ID bits, meaning that Class B networks can support approximately $2^{16}$ or 65,536 computers. In practice the actual maximum number of computers supported is 65,534. In Class B networks the leftmost bit is always on, and therefore is 1; the next bit is always off, and therefore is 0, but the remaining 30 bits can contain either 0 or 1 bits.

> Some combinations of addresses are unusable. A technique to calculate these addresses is presented in Hour 5.

In Class B networks the leftmost 16 bits comprise the network ID and the rightmost 16 bits comprise the host ID. In the following layout each *x* character represents a variable that could be either a 0 or a 1. The *N* characters represent the bit positions that relate to the network ID, and the *H* characters represent the bit positions that relate to the host ID.

10xxxxxx xxxxxxxx xxxxxxxx xxxxxxxx

NNNNNNNN NNNNNNNN HHHHHHHH HHHHHHHH

The default subnet mask for a Class B network is listed here.

11111111 11111111 00000000 00000000

Notice the 1 bits correspond to the location of the network ID and the 0 bits correspond to the location of the host ID. If you convert the Class B default subnet mask to dotted-decimal notation it appears as 255.255.0.0.

If you convert just the 8 bits that comprise the leftmost octet from the network ID into all the possible combinations, the decimal equivalents fall between 128 and 191. Table 4.2 shows a few entries from the beginning of the range of possible numbers and a few entries from the end.

Remember that for Class B network IDs the two leftmost bits are always 10, so there are 14 network bits that can be manipulated. Notice the first usable network ID is 128 and the last usable network ID is 191.

**TABLE 4.2** BEGINNING AND ENDING CLASS B NETWORK IDs

| Left Two Octets | Decimal Equivalent | Purpose |
| --- | --- | --- |
| 10000000 00000000 | 128.0 | Used to identify this network (all zeros) |
| 10000000 00000001 | 128.1 | First Usable Class B network ID |
| 10000000 00000010 | 128.2 | Usable Class B network ID |
| 10000000 00000011 | 128.3 | Usable Class B network ID |
| 10xxxxxx xxxxxxxx | (all 16,528 intervening) | Usable Class B network IDs |
| 10111111 11111100 | 191.252 | Usable Class B network ID |
| 10111111 11111101 | 191.253 | Usable Class B network ID |
| 10111111 11111110 | 191.254 | Last usable Class B network ID |
| 10111111 11111111 | 191.255 | Used for Broadcast (all ones) |

To summarize Class B networks

- The leftmost octet has a decimal number between 128 and 191.
- Each Class B network supports up to 65,534 hosts.
- Class B network IDs are assigned to entities that need to support a medium number of hosts.

## Class C

A Class C network contains 24 network ID bits and 8 host ID bits. This means Class C networks can support approximately $2^8$ or 256 computers. In practice the actual maximum number of computers supported is 254. Class C networks always have the leftmost two bits on and the third bit off, but the remaining 29 bits can contain either 0 or 1 bits.

> Some combinations of addresses are not usable. A technique to calculate
> unusable addresses is presented in Hour 5.

In a Class C network the leftmost 24 bits comprise the network ID and the rightmost 8 bits comprise the host ID. In the following layout each *x* character represents a variable that can be either a 0 or a 1. The *N* characters represent the bit positions that relate to the network ID, and the *H* characters represent the bit positions that relate to the host ID.

110xxxxx xxxxxxxx xxxxxxxx xxxxxxxx

NNNNNNNN NNNNNNNN NNNNNNNN HHHHHHHH

The default subnet mask for a Class C network is listed here.

11111111 11111111 11111111 00000000

Notice the 1 bits correspond to the location of the network ID and the 0 bits correspond to the location of the host ID. If you convert the Class C default subnet mask to dotted-decimal notation it will appear as 255.255.255.0.

Remember that for Class C network IDs the leftmost three bits are always 110, so there are 21 network bits that can be manipulated. If you convert just the 8 bits that comprise the leftmost octet from the network ID into all the possible combinations, you find that the decimal equivalents fall between 192 and 223. Table 4.3 shows a few entries from the beginning of the range of possible numbers and a few entries from the end.

**TABLE 4.3**  BEGINNING AND ENDING CLASS C NETWORK IDs

| Left Three Octets | Decimal Equivalent | Purpose |
| --- | --- | --- |
| 11000000 00000000 00000000 | 192.0.0 | Used to identify this network (all zeros) |
| 11000000 00000000 00000001 | 192.0.1 | First Usable Class C network ID |
| 11000000 00000000 00000010 | 192.0.2 | Usable Class C network ID |
| 11000000 00000000 00000011 | 192.0.3 | Usable Class C network ID |
| 110xxxxx xxxxxxxx xxxxxxxx | (all 2,097,144 intervening) | Usable Class C network IDs |
| 11011111 11111111 11111100 | 223.255.252 | Usable Class C network ID |
| 11011111 11111111 11111101 | 223.255.253 | Usable Class C network ID |
| 11011111 11111111 11111110 | 223.255.254 | Last usable Class C network ID |
| 11011111 11111111 11111111 | 223.255.255 | Used for Broadcast (all ones) |

To summarize Class C networks

- The leftmost octet has a decimal number between 192 and 223.
- Each Class C network supports up to 254 hosts.
- Class C network IDs are assigned to entities that need to support a small number of hosts.

## Class D

IP addresses from Class D networks are not assigned to hosts as are IP addresses from Class A, B, or C networks. Typically, IP can send a message to one specific destination or it can broadcast to every computer on a network. Suppose I want to send a message to 100 of the 254 computers on a Class C network. I would have to send the same message 100 times, which is not an efficient process for performing this rather simple task.

The four leftmost bits of a Class D network address always start with the binary pattern 1110, which corresponds to decimal numbers 224 through 239.

Class D network addresses are used for multicasting. Using multicasts, a single message can be selectively sent to a subset of all the computers on the network. For instance, in a countywide system, fire stations within established geographic boundaries could be assigned a Class D network address. All stations within a geographic region could then be quickly notified of a major fire by multicasting a message to the appropriate Class D address.

> The Internet Group Management Protocol (IGMP) is an Internet layer proto-
> col used in conjunction with multicasting and Class D addresses.

Multicasting is an advanced topic and is not covered in any greater depth in this book.

## Class E

Class E networks are considered experimental. They are not normally used in any production environment.

The five leftmost bits of a Class E network always start with the binary pattern 11110, which corresponds to decimal numbers 240 through 247.

# Address Resolution Protocol (ARP)

The Address Resolution Protocol is the second key TCP/IP protocol that resides within the Internet layer. The purpose of ARP is to resolve a physical address from an IP address. ARP queries machines on the local network for their physical addresses. ARP also maintains IP to physical address pairs in its cache memory.

Whenever IP needs to communicate with any other computer the ARP cache is first consulted to see if the IP address for the desired local computer or for the router is present in cache. If the IP address is in the ARP cache then the corresponding physical address is used to send a datagram directly to the desired physical network adapter. If the IP address is not in the ARP cache then ARP issues a broadcast on the LAN. The ARP request includes the IP address of the intended local computer or router. Every machine on the LAN examines the IP address contained within the ARP request. If the IP address matches the IP address of one of the computers then that computer will generate an ARP reply that includes the corresponding physical address. ARP then adds the IP to physical address combination to its cache, and IP can proceed and send its datagram directly to the desired network adapter.

To increase efficiency, every computer that receives an ARP request adds the physical/IP address pair to its ARP cache. If there is a need to contact the computer that issued the ARP request, the physical address will already be in ARP cache.

*RARP* stands for Reverse ARP. RARP performs the opposite function as ARP. ARP is used when the IP address is known but the physical address is not known. RARP is used when the physical address is known but the IP address is not known. RARP is also used in conjunction with the BOOTP protocol and is usually used to boot diskless workstations.

4

> *BOOTP (BOOT Prom)*—Many network adapters contain an empty socket for insertion of an integrated circuit known as a Boot Prom. The Boot Prom has a protocol (BOOTP) that starts as soon as the computer is powered on. It loads an operating system into the computer by reading it from a network server instead of a local disk drive. The operating system located on the server is pre-built for a specific IP address. The physical address selects which copy of the operating system to download into the remote boot computer.

# Internet Control Message Protocol (ICMP)

This Internet Control Message Protocol is the third key protocol that resides within the Internet layer. Routers principally use this protocol. Data sent to a remote computer travels through one or more routers; these routers can encounter a number of problems in sending the message to its ultimate destination. Routers use ICMP messages to notify the Source IP of these problems.

The most common ICMP messages are listed here. Quite a few other conditions generate ICMP messages but their frequency of occurrence is quite low.

- Echo Request and Echo Reply—ICMP is often used during testing. When a technician uses the ping command to check connectivity with another host he or she is in fact using ICMP. Ping sends a datagram to an IP address and requests the destination computer to return the data sent in a response datagram. The commands actually being used are the ICMP Echo Request and Echo Reply.

- Source Quench—If a fast computer is sending large amounts of data to a remote computer the volume can overwhelm the router. The router might use ICMP to send a Source Quench message to the Source IP to, in effect, ask it to slow down the rate at which it is shipping data. If necessary, additional source quenches can be sent to the Source IP.

- Destination Unreachable—If a router receives a datagram that cannot be delivered, ICMP returns a Destination Unreachable message to the Source IP. One reason that a router cannot deliver a message is a down network due to equipment failure or maintenance.

- Time Exceeded—ICMP sends a Time Exceeded message to the Source IP if a datagram is discarded because TTL reaches zero. This indicates the destination is too many router hops away to reach with the current TTL value, or it indicates router table problems that cause the datagram to loop through the same routers continuously.

**NEW TERM**  A *routing loop* occurs when a datagram circulates through the same routers continuously and never reaches its destination. Suppose three routers are located in L.A., San Francisco, and Denver. The L.A. router sends datagrams to San Francisco, which sends them to Denver, which sends them back to L.A. again. The datagram becomes essentially trapped and will circulate continuously through these three routers until the TTL reaches zero. A routing loop should not occur, but occasionally does.

- Fragmentation Needed—ICMP sends a Fragmentation Needed message if it receives a datagram with the Don't Fragment bit set and if the router needs to fragment the datagram in order to forward the datagram to the next router or the destination.

# Summary

In this hour you learned that IP, ARP, and ICMP are three of the five key Internet layer protocols. IP uses IP addresses to communicate with other computers using TCP/IP. The Source IP determines if the destination host is local or remote. IP can communicate directly with local hosts. IP communicates with remote hosts via a router. ARP resolves IP addresses to physical addresses, and ICMP is used to send router messages.

You learned how to convert dotted-decimal notation into a 32-bit binary address.

Finally, you learned that IP addresses are assigned based on the needs of the requesting organization. Class A addresses are reserved for extremely large organizations. Class B addresses are for medium-sized organizations. Class C addresses are for small organizations. Class D is for multicasting. Class E addresses are experimental.

# Q&A

**Q  Whom would you contact if you need to acquire a Class C address for your 100-employee company?**

**A**  You should direct this request to your ISP, or if you are your own ISP you can direct the request to IANA.

**Q  What are ones bits in the default subnet mask associated with?**

**A**  The network ID.

**Q  A 32-bit binary number is more easily identified after converting it into what format?**

**A**  Dotted-decimal notation.

**Q  ARP returns what type of information when given an IP address?**

**A**  The corresponding physical address, but only if the IP address is local.

**Q  If a router is unable to keep up with the volume of traffic, what type of ICMP message is sent to the Source IP?**

**A**  A Source Quench message.

**Q  What class does an IP address belong to that starts with the binary pattern 110 as the three leftmost bits?**

**A**  A Class C network.

4

# Workshop

Convert the following binary octets to their decimal number equivalents.

| | |
|---|---|
| 00101011 | Answer = 43 |
| 01010010 | Answer = 82 |
| 11010110 | Answer = 214 |
| 10110111 | Answer = 183 |
| 01001010 | Answer = 74 |
| 01011101 | Answer = 93 |
| 10001101 | Answer = 141 |
| 11011110 | Answer = 222 |

Convert the following decimal numbers to their binary-octet equivalent.

| | |
|---|---|
| 13 | Answer = 00001101 |
| 184 | Answer = 10111000 |
| 238 | Answer = 11101110 |
| 37 | Answer = 00100101 |
| 98 | Answer = 01100010 |
| 161 | Answer = 10100001 |
| 243 | Answer = 11110011 |
| 189 | Answer = 10111101 |

Convert the following 32-bit IP addresses into dotted-decimal notation.

| | |
|---|---|
| 11001111 00001110 00100001 01011100 | Answer = 207.14.33.92 |
| 00001010 00001101 01011001 01001101 | Answer = 10.13.89.77 |
| 10111101 10010011 01010101 01100001 | Answer = 189.147.85.97 |

## Key Terms

Review the following list of key terms:

- Address Resolution Protocol (ARP)—A key Internet layer protocol used to acquire the physical address for a local IP address. ARP maintains a cache of recently resolved IP to physical address pairs.
- Class A, B, C, D, and E—A classification system for dividing IP addresses into groups of large, medium, small, multicast, and experimental networks.

- Host ID—A portion of the IP address that refers to a node on the network. Each node within a network should have an IP address that contains a unique host ID.

- Internet Control Message Protocol (ICMP)—A key Internet layer protocol used by routers to send messages that inform the Source IP of routing problems. Also used by the ping command to determine the status of other hosts on the network.

- Internet Group Management Protocol (IGMP)—A TCP/IP protocol used in conjunction with multicasting and Class D addresses.

- Internet Protocol (IP)—A key Internet layer protocol used for addressing, delivering, and routing datagrams.

- Multicast—Allows datagrams to be delivered to a group of hosts simultaneously.

- Network ID—A portion of the IP address that refers to a given physical network. All computers on a network should contain an IP address with the same network ID.

- Node—A point of contact, each TCP/IP address becomes an end-point for communication. Most computers have one node, but others such as servers and routers might have many IP addresses and therefore many nodes.

- Reverse Address Resolution Protocol (RARP)—A TCP/IP protocol that returns an IP address if given a physical address. This protocol is typically used by diskless workstations that have a remote Boot Prom installed in their network adapter.

4

# HOUR 5

# Internet Layer: Subnetting

*By Bob Willsey*

*Subnetting* is the process of dividing a block of IP addresses assigned as a Class A, B, or C network into multiple, smaller blocks of addresses. After they are divided, you can use these smaller address blocks to more effectively meet your networking needs.

This chapter addresses the needs and benefits of subnetting, as well as the steps and procedures you should follow to generate a subnet mask that fits your needs.

## Goals for this Hour

At the completion of this hour, you will be able to

- Explain how subnets and supernets are used
- Explain the benefits of subnetting

- Develop a subnet mask that meets business needs
- Discriminate between valid and invalid IP addresses

# What Is a Subnet?

Typically companies or organizations request and are assigned a network ID from their ISP, and large ISPs are assigned blocks of Class C and possibly Class B network IDs from the Internet Assigned Number Authority (IANA) (formerly InterNIC). (The IANA is the organization responsible for assigning IP addresses in an efficient manner world-wide.) For example, a company with 100 employees would be assigned a Class C network address. As you recall from our discussion in Hour 4,"The Internet Layer" a Class C address allows for 254 usable nodes, which should be more than enough for 100 people. But what if this company is structured into 10 person offices in 10 cities? How would you connect all 100 people in these distant locations using one network ID? The answer is to subnet. As mentioned in this hour's introduction, subnetting is a technique for dividing Class A, B, or C IP address blocks into multiple, smaller IP address blocks of addresses for more efficient usage.

## Benefits of Subnetting

There are several reasons why you might want or need to subnet a network ID. The preceding scenario is the most common reason for subnetting. However, other compelling reasons exist for you to consider subnetting:

- Reduce congestion—Placing large numbers of users on a single network segment is an invitation for congestion. A 10Base-T network with 254 users typically has many collisions and poor performance. However, 30 users on a 10Base-T network usually works quite well. Subnetting allows you to build network segments that service fewer machines.

 An alternative method for reducing congestion is through the use of *switched hubs*. Switched hubs can reduce congestion without the need for routers or subnets.

- Support different technologies—Suppose your network is part Token Ring, part Ethernet, and part AppleTalk. How could you spread your network ID to cover these different technologies? Subnetting allows you to use one network ID with nodes connected to different technologies.

An alternative method for connecting dissimilar technologies is through the use of networking equipment known as translating bridges. However many network designers prefer routers for this purpose. *Routers* are networking equipment that can forward packets from one network to another network; they are covered in more detail in Hour 9, "Routers, Brouters, and Bridges".

- Handle technology-imposed limits—Technologies place a limit on the maximum number of devices allowed per network segment. For example, the Ethernet specifications impose a 1,024 device limit per network segment. If you have a Class B network with 65,534 IP addresses, you will find a 1,024 device limit to be an unacceptable restriction.

- Security—Routers, by their nature, isolate one network segment from another. This isolation can provide a basic level of security.

- Reduce disruption from broadcasts—Broadcasts are packets directed to every node attached to a network segment. Broadcasts are disruptive because they cause every computer to stop what it is currently doing and spend a few milliseconds deciding whether it needs to respond to the broadcast. Subnets allow you to place fewer computers on a network segment, which reduces the number of computers affected by broadcasts.

- Wide area network support—As mentioned previously, a company or organization with multiple geographically separated locations can use a single network ID across multiple LANs.

## Implementing Subnetting

The process of subnetting should not be taken lightly, as it does require a good amount of forethought, planning, and precision. Many people find the subject daunting, tedious, or even scary. But be assured it doesn't have to be that way. The process is actually very logical and has only a few rules that you must abide by.

If you buy a pie at the local pie shop and take it home, how do you decide how many pieces to cut the pie into? You would probably first determine how many hungry people are present then cut the pie into the appropriate number of slices. If four people are present, each slice is quite large; if 16 people are present everybody is only going to get a sliver.

The pie example is analogous to subnetting. If you divide a block of addresses from a network ID into four groups, each group still has a fairly large number of addresses. If it is divided into 16 or more groups, obviously there are fewer addresses per group.

5

One of the rules of subnetting is you must throw away the first and the last item. You lose two groups of addresses: One group is from the beginning of the block of network addresses while the second group is from the end of the block of network addresses. Returning to the pie example, if the pie is cut into two pieces, and the two pieces are thrown away, nobody eats! If the pie is cut into four slices, half the pie gets thrown away. If the pie is cut into eight slices, then two slices or one quarter of the pie is wasted. If the pie is cut into 16 narrow slices, then only two slices or one eighth of the total is lost, and so on. As you can see, the more slices you make, the less the amount of total waste. The same is true for subnetting. When you subnet a network ID, the amount of loss can range from a small percentage to, in the worse case, roughly half the addresses. As in the pie example the greatest loss from eliminating the first and last group occurs when the number of subnets is small, while the least loss occurs when there are many subnets.

In addition to the losses just described, there are additional losses. You will recall that a Class C network ID has 256 addresses. However two of the addresses, the first and last, are not usable. This leaves 254 usable addresses. When you create subnets, each subnet loses the first and the last address within the subnet. The greatest losses here occur when each group contains a small number of addresses.

Suppose you divide a Class C network with 256 addresses into 16 subnets, with 16 addresses per subnet. You would need to "throw away" two subnets, for example, $2 \times 16 = 32$ addresses. In the 14 remaining subnets you must also throw away two addresses per subnet, for example, $14 \times 2 = 28$ addresses. When combined, for example, $32 + 28 = 60$ you lose a total of 60 addresses from the original 256 due to subnetting.

If you look at the three conversion tables in the next section, you will notice that the least total loss occurs in the middle of the subnet range. You typically want to avoid using the ends of a subnet range if possible.

As you do your planning of how to subnet your network ID, try to find the best balance between the three items listed below. Be sure to plan for future growth so that you will not need to reengineer your subnets anytime soon.

1. A usable number of network segments.
2. A usable number of nodes per segment.
3. Minimal loss of IP addresses.

## Conversion Tables

The following tables show the allowable combinations of network segments and nodes you can derive when subnetting. Using the previous example of a Class C network with 10 locations of 10 people each, you can see that using four subnet bits from the leftmost column of the chart would allow up to 14 subnets with up to 14 nodes per subnetwork. This meets our current needs and allows for some future growth as well. If some offices grow to 20 people for instance, a second subnet can be used to handle the additional users.

At the beginning and end of each table you will notice rows that contain the word "Invalid." This indicates combinations of subnet bits that would yield either zero usable subnets, or zero usable nodes per subnet. These would be analogous to cutting the pie in half where no one would eat, or cutting the pie into such thin slices that again no one would eat. The valid portion of each table ranges from two usable subnets near the top of each chart, to two usable nodes near the bottom of each chart.

A Class C network can be subnetted as shown in Table 5.1.

**TABLE 5.1** CLASS C SUBNETTING

| # of subnet bits | Subnet mask | # of usable subnets | Total loss from first and last subnet | # of bits in node | # of usable nodes per subnet | Total loss from within subnets | Total aggregate IP address loss |
|---|---|---|---|---|---|---|---|
| 0 | 255.255.255.0 | Not Subnetted | 0 | 8 | 254 | NA | 2 |
| 1 | NA | Invalid | NA | 7 | NA | NA | NA |
| 2 | 255.255.255.192 | 1–2 | 128 | 6 | 62 | 4 | 132 |
| 3 | 255.255.255.240 | 1–6 | 64 | 5 | 30 | 12 | 76 |
| 4 | 255.255.255.248 | 1–14 | 32 | 4 | 14 | 28 | 60 |
| 5 | 255.255.255.252 | 1–30 | 16 | 3 | 6 | 60 | 76 |
| 6 | 255.255.255.254 | 1–62 | 8 | 2 | 2 | 128 | 132 |
| 7 | NA | Invalid | | 1 | Invalid | NA | NA |
| 8 | NA | Invalid | | 0 | Invalid | NA | NA |

A Class B network can be subnetted as shown in Table 5.2.

5

**TABLE 5.2**  CLASS B SUBNETTING

| # of subnet bits | Subnet mask | # of usable subnets | Total loss from first and last subnet | # of bits in node | # of usable nodes per subnet | Total loss from within subnets | Total aggregate IP address loss |
|---|---|---|---|---|---|---|---|
| 0 | 255.255.0.0 | Not Subnetted | 0 | 16 | 65534 | NA | 2 |
| 1 | NA | Invalid | NA | 15 | NA | NA | NA |
| 2 | 255.255.192.0 | 1–2 | 32768 | 14 | 16382 | 4 | 32772 |
| 3 | 255.255.224.0 | 1–6 | 16384 | 13 | 8190 | 12 | 16396 |
| 4 | 255.255.240.0 | 1–14 | 8192 | 12 | 4094 | 28 | 8220 |
| 5 | 255.255.248.0 | 1–30 | 4096 | 11 | 2046 | 60 | 4156 |
| 6 | 255.255.252.0 | 1–62 | 2048 | 10 | 1022 | 124 | 2172 |
| 7 | 255.255.254.0 | 1–126 | 1024 | 9 | 510 | 252 | 1276 |
| 8 | 255.255.255.0 | 1–254 | 512 | 8 | 254 | 508 | 1020 |
| 9 | 255.255.255.128 | 1–510 | 256 | 7 | 126 | 1020 | 1276 |
| 10 | 255.255.255.192 | 1–1022 | 128 | 6 | 62 | 2044 | 2172 |
| 11 | 255.255.255.224 | 1–2046 | 64 | 5 | 30 | 4092 | 4156 |
| 12 | 255.255.255.240 | 1–4094 | 32 | 4 | 14 | 8184 | 8216 |
| 13 | 255.255.255.248 | 1–8190 | 16 | 3 | 6 | 16380 | 16396 |
| 14 | 255.255.255.252 | 1–16382 | 8 | 2 | 2 | 32764 | 32772 |
| 15 | NA | Invalid | NA | 1 | Invalid | NA | NA |
| 16 | NA | Invalid | NA | 0 | Invalid | NA | NA |

A Class A network can be subnetted as shown in Table 5.3.

**TABLE 5.3** CLASS A SUBNETTING

| # of subnet bits | Subnet mask | # of usable subnets | Total loss from first and last subnet | # of bits in node | # of usable nodes per subnet | Total loss from within subnets | Total aggregate IP address loss |
|---|---|---|---|---|---|---|---|
| 0 | 255.0.0.0 | Not Subnetted | 0 | 24 | 16777214 | NA | 2 |
| 1 | NA | Invalid | NA | 23 | 8388606 | NA | NA |
| 2 | 255.192.0.0 | 1–2 | 8388608 | 22 | 4194032 | 4 | 8388612 |
| 3 | 255.224.0.0 | 1–6 | 4194034 | 21 | 2097150 | 12 | 4194046 |
| 4 | 255.240.0.0 | 1–14 | 2097152 | 20 | 1048574 | 28 | 2097180 |
| 5 | 255.248.0.0 | 1–30 | 1048576 | 19 | 524286 | 60 | 1048636 |
| 6 | 255.252.0.0 | 1–62 | 524288 | 18 | 262142 | 124 | 524412 |
| 7 | 255.254.0.0 | 1–126 | 262144 | 17 | 131070 | 252 | 262396 |
| 8 | 255.255.0.0 | 1–254 | 131072 | 16 | 65534 | 508 | 131580 |
| 9 | 255.255.128.0 | 1–510 | 65536 | 15 | 32764 | 1020 | 66556 |
| 10 | 255.255.192.0 | 1–1022 | 32768 | 14 | 16382 | 2044 | 34812 |
| 11 | 255.255.224.0 | 1–2046 | 16384 | 13 | 8190 | 4086 | 20470 |
| 12 | 255.255.240.0 | 1–4094 | 8192 | 12 | 4094 | 8184 | 16376 |
| 13 | 255.255.248.0 | 1–8190 | 4096 | 11 | 2046 | 16380 | 20476 |
| 14 | 255.255.252.0 | 1–16382 | 2048 | 10 | 1022 | 32764 | 34812 |
| 15 | 255.255.254.0 | 1–32766 | 1024 | 9 | 510 | 65532 | 65556 |
| 16 | 255.255.255.0 | 1–65534 | 512 | 8 | 254 | 131068 | 131580 |
| 17 | 255.255.255.128 | 1–131070 | 256 | 7 | 126 | 262140 | 262396 |
| 18 | 255.255.255.192 | 1–262142 | 128 | 6 | 62 | 524284 | 524412 |
| 19 | 255.255.255.224 | 1–524286 | 64 | 5 | 30 | 1048572 | 1048636 |
| 20 | 255.255.255.240 | 1–1048574 | 32 | 4 | 14 | 2097148 | 2097180 |
| 21 | 255.255.255.248 | 1–2097150 | 16 | 3 | 6 | 4194300 | 4194316 |
| 22 | 255.255.255.252 | 1–4194302 | 8 | 2 | 2 | 8388604 | 8388612 |
| 23 | NA | Invalid | NA | 1 | Invalid | NA | NA |
| 24 | NA | Invalid | NA | 0 | Invalid | NA | NA |

5

# Subnet Masks

A *subnet mask* is a 32-bit pattern of ones and zeros used to differentiate the network portion of an IP address from the host portion of the IP address.

 | For sanity's sake, it is highly suggested to construct subnet masks with all one bits left-justified and all zero bits right-justified. Trust me, you don't want to work with a subnet mask that violates this convention.

The subnet mask is used during two calculations. One calculation generates a result using the IP addresses of the source computer. The second calculation generates a result using the IP address of the destination computer. After both results have been generated, they are compared. If both results are identical, IP knows that both computers are located on the same network and can be contacted directly. If the results are different it indicates the destination computer is located on a different network segment. This causes IP to send packets to a router in order to leave this network segment.

Each class has its own *default subnet mask*. This mask is used when you are NOT subnetting. Table 5.4 lists the default subnet masks for all three classes.

**TABLE 5.4**   DEFAULT SUBNET MASKS

| Class | Dotted Notation | Binary Pattern |
|-------|-----------------|----------------|
| A | 255.0.0.0 | 11111111 00000000 00000000 00000000 |
| B | 255.255.0.0 | 11111111 11111111 00000000 00000000 |
| C | 255.255.255.0 | 11111111 11111111 11111111 00000000 |

Tables 5.5 and 5.6 show how a default Class C subnet mask is used to generate two results.

**TABLE 5.5** GENERATING RESULTS USING SUBNET MASKS

| Description | Source Host | Destination Host |
|---|---|---|
| | **IP Address** | |
| Dotted notation | 192.59.66.200 | 192.59.66.17 |
| Binary | 11000000 00111011 01000010 11001000 | 11000000 00111011 01000010 00010001 |
| | **Subnet Mask** | |
| Dotted notation | 255.255.255.0 | 255.255.255.0 |
| Binary | 11111111 11111111 11111111 00000000 | 11111111 11111111 11111111 00000000 |
| | **Result** | |
| Dotted notation | 192.59.66.0 | 192.59.66.0 |
| Binary | 11000000 00111011 01000010 00000000 | 11000000 00111011 01000010 00000000 |

In Table 5.5 both results are identical; this indicates that both computers are on the same network and therefore can communicate directly.

**TABLE 5.6** GENERATING RESULTS USING SUBNET MASKS

| Description | Source Host | Destination Host |
|---|---|---|
| | **IP Address** | |
| Dotted Notation | 192.59.66.200 | 192.13.130.12 |
| Binary | 11000000 00111011 01000010 11001000 | 11000000 00001101 10000010 00001100 |
| | **Subnet Mask** | |
| Dotted Notation | 255.255.255.0 | 255.255.255.0 |
| Binary | 11111111 11111111 11111111 00000000 | 11111111 11111111 11111111 00000000 |
| | **Result** | |
| Dotted Notation | 192.59.66.0 | 192.13.130.0 |
| Binary | 11000000 00111011 01000010 00000000 | 11000000 00001101 10000010 00000000 |

In Table 5.6 the results are different; this indicates that these computers are located on different networks and therefore must communicate through a router.

In Table 5.7 notice that both the source and destination computer IP addresses start with 192.59.66. This indicates they both belong to the 192.59.66.0 network. However, notice that this example uses a nondefault subnet mask. The result patterns indicate that these machines need to be remote from each other, even though they belong to the same network.

When you create nondefault subnet masks you are in essence borrowing two or more host bits and asking IP to interpret them as network bits.

In summary, the results indicate that these two IP addresses belong to different subnetworks even though they belong to identical networks. This allows you to create physically separate network segments within your company or organization. These separate segments can be located in different offices, or they can use different technologies such as Ethernet on one segment and Token Ring on another segment.

**TABLE 5.7**  GENERATING RESULTS USING A SUBNET MASK

| Description | Source Host | Destination Host |
| --- | --- | --- |
| **IP Address** | | |
| Dotted Notation | 192.59.66.200 | 192.59.66.13 |
| Binary | 11000000 00111011 01000010 11001000 | 11000000 00111011 01000010 00001101 |
| **Subnet Mask** | | |
| Dotted Notation | 255.255.255.240 | 255.255.255.240 |
| Binary | 11111111 11111111 11111111 11110000 | 11111111 11111111 11111111 11110000 |
| **Result** | | |
| Dotted Notation | 192.59.66.192 | 192.59.66.0 |
| Binary | 11000000 00111011 01000010 11000000 | 11000000 00111011 01000010 00000000 |

Table 5.8 shows the binary pattern equivalents of the dotted notation subnet masks. This table shows all possible subnet mask patterns that are valid and illustrates the need for my left-justified one bits suggestion. The Description column in Table 5.8 tells how many additional one bits are present beyond the one bits present in the default subnet mask. For example, the default Class A subnet mask has eight one bits; the row that displays "2 mask bits" means there are eight plus two or a total of ten one bits present in the subnet mask.

**TABLE 5.8**  SUBNET MASK DOTTED NOTATION TO BINARY PATTERN

| Description | Dotted Notation | Binary Pattern |
|---|---|---|
| **Class A** | | |
| Default Subnet Mask | 255.0.0.0 | 11111111 00000000 00000000 00000000 |
| 2 mask bits | 255.192.0.0 | 11111111 11000000 00000000 00000000 |
| 3 mask bits | 255.224.0.0 | 11111111 11100000 00000000 00000000 |
| 4 mask bits | 255.240.0.0 | 11111111 11110000 00000000 00000000 |
| 5 mask bits | 255.248.0.0 | 11111111 11111000 00000000 00000000 |
| 6 mask bits | 255.252.0.0 | 11111111 11111100 00000000 00000000 |
| 7 mask bits | 255.254.0.0 | 11111111 11111110 00000000 00000000 |
| 8 mask bits | 255.255.0.0 | 11111111 11111111 00000000 00000000 |
| 9 mask bits | 255.255.128.0 | 11111111 11111111 10000000 00000000 |
| 10 mask bits | 255.255.192.0 | 11111111 11111111 11000000 00000000 |
| 11 mask bits | 255.255.224.0 | 11111111 11111111 11100000 00000000 |
| 12 mask bits | 255.255.240.0 | 11111111 11111111 11110000 00000000 |
| 13 mask bits | 255.255.248 0 | 11111111 11111111 11111000 00000000 |
| 14 mask bits | 255.255.252.0 | 11111111 11111111 11111100 00000000 |
| 15 mask bits | 255.255.254.0 | 11111111 11111111 11111110 00000000 |
| 16 mask bits | 255.255.255.0 | 11111111 11111111 11111111 00000000 |
| 17 mask bits | 255.255.255.128 | 11111111 11111111 11111111 10000000 |
| 18 mask bits | 255.255.255.192 | 11111111 11111111 11111111 11000000 |
| 19 mask bits | 255.255.255.224 | 11111111 11111111 11111111 11100000 |
| 20 mask bits | 255.255.255.240 | 11111111 11111111 11111111 11110000 |
| 21 mask bits | 255.255.255.248 | 11111111 11111111 11111111 11111000 |
| 22 mask bits | 255.255.255.252 | 11111111 11111111 11111111 11111100 |
| **Class B** | | |
| Default Subnet Mask | 255.255.0.0 | 11111111 11111111 00000000 00000000 |
| 2 bit mask | 255.255.192.0 | 11111111 11111111 11000000 00000000 |
| 3 bit mask | 255.255.224.0 | 11111111 11111111 11100000 00000000 |
| 4 bit mask | 255.255.240.0 | 11111111 11111111 11110000 00000000 |
| 5 bit mask | 255.255.248.0 | 11111111 11111111 11111000 00000000 |
| 6 bit mask | 255.255.252.0 | 11111111 11111111 11111100 00000000 |
| 7 bit mask | 255.255.254.0 | 11111111 11111111 11111110 00000000 |

5

*continues*

**TABLE 5.8**  SUBNET MASK DOTTED NOTATION TO BINARY PATTERN

| Description | Dotted Notation | Binary Pattern |
| --- | --- | --- |
| 8 bit mask | 255.255.255.0 | 11111111 11111111 11111111 00000000 |
| 9 bit mask | 255.255.255.128 | 11111111 11111111 11111111 10000000 |
| 10 bit mask | 255.255.255.192 | 11111111 11111111 11111111 11000000 |
| 11 bit mask | 255.255.255.224 | 11111111 11111111 11111111 11100000 |
| 12 bit mask | 255.255.255.240 | 11111111 11111111 11111111 11110000 |
| 13 bit mask | 255.255.255.248 | 11111111 11111111 11111111 11111000 |
| 14 bit mask | 255.255.255.252 | 11111111 11111111 11111111 11111100 |
| **Class C** | | |
| Default subnet mask | 255.255.255.0 | 11111111 11111111 11111111 00000000 |
| 2 bit mask | 255.255.255.192 | 11111111 11111111 11111111 11000000 |
| 3 bit mask | 255.255.255.224 | 11111111 11111111 11111111 11100000 |
| 4 bit mask | 255.255.255.240 | 11111111 11111111 11111111 11110000 |
| 5 bit mask | 255.255.255.252 *248* | 11111111 11111111 11111111 11111000 |
| 6 bit mask | 255.255.255.254 *252* | 11111111 11111111 11111111 11111100 |

# Determining Address Validity

After you have decided on a subnet mask, you must calculate what IP addresses are valid and which are invalid. IP addresses are invalid if they have either all zero bits or all one bits within the host portion of the subnet mask. Likewise, when subnetting, those bits that comprise the subnet portion of the subnet mask also cannot be all zeros or all ones.

Obviously you should not use invalid addresses. But you must perform the calculation to first determine which addresses are invalid. You want to ensure that you do not configure any computer with an invalid address.

In addition, as mentioned earlier, the addresses at both the beginning and the end of the range are invalid. Refer to Table 5.9 for an example of the patterns of valid and invalid addresses. Assume the addresses are for a Class C network ID of 192.59.66.0 and a subnet mask of 255.255.255.240.

If you convert the rightmost one bit of the subnet mask into its binary equivalent, you have a starting point for determining valid and invalid addresses. The rightmost one bit in this subnet mask is the 16 bit. This means that addresses that end in the range of 0 through 16 are invalid. (Remember we throw out the first and last number as invalid.) Also, multiples of this number are invalid; for example the numbers 16, 32, 48, 64, 80,

96, 112, 128, 144, 160, 176, 192, 208, 224, and 240 indicate the first address of a subnet and are invalid. Numbers one less than these numbers are also invalid; for example 15, 31, 47, 63, 79, 95, 111, 127, 159, 175, 191, 207, 223, and 239 are invalid. They represent the last address within a subnet, which also is thrown out. Finally the last range of addresses, which spans from 240 through 255, is also invalid.

To summarize, the addresses that are invalid using Table 5.9 are as follows:

- The first range in the table, which includes 16 addresses from 192.59.66.255 through 192.59.66.240 (which relates to the last slice of pie).

- The last range in the table, which includes 16 addresses from 192.59.66.16 through 192.59.66.0 (which equates to the first slice of pie).

- Two addresses, the first and the last address from each remaining range, for a total of 28 additional invalid addresses.

**TABLE 5.9**  DETERMINE VALID ADDRESSES FOR CLASS C AND A SUBNET MASK OF 255.255.255.240

| Invalid Address | Valid Starting Address | Valid Ending Address | Invalid Address |
|---|---|---|---|
| 192.59.66.255 through 192.59.66.240 | | | |
| 192.59.66.224 | 192.59.66.225 | 192.59.66.238 | 192.59.66.239 |
| 192.59.66.208 | 192.59.66.209 | 192.59.66.222 | 192.59.66.223 |
| 192.59.66.192 | 192.59.66.193 | 192.59.66.206 | 192.59.66.207 |
| 192.59.66.176 | 192.59.66.177 | 192.59.66.190 | 192.59.66.191 |
| 192.59.66.160 | 192.59.66.161 | 192.59.66.174 | 192.59.66.175 |
| 192.59.66.144 | 192.59.66.145 | 192.59.66.158 | 192.59.66.159 |
| 192.59.66.128 | 192.59.66.129 | 192.59.66.142 | 192.59.66.143 |
| 192.59.66.112 | 192.59.66.113 | 192.59.66.126 | 192.59.66.127 |
| 192.59.66.96 | 192.59.66.97 | 192.59.66.110 | 192.59.66.111 |
| 192.59.66.80 | 192.59.66.81 | 192.59.66.94 | 192.59.66.95 |
| 192.59.66.64 | 192.59.66.65 | 192.59.66.78 | 192.59.66.79 |
| 192.59.66.48 | 192.59.66.49 | 192.59.66.62 | 192.59.66.63 |
| 192.59.66.32 | 192.59.66.33 | 192.59.66.46 | 192.59.66.47 |
| 192.59.66.16 through 192.59.66.0 | 192.59.66.17 | 192.59.66.30 | 192.59.66.31 |

5

# Supernetting

*Supernetting* is the opposite of subnetting. In subnetting you borrow host bits and interpret them as network bits in order to create smaller network segments. With supernetting you borrow network bits and interpret them as host bits. This process creates larger network segments.

Supernetting is used when a company or organization needs a larger network than is supported by a single class network ID. For example, if a company has 800 employees in one location, the company could request and receive from their ISP four adjacent Class C network IDs. The ISP could provide network IDs similar to the four listed below:

207.43.16.0

207.43.17.0

207.43.18.0

207.43.19.0

To supernet these four networks, the subnet address will appear as 255.255.252.0 and will combine these four networks into one having a total of 1,022 usable addresses.

# Summary

Subnetting is a commonly used technique to better utilize the IP addresses in a Class A, B, or C network. Subnetting provides several benefits, such as security, broadcast resolution, and the capability to place subnetworks at distant locations. Therefore, you should consider subnetting if you have a need for installing and supporting multiple locations with a single network ID.

# Q&A

**Q  What are the maximum number of subnet mask bits for a Class B address?**

**A**  14

**Q  Is IP address 207.13.47.48 a valid or an invalid IP address when using a 255.255.255.248 subnet mask?**

**A**  Invalid

**Q  You have a Class C network address. You also have employees at 10 locations; each location has 12 or fewer people. What subnet mask or masks would enable you to install a workstation for each user?**

**A**  255.255.255.240

# Workshop

## Key Terms

Review the following list of key terms:

Subnet—A network segment that has a portion of the total number of addresses assigned to the network ID.

Subnet mask—Used to differentiate the network portion of an IP address from the host portion of the IP address.

Supernet—Enables you to combine several networks into a larger network.

5

# Hour **6**

# The Transport Layer

*By Joe Casad*

The Transport layer provides an interface for network applications and offers optional error checking, flow control, and verification for network transmissions. This hour describes some important Transport layer concepts and introduces the protocols TCP and UDP. Hour 7, "TCP and UDP," continues with a closer look at the TCP and UDP protocols.

## Goals for this Hour

At the completion of this hour, you will be able to

- Describe the basic duties of the Transport layer
- Define what a connection-oriented protocol is
- Define what a connectionless protocol is
- Explain how Transport layer protocols provide an interface to network applications through ports and sockets

- Define multiplexing and demultiplexing
- Describe the differences between TCP and UDP
- Explain how firewalls block access to network applications

# Introducing the Transport Layer

The TCP/IP Internet layer, as you learned in Hours 4 and 5, is full of useful protocols that are effective at providing the necessary addressing information so that data can make its journey across the network. Addressing and routing, however, are only part of the picture. The developers of TCP/IP knew they needed another layer above the Internet layer that would cooperate with IP by providing additional necessary features. Specifically, they wanted the Transport layer protocols to provide the following:

- An interface for network applications, which is a way for applications to access the network. The designers wanted to be able to target data not just to a destination computer, but to a particular application running on the destination computer.
- A mechanism for multiplexing/demultiplexing. *Multiplexing,* in this case, means accepting data from multiple inputs and directing that data to a single output. In other words, the Transport layer must be capable of simultaneously supporting several network applications and managing the flow of data to the Internet layer. On the receiving end, the Transport layer must accept the data from the Internet layer and direct it to multiple outputs (the network applications). This is known as *demultiplexing.* Another aspect of multiplexing/demultiplexing is that a single application can simultaneously maintain connections with more than one computer.
- Error checking, flow control, and verification. The protocol system needs an overall scheme ensuring delivery of data between the sending and receiving machines.

The last item in the preceding list, error checking, flow control, and verification, is the most open-ended. Questions of quality assurance always balance on questions of benefit and cost. An elaborate quality assurance system can increase your certainty that a delivery was successful, but you pay for it with increased network traffic and slower processing time. For many applications, this additional assurance simply isn't worth it. The Transport layer, therefore, provides two pathways to the network, each with the interfacing and multiplexing/demultiplexing features necessary for supporting applications, but each with a very different approach to quality assurance, as follows:

- Transport Control Protocol (TCP)—TCP provides extensive error checking and flow control to ensure the successful delivery of data. TCP is a connection-oriented protocol.

- User Datagram Protocol (UDP)—UDP provides extremely rudimentary error checking and is designed for situations when TCP's extensive control features are not necessary. UDP is a connectionless protocol.

You'll learn more about connection-oriented and connectionless protocols, and about the TCP and UDP protocols, later in this hour.

# Transport Layer Concepts

Before moving to a more detailed discussion of TCP and UDP, it is worth pausing for a moment to focus on a few of the important concepts:

- Connection-oriented and connectionless protocols
- Ports and sockets
- Multiplexing

These important concepts are essential to understanding the design of the Transport layer. You'll learn about these concepts in the following sections.

## Connection-oriented and Connectionless Protocols

In order to provide the appropriate level of quality assurance for any given situation, developers have come up with two alternative network protocol archetypes:

- A connection-oriented protocol establishes and maintains a connection between communicating computers and monitors the state of that connection over the course of the transmission. In other words, each package of data sent across the network receives an acknowledgment, and the sending machine records status information to ensure that each package is received without errors. At the end of the transmission, the sending and receiving computers gracefully close the connection.
- A connectionless protocol sends a one-way datagram to the destination and doesn't worry about officially notifying the destination machine that data is on the way. The destination machine receives the data and doesn't worry about returning status information to the source computer.

Figure 6.1 shows two people demonstrating connection-oriented communication. These humans, of course, are not intended to show the true complexity of digital communications but simply to illustrate the concept of a connection-oriented protocol.

6

**FIGURE 6.1**

*A connection-oriented
protocol.*

**FIGURE 6.1**

*A connection-oriented
protocol.*

Figure 6.2 shows how the same data would be sent using a connectionless protocol.

**FIGURE 6.2**

*A connectionless
protocol.*

## Ports and Sockets

The Transport layer serves as an interface between network applications and the network
and provides a method for addressing network data to particular applications. In the
TCP/IP system, applications can address data through either the TCP or UDP protocol
module using *port* numbers. A port is a predefined internal address that serves as a pathway from the application to the Transport layer or from the Transport layer to the application (see Figure 6.3). For instance, a client computer typically contacts a server's FTP
application through TCP port 21.

## FIGURE 6.3

*A port address targets
data to a particular
application.*

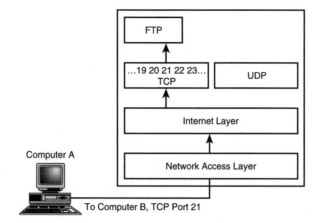

A closer look at the Transport layer's application-specific addressing scheme reveals that TCP and UDP data is actually addressed to what is called a *socket*. A socket is an address formed by concatenating the IP address and the port number. For instance, the socket number 111.121.131.141.21 refers to port 21 on the computer with the IP address 111.121.131.141.

Figure 6.4 shows how computers using TCP exchange socket information when they form a connection. Hour 7 describes the process of establishing a TCP connection in greater detail.

## FIGURE 6.4

*Exchanging the source
and destination socket
numbers.*

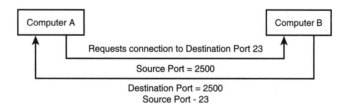

An example of how a computer accesses an application on a destination machine through a socket follows:

1. Computer A initiates a connection to an application on Computer B through a *well-known* port. Well-known ports are port numbers that are assigned to specific applications by IANA. See Tables 6.1 and 6.2 for lists of well-known TCP and UDP ports. Combined with the IP address, the well-known port becomes the destination socket address for Computer A. The request includes a data field telling Computer B which socket number to use when sending back information to Computer A. This is Computer A's source socket address.

6

2. Computer B receives the request from Computer A through the well-known port and directs a response to the socket listed as Computer A's source address. This socket becomes the destination address for messages sent from the application on Computer B to the application on Computer A.

You'll learn more about how to initiate computers to a TCP connection in Hour 7.

**TABLE 6.1** WELL-KNOWN TCP PORTS

| Service | TCP Port Number | Brief Description |
| --- | --- | --- |
| tcpmux | 1 | TCP Port Service Multiplexor |
| compressnet | 2 | Management Utility |
| compressnet | 3 | Compression Utility |
| echo | 7 | Echo |
| discard | 9 | Discard or Null |
| systat | 11 | Users |
| daytime | 13 | Daytime |
| netstat | 15 | Network status |
| qotd | 17 | Quote of the Day |
| chargen | 19 | Character generator |
| ftp-data | 20 | File Transfer Protocol Data |
| ftp | 21 | File Transfer Protocol Control |
| telnet | 23 | Terminal Network Connection |
| smtp | 25 | Simple Mail Transport Protocol |
| nsw-fe | 27 | NSW User System |
| time | 37 | Time server |
| name | 42 | Host name server |
| whois | 43 | NIC name |
| domain | 53 | Domain name server (DNS) |
| nameserver | 53 | Domain name server (DNS) |
| gopher | 70 | Gopher service |
| rje | 77 | Remote Job Entry |
| finger | 79 | Finger |
| http | 80 | WWW service |
| link | 87 | TTY link |
| supdup | 95 | SUPDUP Protocol |

| Service | TCP Port Number | Brief Description |
|---|---|---|
| hostnames | 101 | SRI-NIC host name server |
| iso-tsap | 102 | ISO-TSAP |
| x400 | 103 | X.400 Mail service |
| x400-snd | 104 | X.400 Mail Send |
| pop | 109 | Post Office Protocol |
| pop2 | 109 | Post Office Protocol 2 |
| pop3 | 110 | Post Office Protocol 3 |
| sunrpc | 111 | SUN RPC service |
| auth | 113 | Authentication service |
| sftp | 115 | Secure FTP |
| path | 117 | UUCP Path service |
| uucp-path | 117 | UUCP Path service |
| nntp | 119 | USENET Network News Transfer Protocol |
| nbsession | 139 | NetBIOS Session service |
| news | 144 | News |
| tcprepo | 158 | TCP repository |

**TABLE 6.2** WELL-KNOWN UDP PORTS

| Service | UDP Port Number | Description |
|---|---|---|
| echo | 7 | Echo |
| discard | 9 | Discard or Null |
| systat | 11 | Users |
| daytime | 13 | Daytime |
| netstat | 15 | Network status |
| qotd | 17 | Quote of the Day |
| chargen | 19 | Character generator |
| time | 37 | Time server |
| name | 42 | Host name server |
| whois | 43 | NIC name |
| domain | 53 | Domain name server (DNS) |
| nameserver | 53 | Domain name server (DNS) |
| bootps | 67 | Bootstrap Protocol Service/DHCP |

6

*continues*

TABLE 6.2 CONTINUED

| Service | UDP Port Number | Description |
|---|---|---|
| bootpc | 68 | Bootstrap Protocol Client/DHCP |
| tftp | 69 | Trivial File Transfer Protocol |
| sunrpc | 111 | SUN RPC service |
| ntp | 123 | Network Time Protocol |
| nbname | 137 | NetBIOS name |
| nbdatagram | 148 | NetBIOS datagram |
| snmp | 161 | Simple Network Management Protocol |
| snmp-trap | 162 | Simple Network Management Protocol trap |

## Multiplexing/Demultiplexing

The socket addressing system enables TCP and UDP to perform another important Transport layer task: multiplexing/demultiplexing. As described earlier, multiplexing is the act of braiding input from several sources into a single output, and demultiplexing is the act of receiving input from a single source and delivering it to multiple outputs (see Figure 6.5).

FIGURE 6.5

*Multiplexing and demultiplexing.*

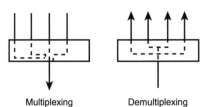

Multiplexing          Demultiplexing

Multiplexing/demultiplexing enables the lower levels of the TCP/IP stack to process data without regard to which application initiated that data. All associations with the originating application are settled at the Transport layer, and data passes to and from the Internet layer in a single, application-independent pipeline.

The key to multiplexing and demultiplexing is the socket address. Because the socket address combines the IP number with the port number it provides a unique identifier for a specific application on a specific machine. See the Telnet server depicted in Figure 6.6. All client machines use the well-known port address TCP 23 to contact the Telnet server, but the destination socket for each of the connecting PCs is unique. Likewise, all network applications running on the Telnet server use the server's IP address, but only the Telnet service uses the socket address consisting of the server's IP address plus TCP port 23.

**FIGURE 6.6**

*The socket address uniquely identifies an application on a particular server.*

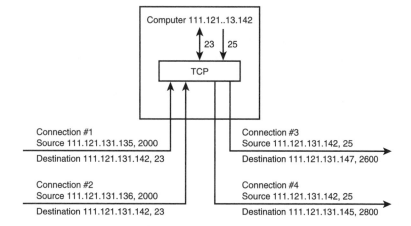

# Introducing TCP and UDP

The concepts described in this chapter provide some background for understanding the TCP and UDP Transport protocols. As this chapter has already mentioned, TCP is a connection-oriented protocol that provides extensive error checking and flow control; and UDP is a connectionless protocol with much less sophisticated error checking. You might say that TCP is built for reliability and UDP is built for speed. Applications that must support interactive sessions, such as Telnet and FTP, tend to use TCP. Applications that do their own error checking or that don't need much error checking tend to use UDP.

A software developer designing a network application can choose whether to use TCP or UDP as a transport protocol. UDP's simpler control mechanisms should not necessarily be considered limiting. First of all, lesser quality assurance does not necessarily mean less quality. The extra checks and controls provided by TCP are entirely unnecessary for many applications. In cases where error checking and flow control are necessary, some developers prefer to provide those control features within the application itself—where they can be customized for specific needs—and to use the leaner UDP transport for network access. UDP-based services such as TCP/IP's Remote Procedure Call (RPC) can support advanced and sophisticated applications, but those applications must take responsibility for more error checking and flow control tasks than if they reached the stack through TCP.

You'll learn more of the details of TCP and UDP in Hour 7. In the meantime, the following sections summarize some of the features of TCP and UDP.

6

## TCP: The Connection-oriented Transport Protocol

This chapter has already described TCP's connection-oriented approach to communication. TCP has a few other important features that warrant mentioning here:

- Stream-oriented processing—TCP processes data in a stream. In other words, TCP can accept data a byte at a time rather than as a preformatted block. TCP formats the data into *variable-length* segments, which it will pass to the Internet layer.

- Resequencing—If data arrives at the destination out of order, the TCP module is capable of resequencing the data in order to restore the original order.

- Flow control—TCP's flow control feature ensures that the data transmission won't outrun or overrun the destination machine's capability to receive the data. This is especially critical in a diverse environment in which there may be considerable variation of processor speeds and buffer sizes.

- Precedence and security—The Department of Defense specifications for TCP call for optional security and priority levels that can be set for TCP connections. Many TCP implementations, however, do not provide these security and priority features.

- Graceful close—TCP is as careful about closing a connection as it is about opening a connection. The graceful close feature ensures that all segments have been sent and received before a connection is closed.

You'll learn more about these features in Hour 7, which takes a closer look at TCP.

## UDP: The Connectionless Transport Protocol

UDP is much simpler than TCP and it doesn't perform any of the functions listed in the preceding section. There are, however, a couple observations about UDP that this hour should mention.

First, although UDP is sometimes described as having no error-checking capabilities, in fact, UDP is capable of performing rudimentary error checking. It is best to characterize UDP as having the capability for *limited error checking*. As you'll learn in Hour 7, the UDP datagram includes a checksum value that the receiving machine can use to test the integrity of the data. (Often, this checksum test is optional and can be disabled on the receiving machine to speed up processing of incoming data.) The UDP datagram includes a *pseudoheader* (described in Hour 7) that encompasses the destination address for the datagram, thus providing a means of checking for misdirected datagrams. Also, if the receiving UDP module receives a datagram directed to an inactive or undefined UDP port, it returns an ICMP message notifying the source machine that the port is unreachable.

Second, UDP does not offer the *resequencing* of data provided by TCP. Resequencing is most significant on a large network, such as the Internet, where the segments of data might take different paths and experience significant delays in router buffers. On local networks, the lack of a resequencing feature in UDP typically leads to unreliable reception.

> UDP's lean, connectionless design makes it the protocol of choice for network broadcast situations. A broadcast is a single message that will be received and processed by all computers on the subnet. Understandably, if the source computer had to simultaneously open a TCP-style connection with every computer on the subnet in order to send a single broadcast, the result could be significant erosion of network performance.

# A Note About Firewalls

A *firewall* is a system that protects a local network from attack by unauthorized users attempting to access the LAN from the Internet. The word firewall has entered the lexicon of Internet jargon, and it is one of many computer terms that can fall within a wide range of definitions. However, one of the most basic features of a firewall is something that is pertinent to this chapter.

That important feature is the capability of firewalls to block off access to specific TCP and UDP ports. The word *firewall*, in fact, is sometimes used as a verb, meaning *to close off access to a port*.

For example, to initiate a Telnet session with the server, a client machine must send a request to Telnet's well-known port address, TCP port 23. (*Telnet* is a utility that lets the client computer serve as a terminal for the server. You'll learn more about Telnet in Hour 13, "Remote Access Utilities.") Unauthorized use of Telnet can sometimes pose a security threat. To increase security, the server can be configured to stop using port 23 to access Telnet; or for that matter, the server can simply stop using the Telnet application, but that extreme solution would prohibit authorized users on the LAN from using Telnet for authorized activities. (Why have it if you're not going to use it?) An alternative would be to install a firewall as shown in Figure 6.7 and configure that firewall to block access to TCP port 23. The result is that users on the LAN, from *inside* the firewall, have free access to TCP port 23 on the server. Users from the Internet, *outside* the LAN, do not have access to the server's TCP port 23 and therefore cannot access the server through Telnet. In fact, users from the Internet cannot use Telnet at all to access any computer on the LAN.

6

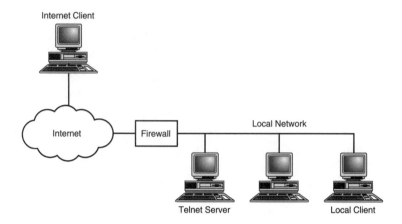

**FIGURE 6.7**

*A typical firewall scenario.*

This scenario uses Telnet and TCP port 23 as an example. Firewalls typically block access to any or all ports that may pose a security threat. Network administrators often block access to all ports except those that are absolutely necessary, such as a port that handles incoming email. You often find devices that provide the company's Internet presence, such as a Web server, placed outside the firewall, so that access to the Internet device will not result in unauthorized access to the LAN.

## Summary

This hour covers some key features of TCP/IP's Transport layer. You learned about connection-oriented and connectionless protocols, multiplexing and demultiplexing, and ports and sockets. This hour also introduces TCP/IP's Transport layer protocols, TCP and UDP, and describes some important TCP and UDP features. The next hour takes a closer look at TCP and UDP.

## Q&A

**Q  Why is multiplexing/demultiplexing necessary?**

**A  If TCP/IP did not provide multiplexing/demultiplexing, only one application could use the network software at a time and only one computer could connect to a given application at a time.**

**Q  Why would a software developer opt to use UDP for a transport protocol when TCP offers better quality assurance?**

**A  TCP's quality assurance comes at the price of slower performance. If the extra error checking and flow control of TCP are not necessary, UDP is a better choice because it is faster.**

**Q** **Why do applications that support interactive sessions, such as Telnet and FTP, tend to use TCP rather than UDP?**

**A** TCP's control and recovery features provide the reliable connection necessary for an interactive session.

**Q** **Why would a network administrator want to use a firewall to intentionally close off Internet access to a TCP or UDP port?**

**A** Internet firewalls close off access to specific ports in order to deny Internet users access to the applications that use those ports.

# Workshop

## Key Terms

Review the following list of key terms:

- Connection-oriented protocol—A protocol that manages communication through a connection between the communicating computers.
- Connectionless protocol—A protocol that transmits data without operating through a connection.
- Demultiplexing—Directing a single input to several outputs.
- Firewall—A device that protects a network from unauthorized Internet access.
- Multiplexing—Combining several inputs into a single output.
- Port—An internal address that provides an interface from an application to a Transport layer protocol.
- Resequencing—Assembling incoming TCP segments so that they are in the order in which they were actually sent.
- Socket—The network address for a particular application on a particular computer, consisting of the computer's IP address followed by the port number of the application.
- Stream-oriented input—Continuous (byte by byte) input, rather than input in predefined blocks of data.
- TCP—A connection-oriented Transport protocol in the TCP/IP suite.
- UDP—A connectionless transport protocol in the TCP/IP suite.
- Well-known port—Predefined standard port numbers for common applications. Well-known ports are specified by the IANA.

6

# Hour 7

# TCP and UDP

*By Joe Casad*

The preceding hour introduced TCP and UDP, the protocols operating at TCP/IP's Transport layer. In this hour, you'll get a closer look at TCP and UDP. You'll learn how TCP transmits data, and you'll learn how two computers establish a TCP connection. You'll also learn about TCP and UDP data formats.

## Goals for this Hour

At the completion of this hour, you will be able to

- Identify the fields that comprise the TCP header
- Describe how TCP sequences and acknowledges data transmissions
- Describe how TCP opens a connection
- Describe TCP's *sliding window* flow control method
- Describe how TCP closes a connection
- Identify the four fields that comprise the UDP headers

# Transmission Control Protocol (TCP)

A close look at Transmission Control Protocol (TCP) reveals a complex system of announcements and acknowledgments supporting TCP's connection-oriented structure. The following sections take a closer look at TCP data format, TCP data transmission, and TCP connections. The technical nature of this discussion should reveal how complex TCP really is. This discussion of TCP also underscores the fact that a protocol is more than just a data format: It is a whole system of interacting processes and procedures designed to accomplish a set of well-defined objectives.

As you learned in Hour 2, "How TCP/IP Works," layered protocol systems such as TCP/IP operate through an information exchange between a given layer on the sending machine and the corresponding layer on the receiving machine. In other words, the Network Access layer on the sending machine communicates with the Network Access layer on the receiving machine; the Internet layer on the sending machine communicates with the Internet layer on the receiving machine, and so forth.

The TCP software communicates with the TCP software on the machine to which it has established (or wants to establish) a connection. In any discussion of TCP, if you hear the phrase "Computer A establishes a connection with Computer B" then what that really means is that the *TCP software of Computer A* has established a connection with the *TCP software of Computer B,* both of which are acting on behalf of a local application. The subtle distinction yields an interesting observation concerning the concept of end-node verification that was introduced in Hour 1, "What Is TCP/IP?"

Recall that end nodes are responsible for verifying communications on a TCP/IP network. (The end nodes are the nodes that are actually attempting to communicate—as opposed to the intermediate nodes, which forward the message.) In a typical internet-working situation (see Figure 7.1), the data is passed from the source subnet to the destination subnet by routers. These routers typically operate at the Internet layer—the layer below the Transport layer. (You'll learn more about routers in Hour 9, "Routers, Brouters, and Bridges.") The important point is that the routers are not concerned with the information at the Transport level. They simply pass on the Transport layer data as *cargo* for the IP datagram. The control and verification information encoded in a TCP segment is intended solely for the TCP software of the destination machine. This speeds up routing over TCP/IP internetworks because routers do not have to actively participate in TCP's elaborate quality assurance ritual and at the same time enables TCP to fulfill the Department of Defense's objective of providing a network with end-node verification.

**FIGURE 7.1**

*Routers forward but do not process the Transport layer's data.*

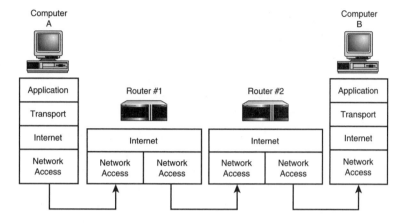

## TCP Data Format

The TCP header format is shown in Figure 7.2. The complexity of this structure reveals the complexity of TCP and the many facets of its functionality.

**FIGURE 7.2**

*TCP segment data format.*

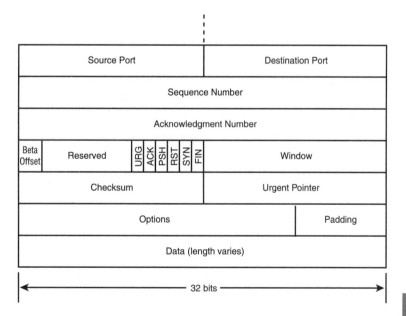

7

The fields are as follows. You'll have a better idea of how these data fields are used after reading the next section, which discusses TCP connections:

- Source Port: (16-bit)—The port number assigned to the application on the source machine.

- Destination Port: (16-bit)—The port number assigned to the application on the destination machine.

- Sequence Number: (32-bit)—The number of the first byte in this particular segment, unless the SYN flag is set to one. If the SYN flag is set to one, the Sequence Number field provides the initial sequence number (ISN), which is used to synchronize sequence numbers. If the SYN flag is set to one, the sequence number of the first octet is one greater than the number that appears in this field (in other words, ISN+1).

- Acknowledgment Number: (32-bit)—The number acknowledges a received segment. The value is the *next* sequence number the receiving computer is expecting to receive; in other words, the sequence number of the last byte received+1.

- Data offset: (4 bits)—A field that tells the receiving TCP software how long the header is and, therefore, where the data begins. The data offset is expressed as an integer number of 32-bit words.

- Reserved: (6 bits)—Reserved for future use. The Reserved field provides room to accommodate for future developments of TCP and must be all zeros.

- Control flags: (1 bit each)—The control flags communicate special information about the segment.

  - URG—A value of one announces that the segment is urgent and the Urgent Pointer field is significant.

  - ACK—A value of one announces that the Acknowledgment number field is significant.

  - PSH—A value of one tells the TCP software to *push* all the data sent so far through the pipeline to the receiving application.

  - RST—A value of one resets the connection.

  - SYN—A value of one announces that sequence numbers will be synchronized, marking the beginning of a connection. See the discussion of the three-way handshake, later in this hour.

  - FIN—A value of one signifies that the sending computer has no more data to transmit. This flag is used to close a connection.

- Window: (16-bit)—A parameter used for flow control. The *window* defines the range of sequence numbers beyond the last acknowledged sequence number that the sending machine is free to transmit without further acknowledgment.

- Checksum: (16-bit)—A field used to check the integrity of the segment. A receiving computer performs a checksum calculation based on the segment and compares the value to the value stored in this field. TCP and UDP include a pseudo-header with IP addressing information in the checksum calculation. See the discussion of the UDP pseudo-header later in this hour.

- Urgent pointer: (16-bit)—An offset pointer pointing to the sequence number that marks the beginning of any urgent information.

- Options—Specifies one of a small set of optional settings.

- Padding—Extra zero bits (as needed) to ensure that the data begins on a 32-bit boundary.

- Data—The data being transmitted with the segment.

TCP needs all these data fields to successfully manage, acknowledge, and verify network transmissions. The next section shows how the TCP software uses some of these fields to manage the tasks of sending and receiving data.

## TCP Connections

Everything in TCP happens in the context of a connection. TCP sends and receives data through a connection, which must be requested, opened, and closed according to the rules of TCP.

As described in Hour 6, "The Transport Layer," one of the reasons for TCP is to provide an interface so that applications can have access to the network. That interface is provided through the TCP ports, and in order to provide a connection through the ports, the TCP interface to the application must be *open*. TCP supports two open states:

- Passive open—A given application process notifies TCP that it is prepared to receive incoming connections through a TCP port. Thus, the pathway from TCP to the application is open in anticipation of an incoming connection request.

- Active open—An application requests that TCP initiate a connection with another computer that is in the passive open state. (Actually, TCP can also initiate a connection to a computer that is in the active open state, in case both computers are attempting to open a connection at once.)

7

In a typical situation, an application wanting to receive connections, such as an FTP *server*, places itself and its TCP port status in a passive open state. On the client computer, the FTP client's TCP state is most likely closed until a user initiates a connection from the FTP client to the FTP server, at which time the state for the client would become active open. The TCP software of the computer that switches to active open (that is, the *client*) then initiates the exchange of messages that lead to a connection. That exchange of information, the so-called three-way handshake, will be discussed later in this hour.

 A *client* is a computer requesting or receiving services from another computer on the network.

 A *server* is a computer offering services to other computers on the network.

TCP sends segments of variable length; within a segment, each byte of data is assigned a sequence number. The receiving machine must send an acknowledgment for every byte it receives. TCP communication is thus a system of transmissions and acknowledgments. The Sequence Number and Acknowledgment Number fields of the TCP header (described in the preceding section) provide the communicating TCP software with regular updates on the status of the transmission.

A separate sequence number is not encoded with each individual byte. Instead, the Sequence Number field in the header gives the sequence number of the first byte of data in a segment. There is one exception to this rule. If the segment occurs at the beginning of a connection (see the description of the three-way handshake, later in this section), the Sequence Number field contains the ISN, which is actually one less than the sequence number of the first byte in the segment. (The first byte is ISN+1.)

If the segment is received successfully, the receiving computer uses the Acknowledgment Number field to tell the sending computer which bytes it has received. The Acknowledgment Number field in the acknowledgment message will be set to the last received sequence number+1. In other words, the Acknowledgment Number field defines which sequence number the computer is prepared to receive next.

If an acknowledgment is not received within the specified time period, the sending machine retransmits the data beginning with the byte after the last acknowledged byte.

## Establishing a Connection

In order for the sequence/acknowledgment system to work, the computers must *synchronize* their sequence numbers. In other words, Computer B must know what initial sequence number (ISN) Computer A used to start the sequence. Computer A must know what ISN Computer B will use to start the sequence for any data Computer B will transmit.

This synchronization of sequence numbers is called a *three-way handshake*. The three-way handshake always occurs at the beginning of a TCP connection. The three steps of a three-way handshake are as follows:

1. Computer A sends a segment with

   SYN=1

   ACK=0

   Sequence Number = X (where X is Computer A's ISN)

   The active open computer (Computer A) sends a segment with the SYN flag set to one and the ACK flag set to zero. SYN stands for *synchronize*. This flag, as described earlier, announces an attempt to open a connection. This first segment header also contains the initial sequence number, which marks the beginning of the sequence numbers for data that Computer A will transmit. The first byte transmitted to Computer B will have the sequence number ISN+1.

2. Computer B receives Computer A's segment and returns a segment with

   SYN = 1 (still in synchronization phase)

   ACK = 1 (the Acknowledgment Number field will contain a value)

   Sequence number = Y, where Y is Computer B's ISN

   Acknowledgment number = M + 1, where M is the last sequence number received from A

3. Computer A sends a segment to Computer B that acknowledges receipt of Computer B's ISN

   SYN=0

   ACK=1

   Sequence number = next sequence number in series (M+1)

   Acknowledgment number = N+1 (where N is the last sequence number received from B)

After the three-way handshake the connection is open, and the TCP modules transmit and receive data using the sequence and acknowledgment scheme described earlier in this section.

# TCP Flow Control

The Window field in the TCP header provides a flow control mechanism for the connection. The purpose of the Window field is to ensure that the sending computer doesn't send too much data too quickly, which could lead to a situation in which data is lost because the receiving computer can't process incoming segments as quickly as the sending computer can transmit them. The flow control method used by TCP is called the *sliding window* method. The receiving computer uses the Window field to define a *window* of sequence numbers beyond the last acknowledged sequence number that the sending computer is authorized to transmit. The sending computer cannot transmit beyond that window until it receives the next acknowledgment.

## Closing a Connection

When it is time to close the connection, the computer initiating the close, Computer A, places a segment in the queue with the FIN flag set to one. The application then enters what is called the *fin-wait state.* In the fin-wait state, Computer A's TCP software continues to receive segments and processes the segments already in the queue, but no additional data is accepted from the application. When Computer B receives the FIN segment, it returns an acknowledgment to the FIN, sends any remaining segments, and notifies the local application that a FIN was received. Computer B sends a FIN segment to Computer A, which Computer A acknowledges, and the connection is closed.

# User Datagram Protocol (UDP)

The primary purpose of the UDP protocol is to expose datagrams to the Application layer. As such, the UDP protocol itself does very little and, therefore, employs a simple header structure. The RFC that describes this protocol, RFC 768, is only three pages in length. As mentioned in Hour 6, UDP does not retransmit missing or corrupted datagrams, sequence datagrams received out of order, eliminate duplicated datagrams, acknowledge the receipt of datagrams, or establish or terminate connections. UDP is primarily a mechanism for application programs to send and receive datagrams without the overhead of a TCP connection.

The UDP header consists of four 16-bit fields. See Figure 7.3 for the layout of the UDP datagram header.

**FIGURE 7.3**

*The UDP datagram header and data payload.*

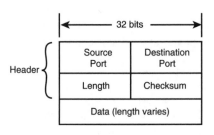

The following list describes these fields:

- Source Port—This field occupies the first 16 bits of the UDP header. This field typically holds the UDP port number of the application sending this datagram. The value entered in the Source Port field is used by the receiving application as a return address when it is ready to send a response. This field is considered optional, and it is not required that the sending application include its port number. If the sending application does not include its port number the application is expected to place 16 zero bits into the field. Obviously if there is no valid source port address, the receiving application will be unable to send a response. However this might be the desired functionality as in the case of an SNMP-trap message, which is a unidirectional message where no response is expected.

- Destination Port—This 16-bit field holds the port address to which the UDP software on the receiving machine will deliver this datagram.

- Length—This 16-bit field identifies the length in octets of the UDP datagram. The length includes the UDP header as well as the UDP data payload. Because the UDP header is eight octets in length, the value will always be at least eight.

- Checksum—This 16-bit field is used to determine whether the datagram was corrupted during transmission. The checksum is the result of a special calculation performed on a string of binary data. In the case of UDP, the checksum is calculated based on the following data: a pseudo-header (explained shortly), the UDP header, the UDP data, and possibly the filler zero octets to build an even octet length checksum input. The checksums generated at the source and verified at the destination allow the client application to determine if the datagram has been corrupted.

Because the actual UDP header does not include the Source or Destination IP addresses, it is possible for the datagram to be delivered to the wrong computer or service. Part of the data used for the checksum calculation is a string of values extracted from the IP header known as the *pseudo-header*. The pseudo-header provides Destination IP addressing information so that the receiving computer can determine whether a UDP datagram has been misdelivered.

# Summary

This hour takes a deeper look at the Transport layer's TCP and UDP protocols. The chapter describes how TCP fulfills the TCP/IP objective of providing end-node verification. It also discusses TCP data format and describes the three-way handshake TCP uses when it opens a connection. This hour also covers TCP's flow control and error recovery features.

7

This chapter also describes the format of a UDP header. For more on TCP and UDP, see the introduction to the Transport layer in Hour 6.

# Q&A

**Q**  **Why don't routers send TCP connection acknowledgments to the computer initiating a connection?**

**A**  Routers operate at the Internet layer (below the Transport layer) and, therefore, do not process TCP information.

**Q**  **Would a functioning FTP server most likely be in a passive open, active open, or closed state?**

**A**  A working FTP server would most likely be in a passive open state—ready to accept an incoming connection.

**Q**  **Why is the third step in the three-way handshake necessary?**

**A**  After the first two steps, the two computers have exchanged ISN numbers, so theoretically, they have enough information to synchronize the connection, however, the computer that sent its ISN in step 2 of the handshake still hasn't received an acknowledgment. The third step acknowledges the ISN received in the second step.

**Q**  **Which field is optional in the UDP header and why?**

**A**  The Source Port field. Because UDP is a connectionless protocol, the UDP software on the receiving machine does not have to know the source port. The source port is provided as an option in case the application receiving the data needs the source port for error checking or verification.

**Q**  **What happens if the source port is equal to 16 zero bits?**

**A**  The application on the destination machine will be unable to send a response.

# Workshop

## Key Terms

Review the following list of key terms:

- ACK— A control flag specifying that the Acknowledgment Number field in the TCP header is significant.

- Acknowledgment Number field—A field in the TCP header specifying the next sequence number the computer is expecting to receive. The acknowledgment number, in effect, acknowledges the receipt of all sequenced bytes prior to the byte specified in the acknowledgment number.

- Active open—A state in which TCP is attempting to initiate a connection.
- Checksum—A 16-bit calculated field used to ensure detection of corrupted datagrams.
- Control flag—A 1-bit flag with special information about a TCP segment.
- Destination Port—The TCP or UDP port number of the application on the destination machine that will be the recipient of the data in a TCP segment or UDP datagram.
- FIN—A control flag used in the process of closing a TCP connection.
- Initial sequence number (ISN)—A number that marks the beginning of the range of numbers a computer will use for sequencing bytes transmitted through TCP.
- Passive open—A state in which the TCP port is ready to receive incoming connections.
- Pseudo-header—A structure derived from fields from the IP header that is used to calculate the TCP or UDP checksum.
- Segment—A package of TCP data and header information.
- Sequence Number—A unique number associated with a byte transmitted through TCP.
- Sliding window—A window of sequence numbers that the receiving computer has authorized the sending computer to send. The sliding window flow control method is the method used by TCP.
- Source Port—The TCP or UDP port number of the application sending a TCP segment or UDP datagram.
- SYN—A control flag signifying that sequence number synchronization is taking place. The SYN flag is used at the beginning of a TCP connection as part of the three-way handshake.
- Three-way handshake—A three-step procedure that synchronizes sequence numbers and begins a TCP connection.

7

# Hour 8

# The Application Layer

*By Joe Casad*

At the top of TCP/IP's stack is the Application layer, a loose collection of networking components perched above the Transport layer. This hour describes some of the kinds of Application layer components and shows how those components help bring the user to the network. Specifically, this hour examines Application layer services, operating environments, and network applications.

## Goals for this Hour

At the completion of this hour, you'll be able to

- Describe what the Application layer is
- Describe some of the Application layer's network services
- Show how NetBIOS over TCP/IP brings TCP/IP networking to NetBIOS environments
- Define IPX tunneling
- List some of TCP/IP's important utilities

# What Is the Application Layer?

The Application layer is the top layer in TCP/IP's protocol suite. In the Application layer, you'll find network applications and services that communicate with lower layers through the TCP and UDP ports discussed in Hour 6, "The Transport Layer," and Hour 7, "TCP and UDP." You might ask why the Application layer is considered part of the stack at all if the TCP and UDP ports form such a well-defined interface to the network. But it is important to remember that in a layer architecture such as TCP/IP, *every* layer is an interface to the network. The Application layer must be as aware of TCP and UDP ports as the Transport layer is and must channel data accordingly.

TCP/IP's Application layer is really an assortment of network-aware software components sending information to and receiving information from the TCP and UDP ports. These Application layer components are not really parallel, in the sense of being logically similar or equivalent. Some of the components at the Application layer are simple utilities that collect information about the network configuration. Other Application layer components might be a user interface system (such as the X Windows interface) or an Application Program Interface (API), such as NetBIOS, that supports a desktop operating environment. Some Application layer components provide services for the network, such as file and print services or name resolution services. (You'll learn more about name resolution in Part IV, "Name Resolution.") This hour shows you some of the kinds of services and applications that populate the Application layer. The actual implementation of these components hinges on details of programming and software design.

But first this hour begins with a quick comparison of the TCP/IP's Application layer with the corresponding layers defined through TCP/IP's counterpart, the OSI model.

# The TCP/IP Application Layer and OSI

As Hour 2, "How TCP/IP Works," mentioned, TCP/IP does not officially conform to the seven-layer OSI networking model. The OSI model, however, has been very influential in the development of networking systems, and the recent trend toward multiprotocol networking has increased reliance on OSI terminology and concepts. The Application layer can draw from a vast range of operating and networking environments, and in many of those environments the OSI model is an important tool for defining and describing network systems. A look at the OSI model will help you understand the processes that take place at the TCP/IP Application layer.

The TCP/IP Application layer corresponds with the OSI Application, Presentation, and Session layers (see Figure 8.1). The extra subdivisions of the OSI model (three layers instead of one) provide some additional organization of features that TCP/IP theorists have traditionally grouped into the heading of "Application-level" (sometimes called Process/Application-level) services.

**FIGURE 8.1**

*OSI and TCP/IP's Application layer.*

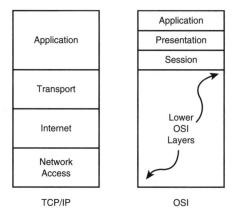

Descriptions of the OSI layers corresponding to TCP/IP's Application layer follow:

- Application layer—OSI's Application layer (not to be confused with TCP/IP's Application layer) has components that provide services for user applications and support network access.
- Presentation layer—The Presentation layer translates data into a platform-neutral format and handles encryption and data compression.
- Session layer—The Session layer manages communication between applications on networked computers. This layer provides some functions related to the connection that aren't available through the Transport layer, such as name recognition and security.

Not all of these services are necessary for all applications and implementations. In the TCP/IP model, implementations are not required to follow the layering of these OSI subdivisions, but overall, the duties defined for OSI's Application, Presentation, and Session layers fall within the range of the TCP/IP Application layer's responsibility.

# Network Services

Many Application-layer components are network services. In earlier hours you might have heard that a layer of the protocol system *provides services* for other layers of the system. In many cases, these services are a well-defined, integral part of the protocol system. In the case of the Application layer, the services are not all required for the operation of the protocol software and are more likely provided for the direct benefit of a user or to link the network with the local operating system.

A few of the services available at the Application layer are as follows:

- File and print services
- Name resolution services
- Redirector services

Other important network services, such as mail services and network management services, are discussed in other hours.

## File and Print Services

The term *server* is now common in networking parlance. A server is a computer that provides services for other computers. Two common types of servers are file servers and print servers. A print server operates a printer and fulfills requests to print documents on that printer. A file server operates a data storage device, such as a hard drive, and fulfills requests to read or write data to that device.

Because file services and print services are such common, everyday networking activities, they are often thought of together. Often the same computer (or sometimes even the same service) provides both file and print service capabilities. Whether or not they're together, the theory is the same. Figure 8.2 shows a typical file service scenario. A request for a file comes across the network and up through the protocol layers to the Transport layer, where it is routed through the appropriate port to the file server service.

**FIGURE 8.2**

*File service.*

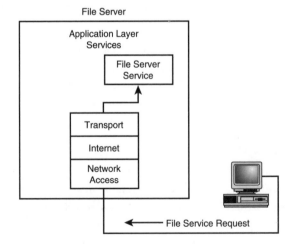

Figure 8.2 is a schematic drawing showing only the basic components as they relate to TCP/IP. In a real protocol and operating system implementation, additional layers or components might assist with forwarding the data to or from the file server service. In a Windows environment, for instance (as you'll learn later in this hour), WinSock provides an interface for the TCP/IP Transport layer with Windows applications.

8

## Name Resolution Services

As you learned in Hour 1, "What Is TCP/IP?" *name resolution* is the process of mapping IP addresses to predefined, user-friendly alphanumeric names. The domain name service (DNS) provides name resolution for the Internet and can also provide name resolution on isolated TCP/IP networks. DNS uses *name servers* to resolve DNS name queries. A name server service runs at the Application layer of the name server computer and communicates with other name servers to exchange name resolution information. Other name resolution systems exist, most notably Microsoft's NetBIOS name resolution through Windows Internet Naming Service (WINS).

Name resolution is an example of an Application-layer service that functions integrally with lower protocol layers and actively participates in the interactions of the protocol stack. DNS or WINS queries are initiated by the protocol software of the client machine, rather than by a user or user application. A user references a domain name and the underlying protocol software resolves that name to an IP address using name resolution. You'll learn more about DNS name resolution in Hours 15 and 16. You'll learn about NetBIOS name resolution in Hour 17.

## Redirectors

In order to integrate the local environment with the network, some network operating systems use a service called a *redirector*. A redirector is sometimes called a requester or a shell.

A Redirector intercepts service requests in the local computer and checks to see whether the request should be fulfilled locally or whether the request should be forwarded to another computer on the network. If the request is addressed to a service on another machine, the redirector redirects the request to the network (see Figure 8.3).

FIGURE 8.3

*A redirector.*

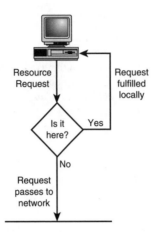

A redirector enables the user to access network resources as if they were part of the local environment. For instance, a remote disk drive could appear as a local disk drive on the client machine.

# Operating Environments and the Application Layer

The local operating system (or the network operating system) might have its own layered components that assist with providing users with access to the network. These components typically function above the TCP and UDP ports and are thus within the province of the Application layer. In some cases, however, the interaction of these components with the protocol stack is so unique that, in effect, the result is best understood as a wholly different stack.

You'll learn about some of the upper-layer user-environment components in the following sections, which cover

- TCP/IP with NetBIOS
- TCP/IP with NetWare

Other network systems provide similar solutions for access to TCP/IP.

It is worth noting that the Application layer isn't the only layer where vendors have contributed additional components in order to adapt TCP/IP to their environments. For instance, lower-level structures related to specifications such as NDIS and ODI (see Hour 2) are common in protocol implementations.

## TCP/IP with NetBIOS

Windows, OS/2, and certain other operating systems use an interface called NetBIOS to access network resources. NetBIOS, which was originally developed by IBM, is a collection of network services and an API designed to give applications access to those services. NetBIOS was originally developed to provide a vendor-neutral program interface for LAN-based proprietary protocols. As TCP/IP became more popular on computer-based LANs, vendors and developers began to see the advantage of providing TCP/IP connectivity to the many NetBIOS-based applications and operating systems. RFCs 1001 and 1002 provide a protocol standard for linking NetBIOS with TCP/IP.

NetBIOS locates computers by *computer name* (often called NetBIOS name). Computer names are the names that appear in Network Neighborhood in Windows 95. To resolve NetBIOS computer names to IP addresses, the network needs an entire name resolution system that is separate from DNS. This NetBIOS-based name resolution is provided in a layer logically located between the Transport layer and the NetBIOS interface called *NetBIOS over TCP/IP* or NBT. You'll learn more about NetBIOS name resolution in Hour 17.

Some Windows or OS/2 applications might need to access the TCP and UDP ports directly. The Windows Sockets (WinSock) interface provides access to the Transport layer protocols for the Windows programming environment. Windows 95, Windows 98, and recent versions of Windows NT include WinSock as part of the operating system.

## TCP/IP with NetWare

Novell NetWare is currently the most popular LAN networking system in the world. Novell had already developed its own protocol suite (called IPX/SPX) before TCP/IP began its rise to prominence. IPX/SPX is a full-featured protocol system with its own error control and logical addressing. With the recent upsurge of interest in TCP/IP, developers and systems engineers started to wonder if it would be possible to integrate IPX/SPX networks with TCP/IP without disturbing the upper NetWare-related layers of the IPX/SPX stack.

An interesting solution emerged known as *IPX tunneling*. IPX tunneling is defined in RFC 1234, "Tunneling IPX Traffic Through IP Networks."

In IPX tunneling, the IPX/SPX stack is basically grafted onto the UDP protocol of the TCP/IP stack (see Figure 8.4). The IPX protocol layer performs logical addressing functions similar to IP for the Novell network. Data passes down from IPX to UDP (see Hours 6 and 7), where it enters the TCP/IP stack and is encoded in an IP datagram and delivered to the physical network.

8

FIGURE **8.4**

*An IP stack supporting*
*IPX.*

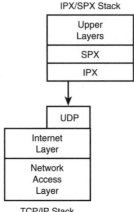

IPX tunneling, and solutions similar to it, produce a sort of hybrid protocol stack that is not easily described with the four-layer TCP/IP model. It is perhaps a matter of opinion whether the IPX superstructure riding above the Transport layer qualifies as an Application layer component or not, and most experts would describe this situation as upper-layer IPX/SPX protocols resting on the IPX/SPX Network layer, resting on TCP/IP's Transport layer. This IPX component, however, supports applications at the top and links to the UDP ports beneath, so if it is included anywhere in this discussion of TCP/IP layering, the Application layer is an appropriate place to mention it. The fact that IPX tunneling is even possible is a tribute to TCP/IP's flexibility and versatility.

Like the rest of the computer industry, Novell is well aware of the emergence of TCP/IP as the dominant routable protocol. Recent versions of NetWare have increased NetWare's support for TCP/IP, and eventually hybrid solutions like IPX tunneling might not be necessary.

# TCP/IP Utilities

Other residents of the Application layer are TCP/IP's utilities. The TCP/IP utilities originally developed around the Internet and early UNIX networks. These utilities are now used to configure, manage, and troubleshoot TCP/IP networks throughout the world, and versions of these utilities are now available with Windows NT Server and other network operating systems.

This book classifies the TCP/IP utilities into four categories: connectivity utilities, file transfer and access utilities, remote access utilities, and Internet utilities (see Table 8.1). The Internet applications (shown in Table 8.1 and discussed in Hour 14, "TCP/IP Internet Utilities") are newer and less UNIX-like than the other applications in Table 8.1, but they are similar in that they provide the user with access to information and resources across a TCP/IP network.

**TABLE 8.1**  TCP/IP UTILITIES

| Utility | Description |
| --- | --- |
| **Connectivity Utilities** | |
| IPConfig | A utility that displays TCP/IP configuration settings. |
| Ping | A utility that tests for network connectivity. |
| ARP | A utility that lets you view the ARP cache of a local or remote computer. The ARP cache contains the physical address to IP address mappings. (See Hour 4.) |
| TraceRoute | A utility that traces the path of a datagram through the internetwork. |
| Route | A utility that lets you add or edit entries in a routing table. (See Hour 9.) |
| Netstat | A utility that displays IP, UDP, TCP, and ICMP statistics. |
| NBTstat | A utility that displays statistics on NetBIOS and NBT. (See Hour 8.). |
| Hostname | A utility that returns the host name of the local host. |
| **File Transfer Utilities** | |
| FTP | A basic file transfer utility that uses TCP. |
| TFTP | A basic file transfer utility that uses UDP. |
| RCP | A remote file transfer utility. |
| **Remote Utilities** | |
| Telnet | A remote terminal utility. |
| Rexec | A utility that runs commands on a remote computer through the rexecd daemon. |
| RSH | A utility that invokes the shell on a remote computer to execute a command. |
| Finger | A utility that displays user information. |
| **Internet Utilities** | |
| Browsers | Utilities that provide access to World Wide Web HTML content. |
| Newsreaders | Utilities that connect with Internet newsgroups. |

*continues*

**TABLE 8.1** CONTINUED

| Utility | Description |
|---------|-------------|
| Email readers | Utilities that provide a means of sending and receiving email. |
| Archie | Legacy Internet utility that provides access to indexes of anonymous FTP sites. |
| Gopher | Legacy menu-based Internet information utility. |
| Whois | A utility that provides access to directories with personal contact information—similar to Internet white pages. |

# Summary

This hour introduces TCP/IP's Application layer and describes some of the applications and services the Application layer supports. You learned about network services and TCP/IP's native utilities. You also learned about some of the ways in which TCP/IP supports network environments such as NetBIOS and NetWare.

# Q&A

**Q  A computer that is acting as a file server is running and is connected to the network, but the users can't access files. What could be wrong?**

**A** Any number of things could be wrong and a closer look at the particular operating system and configuration will yield a more detailed analysis. For purposes of understanding this chapter, the first step would be to check to see whether the computer's file server service is running. A file server is not just a computer; it is a service running on that computer that fulfills file requests.

**Q  The DNS service is running properly on my network, but the computer names of other computers don't appear in Windows 95 Network Neighborhood. What could be wrong?**

**A** Microsoft computer names are NetBIOS names, and DNS does not provide name service for NetBIOS names. You'll need to provide a means of resolving NetBIOS names using NetBIOS over TCP/IP. See Hour 17 for more on NetBIOS name resolution.

**Q  Why does IPX tunneling use the UDP Transport protocol rather than the more reliable TCP protocol?**

**A** IPX essentially grafts the IPX/SPX stack onto TCP/IP. IPX/SPX has its own error control and flow control features, so the error and flow control provided by TCP isn't necessary.

# Workshop

## Key Terms

Review the following list of key terms:

- File service—A service that fulfills network requests to write or read files to or from storage.
- IPX Tunneling—A method of supporting IPX/SPX on TCP/IP networks by interfacing IPX with TCP/IP's Transport layer.
- Name resolution service—A service that maps user-friendly names with network addresses.
- NetBIOS—A collection of network services and an interface to those services used on some computer-based networks.
- NetBIOS over TCP/IP (NBT)—A component that enables NetBIOS to function on TCP/IP networks.
- Print service—A service that fulfills network requests to print documents.
- Redirector—A service that checks local resource requests and forwards them to the network if necessary.
- WinSock—A Windows programming interface that provides access to TCP and UDP ports.

# HOUR **9**

# Routers, Brouters, and Bridges

*By Joe Casad*

Most large networks are divided using connectivity devices to increase network speed and efficiency and to minimize network traffic. As you'll learn in this hour, routers are the most common connectivity devices and certainly the most important for understanding the addressing and delivery systems of TCP/IP. They are an essential part of the Internet and they route and manage traffic on most large TCP/IP networks. Most of this hour focuses on routers and routing protocols, In addition we'll introduce two other connectivity devices: bridges and brouters.

# Goals for this Hour

At the completion of this hour, you'll be able to

- Explain why network administrators subdivide networks
- Define what a bridge is
- Define what a router is
- Describe how routers work
- Describe how routers use routing tables
- Explain the differences between static and dynamic routing
- Describe some of the types of routers found on the Internet

# Divided Networks

As previous hours have mentioned, network access methods such as CSMA/CD (Ethernet) and token passing (token ring) are designed to serve limited numbers of computers. A large network must provide some means of filtering and directing network traffic to prevent an overload of the transmission medium. Large networks are, therefore, divided into smaller segments. Each segment is isolated from the rest of the network by some filtering device.

If the source and the destination of a transmission are within the segment, the filtering device stops the transmission from passing to the greater network (see Figure 9.1). In a practical sense, this segmenting concept stops a considerable amount of traffic, because computers that are in close proximity (and thus on the same segment) are, in many cases, the most likely to be sharing information over the network. Two computers in the same office suite, for example, might regularly exchange files and share a printer and might only occasionally communicate with a third computer on the other end of the building.

**FIGURE 9.1**

*A filtering device.*

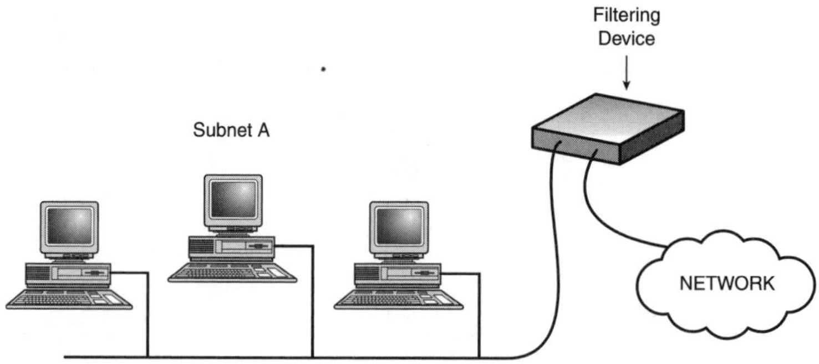

A device that filters traffic (as shown in Figure 9.1) is sometimes called a *connectivity device* (although the term connectivity device is sometimes used more generally to include a device such as a repeater, which doesn't provide filtering capabilities).

The primary uses for connectivity devices are as follows:

- Traffic control—As mentioned previously, a large network needs a means of filtering and isolating network traffic.
- Connectivity—Connectivity devices can connect dissimilar physical networks (for example, an Ethernet and a token ring). Some protocol-translating gateway devices can even connect a network using one protocol suite (such as a NetWare network using IPX/SPX) with a network using another protocol suite (such as the Internet, which uses TCP/IP).
- Hierarchical addressing—A logical addressing scheme such as the IP addressing system (see Hour 4, "The Internet Layer," and Hour 5, "Internet Layer: Subnetting") provides for a hierarchical delivery system in which the network ID is analogous to a street and the host ID is a house on that street. Segmenting the network provides a physical manifestation of this logical addressing concept.
- Signal regeneration—Connectivity devices can regenerate a network signal and thus extend the maximum cabling distance for a network.

Many types of connectivity devices exist, and they all play a role in managing traffic on TCP/IP networks. The following sections examine the these devices:

- Bridges
- Routers
- Brouters

## Bridges

A *bridge* is a connectivity device that filters and forwards packets by physical address. Bridges operate at the OSI Data Link layer (which, as described in Hour 3, "The Network Access Layer," falls within the TCP/IP Network Access layer).

Though a bridge is not a router, a bridge still uses a routing table as a source for delivery information. This physical address-based routing table is considerably different from and less sophisticated than the routing tables described later in this hour.

A modern bridge listens to each segment of the network it is connected to and builds a table showing which physical address is on which segment. When data is transmitted on one of the network segments, the bridge checks the destination address of the data and consults the routing table. If the destination address is on the segment from which the data was received, the bridge ignores the data. If the destination address is on a different segment, the bridge forwards the data to the appropriate segment. If the destination address isn't in the routing table, the bridge forwards the data to all segments except the segment from which it received the transmission.

 It is important to remember that the hardware-based physical addresses used by a bridge are different from the logical IP addresses. See Hours 1–4 for more on the difference between physical and logical addresses.

Bridges are commonly used on LANs as an inexpensive means of filtering traffic and, therefore, increasing the number of computers that can participate in the network. Because bridges use only Network Access layer physical addresses and do not examine logical addressing information available in the IP datagram header, bridges are not very useful for connecting dissimilar networks. Bridges also cannot assist with the IP routing and delivery schemes used to forward data on large networks such as the Internet.

## Routers

Routers are an essential part of any large TCP/IP network. Without routers the Internet could not function. In fact, the Internet never would have grown to what it is today without the development of network routers and TCP/IP routing protocols.

A *router* is a device that filters traffic by logical address. Routers operate at the Internet layer (OSI Network layer) using IP addressing information in the Internet-layer header.

A large network such as the Internet contains many routers that provide redundant pathways from the source to the destination nodes. The routers must work independently, but the effect of the system must be that data is routed accurately and efficiently through the internetwork.

Routers are far more sophisticated than bridges. Routers replace Network-Access header information as they pass data from one network to the next, so a router can connect dissimilar network types. Many routers also maintain detailed information describing the best path based on considerations of distance, bandwidth, and time. (You'll learn more about route-discovery protocols later in this hour.)

## Brouters

A *brouter* is a device that can act as both a bridge and a router. Most modern LANs can support multiple protocol suites concurrently but not all of those suites are routable.

Microsoft's NetBEUI protocol, for instance—a common LAN protocol system—is not routable (meaning that it cannot pass through a router). A brouter routes routable protocols (such as TCP/IP) and bridges non-routable protocols (such as NetBEUI).

> Sometimes a network administrator might not *want* to use a brouter. For traffic control and security reasons, it is sometimes preferable to isolate a non-routable protocol on the local network.

9

# Routing in TCP/IP

Routing in TCP/IP is a subject that has filled 162 RFCs and could easily fill a dozen books. What is truly remarkable about TCP/IP routing is that it works so well. An average homeowner can call up an Internet browser and connect with a computer in China or Finland without a passing thought to the many devices forwarding the request around the world. Even on smaller networks routers play a vital role in controlling traffic and keeping the network fast. The following sections discuss some of the concepts you'll need to be familiar with in order to understand routing in TCP/IP.

## What Is a Router?

The best way to describe a router is to describe how it looks. In its simplest form (or, at least, in its most fundamental form) a router looks like a computer with two network adapters. The earlier routers were actually computers with two or more network adapters (called multihomed computers). Figure 9.2 shows a multihomed computer acting as a router.

**FIGURE 9.2**

*A multihomed computer acting as a router.*

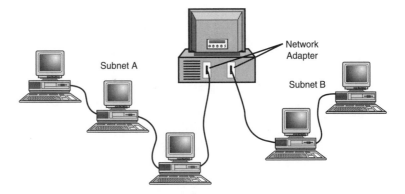

The first step to understanding routing is to remember that the IP address belongs to the adapter and not to the computer. The computer in Figure 9.2 has two IP addresses—one for each adapter. In fact, it is possible for the two adapters to be on completely different IP subnets corresponding to completely different physical networks (as shown in Figure 9.2). In Figure 9.2 the protocol software on the multihomed computer can receive the data from subnet A, check the IP address information to see if the data belongs on subnet B, replace the lower-protocol header information to prepare the data for subnet B (if the data is addressed to subnet B), and transmit the data on to subnet B. In this simple scenario the multihomed computer acts as a router.

If you really want to understand what routers are doing, imagine the scenario in the preceding paragraph with the following complications:

- The router has more than two ports (adapters) and can therefore interconnect more than two networks. The decision of where to forward the data then becomes more complicated and the possibilities for redundant paths increase.

- The networks that the router interconnects are each interconnected with other networks. In other words, the router sees network addresses for networks to which it is not directly connected. The router must have a strategy for forwarding data addressed to networks to which it is not directly attached.

- The network of routers provides redundant paths, and each router must have a way of deciding which path to use.

The simple configuration in Figure 9.2 combined with the preceding three complications offers a more detailed view of the router's role (see Figure 9.3).

**FIGURE 9.3**

*Routing on a complex network.*

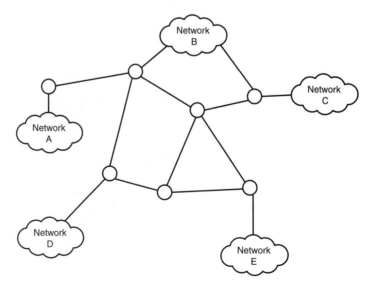

On today's networks, most routers are not multihomed computers. It is more cost-effective to assign routing responsibilities to a specialized device. The routing device is specifically designed to perform routing functions efficiently, and the device does not include all the extra features found in a complete computer.

 One situation in which a multihomed computer is often used as a router is the case of a dial-up server. You'll learn more about dial-up networking in Hour 10, "Dial-up TCP/IP."

9

## How Routing Works

Building on the discussion of the simple router described in the preceding section, a more general description of the router's role is as follows:

1. The router receives data from one of its attached networks.

2. The router passes the data up the protocol stack to the Internet layer. In other words, the router discards the Network Access layer header information and reassembles (if necessary) the IP datagram.

3. The router checks the destination address in the IP header. If the destination is on the network from whence the data came, the router discards the data that has already presumably reached its destination because it was transmitted on the network of the destination computer.

4. If the data is destined for a different network, the router consults a routing table to determine where to forward the data.

5. After the router determines which of its adapters will receive the data, it passes the data down through the appropriate Network Access layer software for transmission through the adapter.

The routing process is shown in Figure 9.4. It might occur to you that the routing table described in step 4 is a rather crucial element. In fact, the routing table and the protocol that builds the routing table are distinguishing characteristics of the router. Most of the discussion about routers is about how routers build routing tables and how the route protocols used to assemble routing table information cause the collection of routers to serve as a unified system.

FIGURE 9.4

*The routing process.*

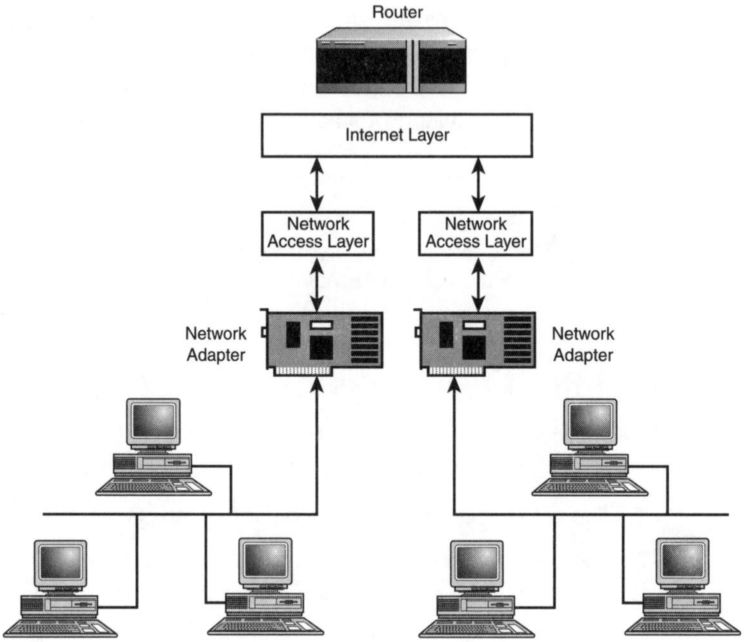

The two primary types of routing are named for where they get their routing table information:

- Static routing—Requires the network administrator to manually enter route information.
- Dynamic routing—Builds the routing table dynamically based on routing information obtained using routing protocols.

Static routing can be useful in some contexts, but as you might have guessed, a system that requires the network administrator to enter routing information manually has some severe limitations. First, static routing does not adapt well to large networks with hundreds of possible routes. Second, static routing on all but the simplest networks requires a disproportionate investment of time from the network administrator, who must not only create but also continually update the routing table information. Also, a static router cannot adapt as quickly to changes in the network, such as a downed router.

## Routing Table Concepts

It is best to focus on a few important concepts before continuing with the discussion of dynamic routing protocols. The role of the routing table and other Internet layer routing elements is to deliver the data to the proper local network. After the data reaches the local network, lower network access protocols will see to the delivery on the local internet. The routing table, therefore, does not need to store complete IP addresses and can simply list addresses by network ID. (See Hours 4 and 5 for a discussion of the host ID and network ID portions of the IP address.)

Conceptually the contents of a typical routing table are as shown in Figure 9.5. A routing table essentially maps destination network IDs to the IP address of the *next hop*—the next stop the datagram makes on its path to the destination network. Note that the routing table makes a distinction between networks directly connected to the router itself and networks connected indirectly through other routers. The next hop can be either the destination network (if it is directly connected) or the next downstream router on the way to the destination network. The Router Port Interface in Figure 9.5 refers to the router port through which the router forwards the data.

**FIGURE 9.5**

*The routing table.*

| Destination | Next Hop | Router Port Interface |
|---|---|---|
| 129.14.0.0 | Direct Connection | 1 |
| 150.27.0.0 | 131.100.18.6 | 3 |
| 155.111.0.0 | Direct Connection | 2 |
| 165.48.0.0 | 129.14.16.1 | 1 |

The next hop entry in the routing table is the key to understanding dynamic routing. On a complex network, several paths to the destination might exist, and the router must decide which of these paths the next hop will follow. A dynamic router makes this decision based on information obtained through routing protocols.

A host computer, such as a router, can have a routing table; because the host does not have to perform routing functions its routing table usually isn't as complicated. Hosts often make use of a *default router* or *default gateway*. The default gateway is the router that receives the datagram if it can't be delivered on the local network or to another router.

## Routing Protocols

In a totally hierarchical system such as the Internet, it is not necessary or useful for all routers to serve the same role. In the ARPAnet system that led to the Internet, a small group of core routers serve as a central backbone for the internetwork, linking individual networks that are configured and managed autonomously. The role of a router in that core backbone network is different from the role of a router within one of the autonomous networks connected to the core.

The routers that connect the autonomous networks to other networks also serve a third role. Figure 9.6 depicts this architecture with its associated router types. Each router type has different needs, and each type uses a different routing protocol to assemble routes. It is also important to note that the routers within one of the autonomous networks might also have a hierarchical configuration. Managers of the autonomous network are free to design a router configuration that works for the network and to choose routing protocols accordingly.

**FIGURE 9.6**

*Internet router archi-*
*tecture.*

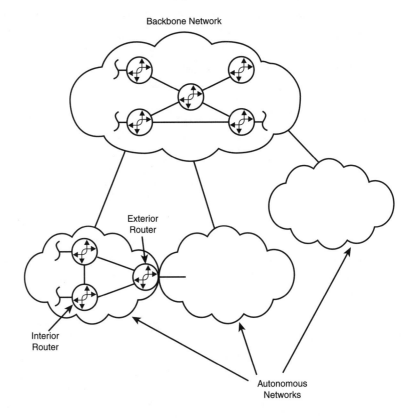

The router types and some examples of their associated protocols are as follows:

- Core routers—Core routers have complete information about other core routers. The routing table is basically a map of where autonomous systems tie into the core network. Core routers do not possess detailed information about routes within the autonomous networks. Examples of core router routing protocols include Gateway-to-Gateway Protocol (GGP) and the more recent routing protocol called SPREAD.

- Exterior routers—Exterior routers are non-core routers between autonomous networks. They maintain routing information about their own and neighboring autonomous networks but do not have a map of the complete internetwork. Exterior routers have traditionally used a protocol called Exterior Gateway Protocol (EGP). The actual EGP protocol is now outdated, but newer routing protocols that serve exterior routers are commonly referred to as EGPs.

- Interior routers—Routers within an autonomous region that "talk" to each other to share routing information are called interior gateways. These routers use a class of routing protocols called Interior Gateway Protocol (IGP). Examples of interior routing protocols include RIP and OSPF. You'll learn more about RIP and OSPF in the following sections.

## Routing Information Protocol (RIP)

RIP is a distance-vector routing protocol, which means that it calculates the next hop entry in the routing table based on the fewest number of hops from the router to the destination network. Each router broadcasts information about itself and the hop count from it to other routers. When a router receives the information from a neighboring router, it increments the hop counts by one and forwards the information to neighboring routers. In this way routers can learn the various hop counts from each of their ports to the destination network and can evaluate the best path based on hop count information.

Other distance-vector routing protocols sometimes include other factors, such as bandwidth and time in their calculation of the best route.

RIP is a common TCP/IP routing protocol that is gradually being replaced by newer protocols, such as OSPF.

## Open Shortest Path First (OSPF)

OSPF is a more recent interior routing protocol that is gradually replacing RIP on many networks. OSPF is a link-state routing protocol.

In a link-state protocol, each router periodically broadcasts information on itself and the status of its links with other routers to which it is directly connected. Each router receives all the link status updates and assembles a map of the network accordingly. The biggest advantage of link-state protocols such as OSPF is that intermediate routers do not have to perform a calculation (increment the hop count) on information obtained from other routers. Also, the total quantity of redundant information is reduced, which reduces the amount of network bandwidth that must be devoted to updating router information. The effect of this is that OSPF can support bigger and busier networks than RIP.

# Summary

This hour introduces the topic of connectivity devices and describes routers, brouters, and bridges. You learned how routing works and you learned about some common router types and router protocols.

# Q&A

**Q** **My friend operates a small subnetwork that is connected to a bigger network using a router. His subnetwork uses both TCP/IP and NetBEUI. I asked him if he wanted a brouter instead of a router so he could forward NetBEUI as well as TCP/IP. He said, "No way!" Why doesn't he want to forward NetBEUI?**

**A** For security as well as capacity reasons some network administrators sometimes choose to use a non-routable protocol for transmissions on the local subnet and a routable protocol for transmissions that must pass to the greater network. Your friend has designed the network to take advantage of NetBEUI's non-routability; if he put in a brouter, NetBEUI services would no longer be isolated.

**Q** **How many legal IP addresses can one network device have?**

**A** A network device can have one IP address for each network adapter.

**Q** **Why don't core Internet routers use static routing?**

**A** It wouldn't be practical for a network administrator to personally type in routing table information for a core router on the wildly complex and amorphous Internet.

# Workshop

## Key Terms

- Bridge—A connectivity device that forwards data based on physical addresses.
- Brouter—A connectivity device that routes routable protocols and bridges non-routable protocols.
- Dynamic routing—A routing method in which routing information is supplied dynamically through routing protocols.
- Multihomed computer—A computer with multiple network adapters.
- OSPF—A common link-state interior routing protocol.
- RIP—A common distance-vector interior routing protocol.

- Router—A connectivity device that forwards data based on logical addresses (IP addresses, in the case of TCP/IP).

- Routing protocol—One of several protocols used by routers to assemble route information.

- Routing table—A table within the router that relates network IDs to network paths.

- Static routing—A routing method in which the routing information is input manually by the network administrator.

9

# Hour **10**

# Dial-up TCP/IP

*By Joe Casad*

One of the most popular methods for connecting to a TCP/IP network is a dial-up connection through a telephone line. This hour introduces modems and TCP/IP modem connectivity. You'll also learn about the two most popular TCP/IP dial-up networking protocols: Serial Line Internet Protocol (SLIP) and Point-to-Point Protocol (PPP).

## Goals for this Hour

At the completion of this hour, you'll be able to

- Describe what a point-to-point connection is
- Describe why dial-up protocols are different from LAN-based network protocols
- Describe the difference between early host dial-up access and today's SLIP and PPP access
- Describe the SLIP data format

- Describe SLIP's characteristics
- List the components that make up PPP
- Describe PPP data format
- Describe PPP characteristics

# A Look at Modems

One of the most common methods for connecting to the TCP/IP network (the Internet) is through a phone line. Telephone access is now an everyday feature of home and traveling computers. Dial-up access is also an option on many office networks, where dial-up service can offer inexpensive Internet access or provide a link for a worker who travels or has an office at home. In most cases this dial-up access is accomplished using a *modem*.

A modem provides network access through a phone line. Engineers created modems because the industry saw the enormous benefit of providing a way for computers to communicate over the world's most accessible transmission medium: the global telephone system. It isn't possible to hook a computer up to a phone cord because the discrete digital signals that come from a computer are entirely different from the sound waves that travel through a phone line, which can display infinite variation in amplitude and frequency. The purpose of a modem is to transform the digital signal from a computer into an analog signal that travels over the line and transforms incoming analog signals from the phone line into a digital signal that the computer understands. The term modem is short for MOdulate/DEModulate.

Not all modems are associated with telephone lines. Another type of modem that has come into vogue recently is the cable modem, which provides network access through a cable TV line.

## Point-to-Point Connections

As you learned in Hour 3, "The Network Access Layer," local networks such as Ethernet and token ring employ elaborate access strategies for enabling computers to share the network medium. By contrast, the two computers at either end of a phone line do not have to compete for the transmission medium with other computers—they only have to share it with each other. This type of connection is called a point-to-point connection (see Figure 10.1).

**Figure 10.1**

*A point-to-point connection.*

A point-to-point connection is simpler than a LAN-based configuration because it doesn't have to provide a means for multiple computers to share the transmission medium. At the same time, a connection through a phone line has some limitations. One of the biggest limitations is that transmission rates over a phone connection are much slower than rates over a LAN-based network such as Ethernet. This reduced transmission speed argues for a protocol that minimizes the data overhead of the protocol itself—less is better. As you'll learn in this hour, as modems have become faster, modem protocols have taken on additional responsibilities.

Another challenge of dial-up protocols is the great diversity of hardware and software configurations they must support. On a local network, a system administrator oversees and controls the configuration of each computer, and the protocol system depends on a high degree of uniformity among the communicating devices. A dial-up connection, on the other hand, can occur from almost anywhere in the world. Dial-up protocols must contend with a wider and more varied range of possibilities regarding the hardware and software of the communicating machines.

## Modem Protocols

You might wonder why this point-to-point connection, with its two computers, even needs the complications of the TCP/IP stack in order to make a connection. The simple answer is that it doesn't.

Early modem protocols were a method for passing information across the phone line, and in that situation the logical addressing and internetwork error control of TCP/IP was not necessary or even desirable. Later, with the arrival of local networks and the Internet, engineers began to think about using a dial-up connection as a means of providing network access. The first implementations of this remote network access concept were an extension of earlier modem protocols. In these first *host dial-up* schemes, the computer attached to the network assumed all responsibility for preparing the data for the network. Either explicitly or implicitly, the remote computer acted more like a terminal (see Figure 10.2), directing the networked host to perform networking tasks and sending and receiving data across the modem line through an entirely separate process.

**10**

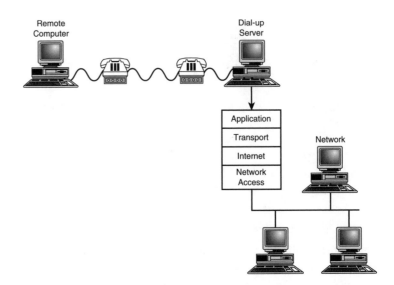

**FIGURE 10.2**

*An early host-dial-up configuration.*

These early host dial-up schemes, however, had some limitations. They reflected an earlier centralized model of computing, which placed huge demands on the computer providing the network access. (Imagine Figure 10.2 with several computers simultaneously connected to the dial-up server.) They also made inefficient use of the processing power of the remote computer.

As TCP/IP and other routable protocols began to emerge, designers began to imagine another solution in which the remote computer would take more responsibility for networking tasks and the dial-up server would act more like a router. This solution (shown in Figure 10.3) was more consistent with the newer, more decentralized paradigm of computer networks and also closer to the true nature of TCP/IP. In this arrangement, the remote computer operates its own protocol stack, with the modem protocol(s) acting at the Network Access layer. The *dial-up* server accepts the data and routes it to the greater network.

Dial-up protocols, therefore, began to work directly with TCP/IP and became an integral part of the stack. This hour covers the two most common TCP/IP modem protocols. You'll learn about

- Serial Line Internet Protocol (SLIP)—An early TCP/IP-based modem protocol, SLIP was simple and, therefore, had some limitations. You'll learn about some of these limitations later in this hour.

- Point-to-Point Protocol (PPP)—Currently the most popular protocol for modem connections, PPP began as a refinement of SLIP. It offers many important features that weren't available with its predecessor.

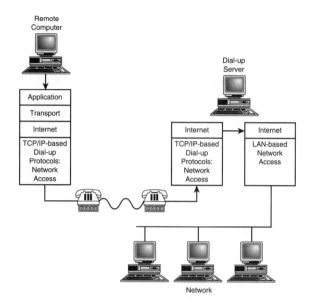

**FIGURE 10.3**

*A true TCP/IP dial-up connection.*

10

PPP is gradually replacing SLIP as the method of choice for dial-up Internet connections. The remainder of this chapter takes a closer look at SLIP and PPP.

 Both SLIP and PPP are built on lower-level serial communications protocols that see to the details of actually modulating and demodulating the signal. These serial communication protocols provide what would be considered OSI Physical layer functions.

# Serial Line Internet Protocol (SLIP)

SLIP was an early attempt at directly integrating modem protocols with TCP/IP. SLIP began with 3COM's UNET TCP/IP. It was later implemented on Berkeley UNIX systems and since then has become widely available, both within the UNIX world and in the world of computer compatibles.

SLIP's technology is now considered somewhat obsolete. There is no question, however, that it works, and in some situations SLIP's simplicity is a benefit. Two reasons SLIP survives to this day are its ties to UNIX and the large investment that some institutions made in SLIP a few years ago when they began to go online.

## What SLIP Does

The purpose of SLIP is to transmit IP datagrams across a modem line. SLIP provides no physical addressing or error control and depends on upper-layer protocols for error control functions. SLIP simply sends the data then sends a signal marking the end of the data.

The SLIP data format is shown in Figure 10.4. A special END character (equivalent to decimal 192) marks the end of the data. If an END character occurs naturally in the data, SLIP includes a special ESC character before the END character so that the receiving computer doesn't prematurely stop receiving the packet.

**FIGURE 10.4**

*The SLIP data format.*

> The ESC character used in SLIP is unrelated to the Esc button on your computer keyboard.

The RFCs do not specify a standard maximum size for a packet of SLIP data, but RFC 1055 recommends a maximum size of 1006 bytes, excluding the characters that mark the end of the frame, when using a Berkeley UNIX SLIP driver.

SLIP implementation developers can set a maximum size and define other configuration settings. Unlike PPP, SLIP does not enable the communicating computers to dynamically negotiate connection configuration settings. Therefore, SLIP configurations are not always compatible.

## Characteristics

SLIP has survived beyond its years, and although it was an innovation in its time, in the context of today's technology a list of SLIP's characteristics looks similar to a list of its shortcomings.

RFC 1055 identifies the following SLIP characteristics/deficiencies:

- Addressing—Both computers have to know each other's IP address. SLIP is incapable of supporting dynamic IP address assignment. This makes SLIP impractical for dial-up accounts with Internet service providers (ISPs), which typically lease IP addresses to dial-up users for the duration of the session. SLIP is incapable of receiving this leased address.

- Type identification—As RFC 1055 puts it, "SLIP has no Type field." Because SLIP offers no means of specifying a protocol type, SLIP is incapable of supporting multiple protocols simultaneously. Unlike PPP, SLIP cannot multiplex/demultiplex other protocol systems with TCP/IP.

- Error correction/detection—SLIP does not provide error correction. As you learned in previous hours, various forms of error checking occur at upper layers, so error checking through the modem protocols is not absolutely essential. Some services, however, are designed with the assumption that network access protocols will check for transmission errors on the physical network. Depending solely on an upper-layer error recovery scheme such as TCP's (refer to Hour 7, "TCP and UDP") can result in a significant amount of retransmission, reducing efficiency over the already slow modem link.

- Compression—Because transmission over a phone line is so slow, any means of reducing the quantity of data is beneficial. Successive TCP and IP headers often contain redundant information, and there are several strategies for compressing header information. SLIP does not support header compression.

The networking industry addressed some of the shortcomings of SLIP through the development of PPP, which you'll learn more about in the following sections.

# Point to Point Protocol (PPP)

When industry experts began to design the PPP standard, they had a much better idea of what features would be useful for the emerging Internet. They also knew that modems and phone lines were getting faster and could support a greater amount of protocol overhead. PPP was an effort to address some of the shortcomings of SLIP.

The designers of PPP also wanted PPP to be capable of dynamically negotiating configuration settings at the beginning of a connection and to be capable of managing the link between the communicating computers throughout the session.

## How PPP Works

PPP is really a collection of protocols that interact to supply a full complement of modem-based networking features. The design of PPP evolved through a series of RFCs. The current PPP standard is RFC 1661; subsequent documents have clarified and extended PPP components. RFC 1661 divides the components of PPP into three general categories:

- A method for encapsulating multiprotocol datagrams. SLIP and PPP both accept datagrams and prepare them for the Internet. But PPP, unlike SLIP, must be prepared to accept datagrams from more than one protocol system.

**10**

- A Link Control Protocol (LCP) for establishing, configuring, and testing the connection. PPP negotiates configuration settings and thus eliminates compatibility problems encountered with SLIP connections.

- A family of Network Control Protocols (NCPs) supporting upper-layer protocol systems. PPP can include separate sublayers that provide separate interfaces to TCP/IP and to alternative suites, such as IPX/SPX.

The following sections discuss these components of PPP.

## PPP Data

The primary purpose of PPP, and SLIP, is to forward datagrams. One challenge of PPP is that it must be capable of forwarding more than one type of datagram. In other words, the datagram could be an IP datagram, or it could be some other OSI network-layer datagram.

> The PPP RFCs use the term *packet* to describe a bundle of data transmitted in a PPP frame. A packet can consist of an IP (or other upper-layer protocol) *datagram*, or it can consist of data formatted for one of the other protocols operating through PPP. The word *packet* is an often imprecise term used throughout the networking industry for a package of data transmitted across the network; for the most part, this book has attempted to use a more precise term, such as *datagram*. Not all PPP data packages, however, are datagrams, so in keeping with the RFCs, this hour uses the term *packet* for data transmitted through PPP.

PPP must also forward data with information relating to its own protocols: the protocols that establish and manage the modem connection. Communicating devices exchange several types of messages and requests over the course of a PPP connection. The communicating computers must exchange LCP packets, used to establish, manage, and close the connection; authentication packets, which support PPP's optional authentication protocols; and NCP packets, which interface PPP with various protocol suites. The LCP data exchanged at the beginning of the connection configures the connection parameters that are common to all protocols. NCP protocols then configure suite-specific parameters relating to the individual protocol suites supported by the PPP connection.

The data format for a PPP frame is shown in Figure 10.5. The fields are as follows:

- Protocol—A one- or two-byte field providing an identification number for the protocol type of the enclosed packet. Possible types include an LCP packet, an NCP packet, an IP packet, or an OSI Network layer protocol packet. IANA maintains a list of standard identification numbers for the various protocol types.

- Enclosed data (zero or more bytes)—The control packet or upper-layer datagram being transmitted with the frame.

- Padding (optional and variable length)—Additional bytes as required by the protocol designated in the protocol field. Each protocol is responsible for determining how it will distinguish padding from the enclosed datagram.

**FIGURE 10.5**

*PPP data format.*

| Protocol 1-2 Byte | Enclosed Data | Padding |
|---|---|---|

If the enclosed data is a datagram of some other protocol suite, it isn't related to TCP/IP, and you won't find it discussed in this book.

## PPP Connections

The life cycle of a PPP connection is as follows:

1. The connection is established using the LCP negotiation process, as described in the next section.

2. If the negotiation process in step 1 specifies a configuration option for authentication, the communicating computers enter an authentication phase. RFC 1661 offers the authentication options Password Authentication Protocol (PAP) and Challenge Handshake Authentication Protocol (CHAP). Additional authentication protocols are also supported, as specified in the Assigned Numbers Standard, RFC 1340.

3. PPP uses NCP packets to specify protocol-specific configuration information for each supported protocol suite (for example, TCP/IP or IPX/SPX).

4. PPP transmits datagrams received from upper-layer protocols. If the negotiation phase in step 1 includes a configuration option for link quality monitoring then monitoring protocols will transmit monitoring information. NCP might transmit information regarding specific protocols.

5. PPP closes the connection through the exchange of LCP termination packets.

## Link Control Protocol (LCP)

Much of PPP's power and versatility comes from the LCP functions that establish, manage, and terminate connections. RFC 1661 identifies three types of LCP packets:

- Link configuration packets
- Link termination packets
- Link maintenance packets

Many PPP features that aren't available with SLIP are a result of LCP. Figure 10.6 describes how LCP configuration packets enable the communicating computers to establish a connection. In Figure 10.6, Computer A sends an LCP configure-request packet to Computer B. The configure-request packet includes a proposal for any connection parameters Computer A would like to negotiate for the connection. These parameters include the Maximum Receive Unit (MRU)—the maximum length for the data enclosed in a PPP frame, the authentication protocol, and the quality control protocol—that defines how the connection monitors for reliable delivery, compression protocol settings, and other configuration choices. RFC 1340, "Assigned Numbers, Std 2," describes the configuration options.

**FIGURE 10.6**

*An LCP connection configuration.*

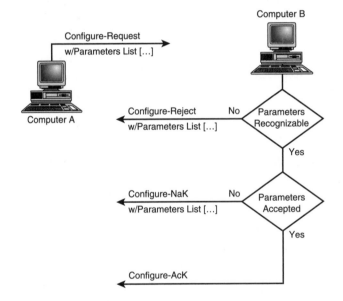

If Computer B accepts all configuration options submitted in the Configure-Request packet, Computer B responds with a Configure-Ack packet (Ack stands for Acknowledge). If all configuration options transmitted with the Configure-Request are recognizable but some are not acceptable to Computer B then Computer B responds with a Configure-Nak packet (Nak stands for not acknowledged) and returns a list of unacceptable parameters with alternative values. Computer A then responds to the Configure-Nak with a new configuration request using adjusted values. This process continues until all values are accepted.

If the Configure-Request packet includes unrecognizable options, Computer B returns a Configure-Reject packet, which lists any unacceptable options.

Figure 10.7 shows the format for an LCP packet. Several other types of LCP packets assist with overseeing the modem connection. The code field in Figure 10.7 identifies the LCP packet type. The Identifier field identifies the packet and helps to match up requests with acknowledgments. The Length filed is the length of the packet. The data transmitted with the packet depends on the type of packet. A list of LCP packet type codes is shown in Table 10.1.

**FIGURE 10.7**

*LCP packet format.*

| Code (1-Byte) | Identifier (1-Byte) | Length (2-Byte) | Data (Varies)... |
|---|---|---|---|

**TABLE 10.1** LCP PACKET TYPE CODES

| Code | Description |
|---|---|
| 1 | Configure-Request |
| 2 | Configure-Ack |
| 3 | Configure-Nak |
| 4 | Configure-Reject |
| 5 | Terminate-Request |
| 6 | Terminate-Ack |
| 7 | Code-Reject |
| 8 | Protocol-Reject |
| 9 | Echo-Request |
| 10 | Echo-Reply |
| 11 | Discard-Request |

As mentioned earlier, LCP tends to maintenance and termination tasks as well as configuration tasks. The Terminate-Request and Terminate-Ack packets are used to request and acknowledge termination of the connection. Code-Reject and Protocol-Reject reject requests for an unknown code or protocol. Echo-Request, Echo-Reply, and Discard-Request provide maintenance, quality assurance, and troubleshooting capabilities.

# Summary

This hour covers some of the basics of dial-up networking. You learned about modems, point-to-point connections, and host dial-up access. This hour also discusses the two most important TCP/IP dial-up protocols: SLIP and PPP. You learned about SLIP data format and some of SLIP's weaknesses. You also learned about the newer and more powerful PPP protocol, which provides dynamic configuration and supports multiple protocol suites.

# Q&A

**Q Why don't SLIP and PPP require a complete physical addressing system such as the system used with Ethernet?**

A A point-to-point connection doesn't require an elaborate physical addressing system such as Ethernet's because only the two computers participating in the connection are attached to the line. SLIP and PPP do, however, provide full support for logical addressing using IP or other Network-layer protocols.

**Q Why does PPP use NCP protocols to configure protocol-specific settings instead of configuring protocol-specific settings during the LCP connection establishment phase?**

A LCP only undertakes configuration tasks that are common to all protocols. Individual protocols are then configured through NCP packets. This modular arrangement minimizes startup time because only the protocol settings that are actually necessary will be configured.

**Q Why wouldn't SLIP be a good choice for a typical dial-up Internet service connection?**

A Most ISPs assign temporary IP addresses at connect time. SLIP doesn't support dynamic IP address assignment, so SLIP wouldn't be a good choice for a typical dial-up account.

# Workshop

## Key Terms

Review the following list of key terms:

- Link Control Protocol (LCP)—A protocol used by PPP to establish, manage, and terminate dial-up connections.
- Maximum Receive Unit (MRU)—The maximum length for the data enclosed in a PPP frame.
- Modem—A device that translates a digital signal to or from an analog signal.
- Network Control Protocol (NCP)—One of a family of protocols designed to interface PPP with specific protocol suites.
- Point-to-point connection—A connection consisting of exactly two communicating devices sharing a transmission line.
- Point-to-Point Protocol (PPP)—A TCP/IP dial-up protocol. PPP is newer and more powerful than SLIP.
- Serial Line Internet Protocol (SLIP)—An early TCP/IP-based dial-up protocol.

# PART III

# TCP/IP Utilities

## Hour

# HOUR 11

# TCP/IP Connectivity Utilities

*By Bob Willsey*

This hour introduces you to 10 utilities that you can use when troubleshooting and configuring TCP/IP. The utilities presented here are tools that you will find indispensable when you need to identify connectivity problems, test communication between network nodes, and check the TCP/IP settings of computers on your network. By becoming familiar with how these utilities function in a properly working environment, you will be able to use them to isolate problems when they occur.

By using various utilities and determining which utilities work correctly and which do not, and by identifying the path through which data flows for each utility, you can often zero in on problem areas. Possible problem areas are indicated by unique paths taken by data in the not-fully functioning utility, which may help you narrow the list of problems.

The section titled, "Using Connectivity Utilities to Troubleshoot," later in this chapter introduces several techniques to help you zero in on problems.

Companies that write TCP/IP software might implement the utilities presented in this chapter differently, or not at all. Generally speaking these utilities are not covered by RFC specifications, which explains the latitude in implementation. Unless otherwise noted the options and screen shots presented are based on Windows NT 4.0 Server. You should check the documentation accompanying your TCP/IP software to determine the actual optional parameters and expected display output for utilities in your system.

## Goals for this Hour

At the completion of this hour, you will be able to

- Identify the uses and types of responses you should expect from the following utilities:
    - IPConfig
    - Ping
    - Address Resolution Protocol (ARP)
    - TraceRoute
    - Route
    - Hostname
    - NetStat
    - Net Use/View
    - NBTStat
    - Network Monitor
- Use connectivity utilities to troubleshoot problems

## IPConfig

The IPConfig utility and its GUI Windows95/98 counterpart WinIPCfg display current TCP/IP configuration settings. This information is useful to verify that manually configured settings are actually implemented correctly. However, this utility is even more useful if your computer leases its IP address and related parameters from a Dynamic Host Configuration Protocol (DHCP) Server. Here IPConfig allows you to see whether or not your computer has successfully leased an IP address, and if it has, what address it is currently assigned. Knowing a computer's current IP address, subnet mask, and default gateway are virtually required items for testing and troubleshooting. Here are some of the most useful options:

- Default (no options)—When IPConfig is used without options it displays the IP address, subnet mask, and default gateway values for each configured interface, as shown in the upper portion of Figure 11.1.

- All—When the all option IPConfig/all is used, IPConfig displays additional information such as the IP addresses for the DNS and WINS server(s) it is configured to use, as well as the physical address burned into local network adapters. If addresses were leased from a DHCP server, IPConfig will display the IP address of the DHCP server and the date the lease is scheduled to expire. (Setting up a DHCP server is an advanced topic that is covered in Hour 21, "Dynamic Host Configuration Protocol.")

**Figure 11.1**

ipconfig *and* ipconfig/all *commands and responses.*

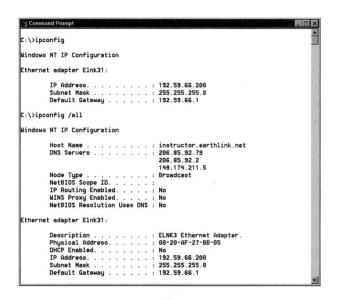

11

- release and renew—These two additional switch options only work on computers that leased their IP address from a DHCP server. If you enter ipconfig/release then the leased IP addresses for all interfaces are released back to the DHCP server(s). Conversely, if you enter ipconfig/renew then the local computer attempts to contact a DHCP server and lease an IP address. Be aware that in many cases the network adapter(s) will be reassigned the same IP addresses previously assigned.

A variation on the release and renew commands can be used to release or renew one adapter at a time in a computer that contains multiple network adapters. Assuming one of the computers adapters is named Elnk31, this one adapter can be released or renewed by using the following commands ipconfig/release Elnk31 or ipconfig/renew Elnk31.

If you are using Windows 95 or 98 then you use the command winipcfg instead of ipconfig; this displays a graphical interface with the same information as displayed by ipconfig, and it provides the same options for releasing and renewing IP addresses. Windows NT also has a graphical replacement that is included if you purchase the Windows NT Resource Kit; this utility is named WNTIPCfg. See Figure 11.2 for an example of these graphical equivalents. On UNIX or UNIX-like systems you can use the IFConfig utility to output TCP/IP configuration information. For more information see Hour 18, "Using TCP/IP in UNIX and Linux."

**FIGURE 11.2**

*The graphical interface equivalent for IPConfig.*

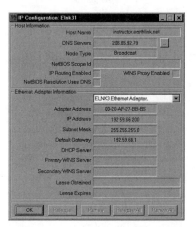

# Ping

The Ping utility is used to determine if the local host is capable of exchanging (sending and receiving) datagrams with another host. Using this information you can infer that certain TCP/IP configuration parameters are correctly configured and operating properly. However, don't fall into the trap of thinking that by successfully pinging another host once or twice that TCP/IP is properly configured. You need to perform a number of pings of both local and remote hosts in order to gain a level of confidence.

Ping is a term based on the sonar technology used by submarines and ships to locate other objects. Ping is an acronym for Packet Internet Groper.

Ping is a great utility to use as a starting point in checking a computer's capability to communicate. It only requires that the bottom two layers of the TCP/IP stack are operational. You could have problems with TCP, UDP, or applications in the upper two layers and Ping would still operate. For instance, if Ping operates correctly you can largely rule out problems with items such as the Network Access layer, the network adapter, cabling, and even routers, thus narrowing your focus as to where the problem lies.

Ping sends datagrams to a specific host using the ICMP echo request command. (For more information on ICMP, see Hour 4, "The Internet Layer.") If the station is present and operational it responds using the ICMP echo reply. Ping displays statistics such as the number of lost datagrams and the amount of time in milliseconds it takes for the response to return.

Ping, by default on Windows NT, sends four ICMP echo requests with 32 bytes of data; you should expect four echo replies if everything is working correctly. However, it is not uncommon to send four echo requests and to receive three or even fewer responses to a ping. You should not consider the occasional dropped datagram as a failure, as IP does not guarantee delivery but makes its best effort to deliver datagrams. On the other hand if datagrams are being dropped on a fairly consistent basis this is an indication that even under normal use TCP/IP will be required to resend datagrams, which obviously slows throughput and increases network traffic.

Ping displays the time in milliseconds from the time the echo request was sent until the echo reply is returned. Short response times indicate that a datagram does not have to pass through too many routers or through slow networks.

Ping also displays the TTL (Time to Live) value, which lets you know how many additional routers this packet could pass through before it would be discarded. You can also use TTL to make an educated guess as to how many routers the packet has passed through. For instance, if you see packets are returning with a TTL of 119 you would probably be correct in assuming the TTL started as 128 (being the next higher multiple of the power of 2) when the packet first left the source. Subtracting to find the difference 128-119= 9 you could assume the source is 9 router hops away. The TraceRoute utility, which is covered later, can be used to verify your assumption.

If pings are returning with a TTL near zero, for example values of one or two, it might be an indication of network errors and retries. For example, suppose I ping an IP address in Hong Kong and the computer I am pinging sends packets with a TTL of 32. Suppose the most direct path from Hong Kong to my computer passes through 30 routers and the datagrams which travel that path arrive with a TTL value of two. Because each datagram might follow a separate path as it travels from source to destination, other datagrams might travel through the next most direct path, which contains 35 routers. Datagrams sent through this longer path expires before ever reaching my computer. This would likely cause the source to resend the datagram additional times until one of the datagrams took the shortest path.

Normally when you use Ping to troubleshoot problems or to verify operation, you use a number of ping statements. If all pings work correctly you can gain confidence in basic connectivity and the configuration parameters. If on the other hand some of the ping commands fail, it can indicate where to look for problems.

The following list identifies a typical order for using ping commands to troubleshoot and describes what information you can derive from the responses. Typically you perform an ipconfig prior to the ping commands to display the IP address of the computer and of the default gateway. Both of these addresses are used during this process. In the examples shown the local computer was configured with an IP address of 207.217.151.5 and a default gateway of 207.217.151.1. Be sure to substitute your actual parameters in place of those shown in the example.

A successful ping returns four replies, while pings that return one, two, or three replies fall into a gray area that might indicate an intermittent problem. A ping that returns zero replies is definitely a failure. Figure 11.3 displays a few ping commands.

FIGURE **11.3**

ping *commands of*
*specific IP addresses.*

```
 ; Command Prompt                                                    _ □ ×
C:\>ping 127.0.0.1

Pinging 127.0.0.1 with 32 bytes of data:

Reply from 127.0.0.1: bytes=32 time<10ms TTL=128
Reply from 127.0.0.1: bytes=32 time<10ms TTL=128
Reply from 127.0.0.1: bytes=32 time<10ms TTL=128
Reply from 127.0.0.1: bytes=32 time<10ms TTL=128

C:\>ping 207.217.151.5

Pinging 207.217.151.5 with 32 bytes of data:

Reply from 207.217.151.5: bytes=32 time<10ms TTL=128
Reply from 207.217.151.5: bytes=32 time<10ms TTL=128
Reply from 207.217.151.5: bytes=32 time<10ms TTL=128
Reply from 207.217.151.5: bytes=32 time<10ms TTL=128

C:\>ping 207.217.151.1

Pinging 207.217.151.1 with 32 bytes of data:

Reply from 207.217.151.1: bytes=32 time=431ms TTL=127
Reply from 207.217.151.1: bytes=32 time=410ms TTL=127
Reply from 207.217.151.1: bytes=32 time=421ms TTL=127
Reply from 207.217.151.1: bytes=32 time=410ms TTL=127
```

- `ping 127.0.0.1`—This ping is directed to the local computer IP software. The ping never leaves the computer. If this fails it indicates basic problems with the installation or operation of TCP/IP.

- `ping 207.217.151.5`—This ping is directed to the IP address of your computer. Your computer should always answer this ping, so if this fails it could indicate local configuration or installation problems. If this fails, disconnect the network cable then try the command again. If it works correctly with the network cable disconnected it indicates another computer might be configured with the same IP address. `ipconfig, ping 127.0.0.1`, and this command should all work—even with the network cable disconnected.

- `ping the IP address of a computer on the local network that you know is functioning properly`—This ping should leave your computer, travel through the network cabling to that computer, and then return. Echo replies here are an indication that the network adapter and media in the local network are working correctly. However, if you receive zero echo replies, it points to an incorrect subnet mask, an incorrectly configured network adapter, or cabling problems.

- `ping the computer by hostname`—This checks the capability to resolve a name to an IP address, which must occur before the actual echo requests are sent. A failure here could point to DNS or Hosts file problems. (You'll learn about host files and DNS in Hour 15, "Host and Domain Resolution.")

 The following ping commands require a router and IP to be configured with a default gateway or other route information.

- `ping 207.217.151.1`—Pings the IP address of your default gateway. Successful replies indicate that the router is up and capable of responding.

- `ping 198.137.240.92`—Pings the IP address of a remote computer, as shown in Figure 11.4. Four replies here indicate the successful use of a default gateway (unless custom route information has been loaded with the route command, which is discussed in a moment).

- `ping localhost`—The name *localhost* is reserved and is an alias for 127.0.0.1; every computer should resolve this name to this address. Failure here might indicate a problem in the Hosts file (see Hour 15 for information on host name resolution).

- `ping www.whitehouse.gov`—Pinging a domain name such as this requires your computer to first resolve the name to an IP address (see Figure 11.4), usually a DNS server. A failure here might point to an incorrectly configured DNS server IP address.

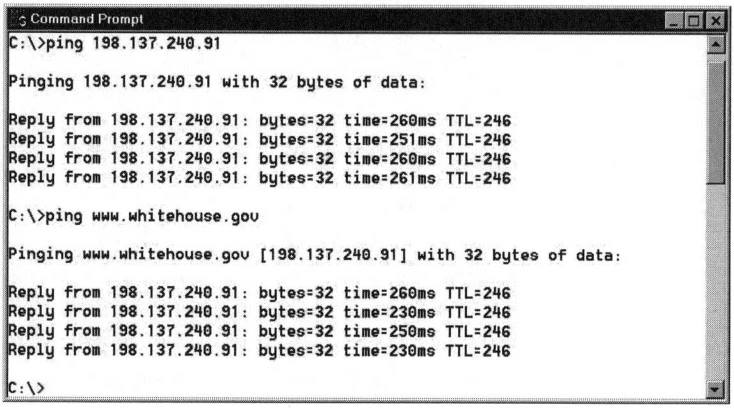

FIGURE **11.4**

*Ping a remote comput-er using both the IP address and domain name.*

```
Command Prompt                                                          _ □ ×
C:\>ping 198.137.240.91

Pinging 198.137.240.91 with 32 bytes of data:

Reply from 198.137.240.91: bytes=32 time=260ms TTL=246
Reply from 198.137.240.91: bytes=32 time=251ms TTL=246
Reply from 198.137.240.91: bytes=32 time=260ms TTL=246
Reply from 198.137.240.91: bytes=32 time=261ms TTL=246

C:\>ping www.whitehouse.gov

Pinging www.whitehouse.gov [198.137.240.91] with 32 bytes of data:

Reply from 198.137.240.91: bytes=32 time=260ms TTL=246
Reply from 198.137.240.91: bytes=32 time=230ms TTL=246
Reply from 198.137.240.91: bytes=32 time=250ms TTL=246
Reply from 198.137.240.91: bytes=32 time=230ms TTL=246

C:\>
```

If all the `ping`s listed previously work correctly, you should have a basic level of confidence in your computer' capability to communicate both locally and remotely. However, success on all of these listed items is not a guarantee that everything is configured correctly; it is possible for the subnet mask to be incorrect and still have all these items work.

You can end up with an incorrect subnet mask in either of two ways. One possibility is that the subnet mask was calculated incorrectly; see Hour 5, "Internet Layer: Subnetting," for how to correctly calculate a subnet mask. The other way is that the subnet mask was incorrectly configured and does not match the calculated subnet mask. For this you can use the IPConfig or WinIPCfg utilities to verify that the subnet mask matches the value that was intended for this network.

Ping has a number of options that can be used with any of the `ping` commands listed earlier; the following list describes a few that are commonly used.

- `ping 207.217.151.1 -t`—Pings continuously until interrupted. Usually Ctrl-C is used to break out of this continuous `ping` sequence.
- `ping 207.217.151.1 -n 10`—Pings a specific number of times then stops. In this example 10 `ping` commands will be issued.
- `ping 207.217.151.1 -l 1000`—The length of the data in the `ping` is 1,000 bytes instead of the default 32 bytes.

# Address Resolution Protocol (ARP)

The ARP is a key TCP/IP protocol and is used to determine the physical address that corresponds to an IP address. The arp command allows you to view the current contents of the ARP cache of either the local computer or of another computer. Additionally the arp command allows you to manually enter desired physical/IP address pairs permanently. You might want to do this for commonly used hosts such as the default gateway and local servers. This helps reduce traffic on the network.

Entries in the ARP cache are by default dynamic; entries are automatically added by ARP whenever a directed datagram is sent and a current entry does not exist in cache. The cache entries start to expire as soon as they are entered—for example, in Windows NT, the physical/IP address pairs expire within 2 to 10 minutes if there is no further use beyond the initial entry. Therefore, don't be surprised if there are few or no entries in the ARP cache. Entries can be added by performing pings of another computer or router. The following arp commands can be used to view cache entries:

- arp -a—Use this command to view all ARP cache entries.
- arp -g—Use this command to view all ARP cache entries.

> You can use either arp -a or arp -g. The -g option has for many years been the option used on UNIX platforms to display all ARP cache entries. Windows NT uses arp -a (think of -a as all) but it also accepts the more traditional -g option. On Windows NT both supply options provide identical results. If however you are working on another platform you might only have one option to display all entries, which is most likely the -g option.

- arp -a plus IP address—If you have multiple network adapters you can see just the ARP cache entries associated with one interface by using arp -a plus the IP address of the interface, for example: arp -a 192.59.66.200.
- arp -s plus IP address plus physical address—You can manually add a permanent static entry to the ARP cache. This entry remains in effect across boots of the computer or is updated automatically if errors occur using manually configured physical addresses. For example, to manually add an entry for a server using IP address 192.59.66.250 with a physical address of 0080C7E07EC5 enter arp -s 192.59.66.250 00-80-C7-E0-7E-C5.
- arp -d plus IP address—Use this command to manually delete a static entry. For example, enter arp -d 192.59.66.250.

See Figure 11.5 for examples of arp commands and responses.

11

**Figure 11.5**

arp *commands and*
*responses.*

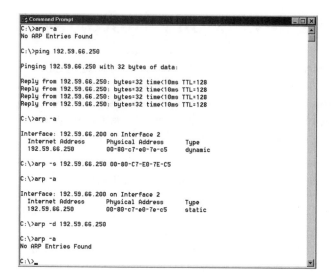

# TraceRoute

The traceroute command is used to trace the route (path) taken by datagrams as they travel from your computer through multiple gateways to their destination. The path traced by this utility is one path between the source and destination; there is no guarantee or assumption that datagrams will always follow this path. If you are configured to use DNS, you can often derive names of cities, regions, and common carriers from the responses. traceroute is a slow command; you need to give it approximately 15 seconds per router.

TraceRoute works by leveraging an ICMP message in which a router sends a time exceeded message to the Source IP when a TTL datagram at the router reaches 0. TraceRoute sends the first datagram with a TTL of 1. When this datagram expires in the first router, the router sends a time exceeded message to the Source IP, and as a result TraceRoute learns the IP address of the first router. TraceRoute then sends the second datagram with a TTL of 2, which expires in the second router and then sends a time exceeded message so that TraceRoute now learns the IP address of the second router. This process continues until a datagram either reaches its destination or a maximum number of routers have been reached. The syntax for TraceRoute is simply traceroute followed by an IP address, or traceroute followed by a URL. For example, traceroute 198.137.240.91, or traceroute www.whitehouse.gov.

Microsoft operating systems uses `tracert` for this command instead of `traceroute`.

TraceRoute is useful for showing you the path and how many router datagrams traverse on the way to their destination. TraceRoute can also provide some diagnostic capabilities. For example, one Saturday when I was working at a large company I could not get on the Internet. I ran a `traceroute` to `www.whitehouse.gov` to see where the hold-up was. The path worked from the router in the building where I worked to routers in three successive states and finally to the city where the corporate networks converge and the company's firewall to the Internet resides. At that point TraceRoute stopped reporting useful information. While TraceRoute did not fix anything, it did let me know where the problem resided. In this instance it was simply the case of a planned outage to load new network configurations to communications processors and routers.

**NEW TERM** A *firewall* is a program that runs on the computer where a private network connects to public networks (for example, the Internet). Firewalls are used to protect internal computers from access or attack by external computers.

# Route

Most hosts reside on network segments that have only one router connected. With only one router there is no question as to which router to use to send datagrams destined for a remote computer. The IP address of this router can be entered as the default gateway for all computers on that network segment.

But when a network has two or more routers, you don't necessarily want to rely solely on a default gateway. You might in fact want certain remote IP addresses to be routed through one particular router while other remote IP addresses are routed through another router.

In this case, you need routing information, which is stored in routing tables. Each host and each router contains its own unique routing table. Most routers use special router protocols to exchange and dynamically update route tables between routers. However, there are many times when it is necessary to manually add entries to route tables on routers as well as host computers. The route command is used to manually add, delete, and change entries in routing tables. It can also be used to print (display) entries that have been entered or changed automatically or manually.

- route print—This command displays the current entries in the routing table. See Figure 11.6 for a sample output from a route print command. As you can see several entries refer to various networks, for example 0.0.0.0, 127.0.0.0, and 192.59.66.0; some are used for broadcasting 255.255.255.255 and 207.168.243.255, whereas others are for multicasting 224.0.0.0. All of these entries were added automatically as a result of configuring network adapters with IP addresses.

**FIGURE 11.6**

*A route print command and its response.*

```
Command Prompt                                                    _ □ ×
C:\>route print

Active Routes:

Network Address          Netmask  Gateway Address      Interface  Metric
        0.0.0.0          0.0.0.0      192.59.66.1  192.59.66.200       1
      127.0.0.0          255.0.0.0      127.0.0.1      127.0.0.1       1
    192.59.66.0    255.255.255.0    192.59.66.200  192.59.66.200       1
  192.59.66.200  255.255.255.255      127.0.0.1      127.0.0.1       1
  192.59.66.255  255.255.255.255  192.59.66.200  192.59.66.200       1
      224.0.0.0        224.0.0.0  192.59.66.200  192.59.66.200       1
255.255.255.255  255.255.255.255  192.59.66.200  192.59.66.200       1

C:\>
```

- route add—Use this command to add a new route entry to a routing table. For example, to specify a route to destination network 207.34.17.0 that is five router hops away and passing first through a router with an IP address on the local network of 192.59.66.5 and the subnet mask of 255.255.255.224, you would enter the following command:

```
route add 207.34.17.0 mask 255.255.255.224 192.59.66.5 metric 5
```

In this example, the term *metric* designates the number of routers that must be passed through to reach the destination. In essence, metric is a weighting system. When you drive to work there are a number of possible paths you could take; you probably take the shortest, most direct path. This is the path with the lowest metric. However, if a bridge you cross on the shortest route is under repair you probably decide on the next shortest path, that is the path with the next lowest metric. Routers operate in much the same manner; they usually contain multiple routes to a network. The router generally selects the lowest cost route (lowest metric) when routing datagrams.

The route information added in this way is volatile and is lost if the computer reboots. Often a series of route add commands such as this are contained in startup scripts so that they are reapplied every time the computer boots.

- `route change`—You can use this command to change the routing of data, however, you cannot use the command to change the destination of the data. The following example changes the routing of the data to a different router that has a more direct three-hop path to the destination.

  ```
  route change 207.34.17.0 mask 255.255.255.224 192.59.66.7 metric 3
  ```

- `route delete`—Use this command to delete a route from the routing table. For example:

  ```
  route delete 207.34.17.0
  ```

# Hostname

The Hostname utility is a miniscule command that returns the host name of the local computer. There are no options or parameters to hostname. Simply enter the word `hostname` and view the one word response.

# NetStat

The NetStat utility displays statistics related to the IP, TCP, UDP, and ICMP protocols. The statistics display numerical counts for items such as datagrams sent, datagrams received, and a wide variety of errors that could have occurred.

You should not be surprised if your computer occasionally receives datagrams that cause errors, discards, or failures. TCP/IP is tolerant of these types of errors and automatically resends the datagram. Discards occur when a datagram is delivered to the wrong location. If your computer acts as a router it will also discard datagrams when TTL reaches zero on a routed datagram. Reassembly failures occur when all the fragments fail to arrive within a time period based on the TTL value in received fragments. Again, like errors and discards, occasional reassembly failures should not be a reason for concern. In all three cases, accumulated counts that are a significant percentage of the total IP packets received, or that rapidly accumulate should cause you to investigate why this is occurring.

The following list describes various `netstat` options:

- `netstat -s`—This option displays statistics on a protocol by protocol basis. If user applications such as Web browsers seem unusually slow or are incapable of displaying data such as Web pages, you might want to use this option to see what information is displayed. You can look through the rows of statistics for rows that include the words error, discard, or failure. If the counts in these rows are significant relative to the IP packets received, then this should serve as a flag to prompt further investigation.

11

- `netstat -e`—This option displays statistics about Ethernet. Items listed include total bytes, errors, discards, number of directed datagrams, and number of broadcasts. These statistics are provided for both sent and received datagrams.

- `netstat -r`—This option displays information about the routing table similar to what was seen with the `route print` command. In addition to displaying the active routes, current active connections are also displayed.

- `netstat -a`—This option displays the list of all active connections including both established connections as well as those that are listening for a connection request.

  The following three options provide subset information of what is displayed with the `-a` option.

- `netstat -n`—This option displays all established active connections.

- `netstat -p TCP`—This option displays established TCP connections.

- `netstat -p UDP`—This option displays established UDP connections.

See Figure 11.7 for an example of the statistics displayed by using netstat `-s`.

**FIGURE 11.7**

`netstat` *displays protocol by protocol statistics.*

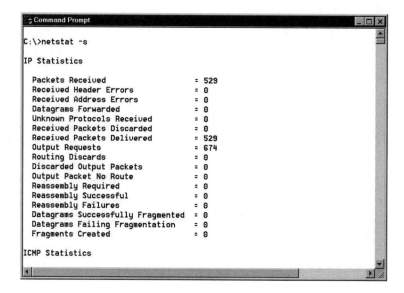

# Net Use/View

Net Use and Net View are utilities that use and verify NetBIOS connections between computers. We'll cover NetBIOS in more detail in Hour 17, "NetBIOS Name Resolution," but basically it is a method computers (primarily Microsoft Windows-based computers) use to find and communicate with each other on a network.

NetBIOS uses the Universal Naming Convention (UNC) to identify a computer name and access a share point. A share point is the location where client computers can connect with the computer.

UNC names always start with a double backslash followed by the name of the computer. For instance \\Staffserver can be used as a UNC identification of a server named Staffserver. To access a share point, you follow the server name with another backslash followed by the share point name. For instance the UNC designation \\Staffserver\public identifies a directory of the computer named Staffserver that has been shared with the name public.

You can use the net commands as a quick test to see whether NetBIOS is functional. For these Application layer commands to be used the application must use NetBIOS conventions and the Network Access, Internet, and Transport layers must be operational.

The net commands have a number of functions, but for this discussion we focus on net view and net use functions. These commands allow you to view, establish, and break connections to share points on computers that are running a Server Message Block (SMB) server service. An SMB server service is an Application layer service that allows computers to share directories with other computers via the network.

**11**

- net view—This command allows you to view the share point names on a server. Anybody can issue a net view command—unlike the net use command, it does not require a user ID or password. For this reason it is best to start by using the net view command. As a basic test of NetBIOS you can enter net view \\servername to see if NetBIOS is functional and the server computer is reachable. If it is functional, you should see a list of share points.

- net use—This command is used to establish or drop a mapped drive letter connection to a specific share point. (You might need to provide a valid user ID and password to use this command.) For example, you would enter net use F:\\Staffserver\public to map a connection to the share called public on the computer Staffserver. This assumes you are not currently using the drive letter. If the drive mapping works successfully you can access the public shared directory on Staffserver by accessing the P: drive.

# NBTStat

The NBTStat (NetBIOS over TCP/IP statistics) utility provides statistics about NetBIOS. NBTStat allows you to view the NetBIOS name table on the local computer or on remote computers.

The following options are used in relation to the local computer.

- nbtstat  -r—This command causes the NetBIOS name cache to be purged and reloaded. This is done to load recently added entries to the LMHosts file. (LMHosts entries are covered in Hour 16, "The Domain Name System.")

- nbtstat  -n—This command displays the names and services registered on the local computer.

- nbtstat  -c—This command displays the contents of the NetBIOS name cache that holds the NetBIOS names to IP address pairs of other computers with which this computer has had recent communication.

- nbtstat  -r—This command lists the count of registrations and resolved names of other computers and whether they were registered or resolved by broadcast or by a name server.

See Figure 11.8 for examples of these outputs.

**FIGURE 11.8**

nbtstat *commands and responses.*

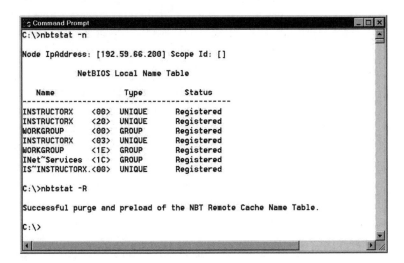

Two commands allow you to view the NetBIOS name table of remote computers. The output from these two syntaxes is similar to the nbtstat  -n on the local computer.

- nbtstat  -A plus IP address—Displays the name table including physical addresses from another computer by using its IP address.

- nbtstat  -a plus NetBIOS name—Displays the name table including physical addresses from another computer by using its NetBIOS name.

Similarly two other syntaxes allow you to view the list of NetBIOS connections that a remote computer has open. This list is called a connections table.

- `nbtstat -S` plus IP address—Displays the NetBIOS connections table of another computer using its IP address.

- `nbtstat -s` plus NetBIOS name—Displays the NetBIOS session table of another computer using its NetBIOS name.

# Network Monitor

Network Monitor is a utility included with Windows NT Server. It is representative of a class of utilities known as *sniffers*. These utilities capture datagrams from the network into a buffer or a file. After they are captured you can display the contents of datagrams one at a time. Network Monitor allows you to examine each datagram from its lowest layer (an Ethernet frame for example) successively up through each layer so you can see its activity at each step of its travels from source to host.

For example, at the lowest layer, you can use Network Monitor to check the physical address of the datagram's source and destination, and to find out how many bytes of data the Ethernet frame is carrying. At the Internet layer you can see a detailed breakdown of the headers in that layer, and so on up through the Application layer.

Sniffer programs can provide a wealth of information as to what is actually inside a datagram and can be a powerful tool when learning about networking as well as when troubleshooting problems.

Figure 11.9 shows the sequence of 10 datagrams that was initiated by entering a `ping` command. The top window shows the 10 datagrams starting with an `arp` request and an `arp` reply followed by four ICMP request/reply pairs. The middle window decodes the ICMP header, and in the bottom frame you can see the 32 bytes of data in the datagram. The data includes the complete alphabet followed by letters abcdef for a total of 32 bytes of data.

# Using Connectivity Utilities to Troubleshoot Problems

By trying various applications that use TCP or UDP and that use either a sockets interface or a NetBIOS interface and by determining what works and what doesn't work you can often zero in on which component in the TCP/IP stack is causing a problem.

11

**FIGURE 11.9**

*A view of traffic cap-
tured by Network
Monitor following a*
`ping` *command.*

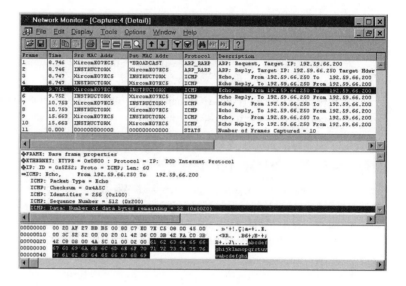

As mentioned when discussing the Ping utility, there is a definite order that you should
follow when troubleshooting network problems. Networking problems can be extremely
varied, but are usually manifested by some application such as a Web browser being
incapable of displaying Web pages. Typically in troubleshooting you start with simple
basic commands. If these work as expected you then continue to build on what you know
to be working by using commands that require progressively more network functionality.
To troubleshoot a network problem, follow these steps:

1. Start with the `ipconfig` to ensure you know the current IP address, subnet mask,
   and default gateway parameters.

2. Then move on to the `ping` command and follow the sequence of `ping` commands
   described earlier. If the `ping` commands work as expected, you have gained some
   confidence in the two lower layers including the network adapter and the network
   cabling.

3. Next use an application such as a Web browser to access a Web server. If this
   works you know that TCP and the sockets interface work; if this doesn't work try
   another application that uses TCP and sockets such as the FTP client. If this
   doesn't work either, you would probably want to concentrate on TCP or sockets as
   a source of the problem.

4. Finally, try NetBIOS-based applications such as `net view`, `net use`, Network
   Neighborhood, or File Manager, which uses NetBIOS over TCP/IP. (Network
   Neighborhood and File Manager are NetBIOS-based applications in Windows NT.)

# Summary

The utilities presented in this chapter give you a number of tools for identifying the state of TCP/IP communication on your network and troubleshooting breakdowns of that communication. Each utility displays only a small amount of information about the activity on your network. However, when the results of these utilities are combined in a useful manner they can provide a more complete picture of the operation of TCP/IP on your computer.

# Q&A

**Q** **Which utility defines a path taken by datagrams?**

**A** TraceRoute.

**Q** **Which utility type is used to examine the contents of datagrams?**

**A** A network sniffer.

**Q** **Which utility displays statistics for TCP/IP protocols?**

**A** NetStat.

**Q** **Which utility displays statistics for NetBIOS-based networks?**

**A** NBTStat.

**Q** **Which utility allows you to generate datagrams to a specific IP address?**

**A** Ping.

**Q** **Which utility displays the host name of your computer?**

**A** Hostname.

**Q** **Which utility would you use if your network contained several routers?**

**A** Route.

**11**

# Workshop

Perform the following commands and view the responses on your computer.

| | |
|---|---|
| `ipconfig/all or winipcfg` | Not all TCP/IP stacks implement these. |
| `ping 127.0.0.1` | |
| `ping w.x.y.z` | Replace w.x.y.z with the IP address of your computer. |
| `ping w.x.y.z` | Replace w.x.y.z with the IP address of another local computer. |

| | |
|---|---|
| `ping w.x.y.z` | Replace w.x.y.z with the IP address of your default gateway. |
| `ping w.x.y.z` | Replace w.x.y.z with the IP address of a remote computer. |
| `ping localhost` | |
| `ping http://www.whitehouse.gov` | If you are connected to the Internet and have a DNS server. |
| `hostname` | |
| `ping <hostname>` | Replace *<hostname>* with your actual host name. |
| `arp -a or arp -g` | One or both might work. Wait a few minutes then repeat. |
| `netstat -s` | |
| `nbtstat -n` | Not all TCP/IP stacks implement `nbtstat`. |

## Key Terms

Review the following list of key terms:

- Network sniffer—A class of diagnostic applications that can capture and display the contents of datagrams.
- Server Message Block (SMB)—An Application layer service that enables computers to share directories with other computers via the network.
- Share point—A named location on a computer with a SMB server service. A share point is a location to which client computers can connect.

# HOUR 12

# TCP/IP File Transfer and Access Utilities

*By Bob Willsey and Walter Glenn*

One of the greatest things about TCP/IP is that it provides a very flexible environment in which systems of many different types can communicate. Regardless of what hardware or operating systems are in use, two hosts on a TCP/IP network can talk to one another if they use the same protocols. Usually these two hosts need access to special utilities, as well.

File access and transfer is usually one of the biggest uses of any network. TCP/IP contains a couple of protocols that are used specifically for file access and transfer. Most operating systems also provide built-in utilities designed to take advantage of these protocols. This hour discusses the File Transfer Protocol (FTP), Trivial File Transfer Protocol (TFTP), and the Remote Copy (rcp) command. I also explain the network file system.

# Goals for this Hour

At the completion of this hour you will be able to

- Explain the purpose and use of FTP
- Initiate an FTP session and use `ftp` commands to traverse remote directory structures, transfer files to or from the remote system, and create or remove directories
- Explain the purpose and use of the TFTP
- Construct a command to transfer a file using TFTP
- Explain the purpose and use of `rpc` command
- Explain the purpose and use of NFS

# File Transfer Protocol (FTP)

FTP is a widely used utility that allows a user to transfer files between two computers on a TCP/IP network, regardless of the type of computer or operating systems in use. The user runs an FTP client program on one computer while the other computer runs an FTP server program such as the `ftpd` (FTP daemon) on a UNIX box, or an FTP service on other platforms. Most FTP client programs are command-line based, but graphical versions are available as well. FTP is primarily used to transfer files, although it can perform other functions such as creating directories, removing directories, and listing files. When FTP is used to transfer files it only transfers one file at a time.

**NEW TERM** *Daemons* are UNIX processes that run idly in the background and provide a service to other users or other computers when needed.

On most computers you start an FTP session by entering `ftp` at a command prompt. FTP then prompts you for a user ID and a password, which are used by the FTP server to validate you as an authorized user and determine your rights, such as read-only or read/write. Many FTP servers are available for public use and allow you to log on using a user ID called *anonymous*. When the anonymous account is used as the user ID you can enter virtually any password, however, it is customary to enter your email account name as the password. When FTP servers are not intended for general public use, the servers are configured to not allow anonymous access. In this case you must enter a user ID and password to gain access. The user ID and password are typically set up and provided by the FTP server administrator.

Many FTP client implementations allow you to enter either UNIX-based commands or DOS-based commands. The actual commands available depend on the client software being used. When you transfer files using FTP you must specify to FTP the type of file that you are about to transfer; the most commonly used choices are binary and ASCII.

Choose ASCII when the type of file you want to transfer is textual. Choose binary when the type of file you want to transfer is either a program or graphic. The default file transfer mode is ASCII.

Be aware that many FTP servers reside on UNIX boxes. Because UNIX is case-sensitive—that is it distinguishes between uppercase and lowercase letters—you must match the case exactly when entering file names. The current directory on the local computer from which you start an FTP session is the default location where files are transferred to or from.

Following is a list of commonly used FTP commands and explanations of these commands. When UNIX commands and DOS commands perform the same function, both are introduced at the same point in the list.

- ftp—The ftp command is used to start the FTP client program. You can enter ftp by itself or you can follow it with an IP address or domain name. In Figure 12.1 an FTP session to rs.internic.net was started by typing ftp rs.internic.net. As you can see, a lot of information was returned.

  The first line tells you that you are connected. All of the lines between and including those preceded by 220 are a customized logon message presented to all users. The next line asks for a user ID; here it is entered as anonymous. The line preceded by 331 is a customized system message requesting your email address as a password. A number always precedes system messages. As you can see by the final line, the password is not displayed when typed.

**FIGURE 12.1**

*Starting an FTP session.*

**12**

- user—The user command is used to change the user ID and password information of the current session. You will be prompted to enter a new user ID and password, exactly as when you used the ftp command. This command is effectively the same as quitting FTP and starting again as a new user.

- help—the help command displays the ftp commands that are available on your FTP client.

- ls; dir—the UNIX ls or ls -l commands, or the DOS dir command are used to list the contents of a directory. The response from these commands lists the file-names and directory names contained within the current working directory on the FTP server. The results of the ls command are shown in Figure 12.2. Between the two system messages (the lines preceded by 150 and 226) is the actual directory listing, which contains all of the files and subdirectories within the current working directory. The ls -l command is similar to the ls command but lists additional details such as read and write permissions and file creation dates.

**FIGURE 12.2**

*The ls command.*

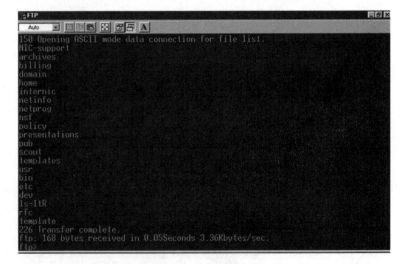

- pwd—The pwd command is used to print the name of the current working directory.

- cd—The cd command is used to change the current working directory on the FTP server where the command is to change to the Policy directory.

- mkdir; md—the UNIX mkdir command or the DOS md command is used to create a directory on the FTP server inside the current working directory. This command is typically not allowable during an anonymous FTP session.

- rmdir; rd—The UNIX rmdir command or the DOS rd command is used to remove a directory on the FTP server from the current working directory. This command is typically not allowable during an anonymous FTP session.

- binary—The binary command is used to switch the FTP client to binary transfer mode from ASCII transfer mode. Binary mode is useful when transferring binary files, such as programs and graphics, using a get or put command.

- ascii—The ascii command is used to switch the FTP client to ASCII transfer mode from binary mode. ASCII is the default transfer mode and is used when transferring textual files.

- type—The type command displays the current mode (ASCII or binary) for file transfer.

- status—The status command displays information about the various settings on the FTP client. Such settings include the mode (binary or ASCII) the client is set to, whether the client is set to display verbose system messages, and more.

- get—The get command is used to retrieve a file from an FTP server to an FTP client. Using the get command followed by a single filename will copy that file from the FTP server to the working directory on the FTP client. If the get command is followed by two filenames; the second name is used to designate the name of the new file created on the client.

- put—Use the put command to transfer a file from the FTP client to the FTP server by using the put command followed by a single filename. If the put command is followed by two filenames, the second name is used to designate the name of the new file created on the server.

- open—The open command allows you to establish a new session with an FTP server. This is essentially a shortcut to quitting FTP and starting it again. The open command can be used to open a session with an entirely different FTP server or to reopen a session with the current server.

- close—The close command is used to end the current session with an FTP server. The FTP client program remains open, and you can start a new session with the server by using the open command.

- bye; quit—These commands close the current FTP session and terminate the FTP client.

Although the preceding list does not include every ftp command, it gives you an idea of the commands used most often during an FTP session. To learn more about the FTP protocol see RFC 959.

12

# Trivial File Transfer Protocol (TFTP)

TFTP is used to transfer files between the TFTP client and a TFTP server, which is a computer running the `tftpd` TFTP daemon. This protocol uses UDP as a transport and, unlike FTP, does not require a user to log on in order to transfer files. Because TFTP does not require a user logon it is often considered a security hole, especially if the TFTP server permits writing.

The TFTP protocol was designed to be small so that both it and the UDP protocol could be implemented on a PROM (Programmable Read Only Memory) chip. The TFTP protocol is limited (hence the name trivial) when compared to the FTP protocol. The TFTP protocol can only read and write files; it cannot list the contents of directories, create or remove directories, or allow a user to log on as the FTP protocol allows. The TFTP protocol is primarily used in conjunction with the RARP and BOOTP protocols to boot diskless workstations. The TFTP protocol can transfer files using either an ASCII format known as netascii or a binary format known as octet; a third format known as mail is no longer used.

When a user enters a `tftp` statement on a command line it initiates a connection to the server and performs the file transfer; at the completion of the file transfer the session is closed and terminated. The syntax of the TFTP statement follows:

```
TFTP [-i] host [get ¦ put] <source file name> [<destination file
➥name>]
```

To learn more about the TFTP protocol see RFC 1350.

# Remote Copy (RCP)

The `rcp` command provides an alternative to `ftp`, it allows users to copy files to or from UNIX boxes. The `rcp` command is the remote version of the UNIX `cp` (copy) command. When using the `rcp` command, you do not need to supply a user ID or password; this might be considered a security hole. However, a level of security is provided by the fact that the name of your computer must reside in either of two server-based files named rhosts and hosts.equiv. The `rcp` command allows a user to copy files between a local computer and the host server or between two remote computers. The syntax for the `cp` command appears as follows:

```
Rcp [hostname1]:filename1 [hostname2]:filename2
```

- `hostname1`—Optionally indicates the hostname or Fully Qualified Domain Name (FQDN) of the source computer. Use this hostname if the source file is located on a remote computer. You'll learn more about hostnames and FQDNs in Hour 15, "Host and Domain Name Resolution."

- `filename1`—Indicates the path and filename of the source file.
- `hostname2`—Optionally indicates the hostname or FQDN of the destination computer. Use this hostname if the destination file is located on a remote computer.
- `filename2`—Indicates the path and filename of the destination file.

Following are three examples using the `rcp` command.

This example copies a file from the remote UNIX computer to the local host:

```
rcp server3.corporate.earthquakes.txt  earthquakes.txt
```

This example copies a file from the local host to a remote computer:

```
rcp earthquakes.txt  server3.corporate.earthquakes.txt
```

This example copies a file between two remote UNIX computers:

```
rcp server3.corporate.com:earthquakes.txt
➥server4.corporate.com:earthquakes.text
```

The `rcp` command is a UNIX command and as such information regarding `rcp` is not contained in RFC specifications.

# Network File System (NFS)

The NFS is supported on UNIX and other systems. The NFS file system allows users to transparently access (read, write, create, and delete) directories and files located on a remote computer as if those directories and files were located on the local computer. Because NFS is designed to provide a transparent interface between local file systems and remote file systems and because it is implemented within the operating system of both computers, it does not require any changes to application programs. Programs are capable of accessing both local files and remote files and directories via NFS without any recompilation or other changes. To the user, all files and directories appear and operate as if they exist only on the local file system.

The original implementation of NFS used the UDP protocol for its transport and was intended for use on a LAN. However, later revisions now allow use of the TCP protocol; the additional reliability of TCP over UDP allows for expanded capabilities of NFS, which can now operate in a WAN.

The NFS file system is designed to be independent of operating systems, transport protocols, and physical network architecture. This allows an NFS client to interoperate with

**12**

any NFS server. This independence is achieved by using Remote Procedure Calls (RPCs) between the client and server computers. RPC is a process that allows a program running on one computer to make calls on code segments inside a program running on another computer. It has been around for many years and is supported on many operating systems. In the case of NFS, the operating system on the client issues an RPC call to the operating system on the server. Because RPCs reside at a higher level on the protocol stack than the transport protocols, it can work with either TCP or UDP and of course lower-level implementations such as Ethernet and token ring.

Before remote files and directories can be used on the NFS file system, they must first go through a process known as *mounting*. After mounted, the remote files and directories appear and operate as if they were located on the local file system.

For additional information on the NFS protocol see RFC 1094, which addresses implementation of NFS version 2, also see RFC 1813 for updates relative to NFS version 3.

# Summary

A number of TCP/IP-based utilities allow the user to transfer files to or from a remote computer, or to access files located on the remote computer as if they were local. Of these, the FTP protocol is the most commonly used; it allows a user to either connect to a remote system anonymously or to connect using a specific user ID and password. With the proper permissions the user can use `ftp` commands to copy files, create or remove directories, and traverse the directory structure on the remote computer.

The TFTP protocol provides basic file transfer capability using the UDP protocol; it does not require a user login and is rarely used directly by users. The TFTP protocol is primarily used to boot diskless workstations.

The RCP protocol provides an alternative to the FTP protocol and allows the user to copy files between a UNIX computer and a local computer, or between two UNIX computers.

The NFS protocol allows a user to access a portion of a remote file system as if it were a local file. In fact, the user might be unaware that some of the files are actually located on a remote computer.

# Q&A

**Q  What is the default representation (transfer type) for FTP?**

**A  ASCII.**

**Q What ftp command displays your current working directory?**

**A** pwd (print working directory).

**Q What ftp commands are typically *not* allowed when a user is connected using the anonymous account?**

**A** put, mkdir, md, rmdir, rd.

**Q Can you list the files in the directory using TFTP?**

**A** No. TFTP can only transfer files, nothing else.

**Q What advantages does rcp have over ftp?**

**A** Easier syntax and a login is not required in order to copy files.

**Q What is the main use of TFTP?**

**A** To boot diskless workstations.

**Q What is the main functional difference between FTP and NFS?**

**A** FTP is used to transfer files, whereas NFS is used to provide access to files.

# Workshop

In this workshop you connect to an FTP server, view directory listings, traverse the directory structure, and copy files to your computer.

1. Gain access to the Internet either by dialing in to your ISP or connecting through a network connection.

2. Start an FTP session and login to rs.internic.net using the anonymous account. Enter your complete email address as your password.

3. Use the ls, the ls -l, and the dir commands. Compare the different ways they display the names and files and directories.

4. Use the cd netinfo command to change your current working directory to the netinfo directory, then list the contents of this directory.

5. Use the pwd command to display the path to your current working directory.

6. Use the cd command to change your current working directory to the parent directory.

7. Use the type command to display the default representation format.

8. Use the binary command to change the representation to binary (image).

9. Display the current representation format.

10. Change the current working directory to the policy directory.

12

11. List the files in the policy directory.

12. You should see a number of text files for RFCs. Set and check the representation type for transferring textual files.

13. Use the `get` command to transfer one of the text files to your local computer.

14. Use the `status` command to display the current status of your FTP client.

15. Use the `close` command to terminate the session with `rs.internic.net`.

16. Use the `open` command to initiate a new session with `rs.internic.net`.

17. Use the `help` command to see the other commands that are available with your FTP client software.

18. Use the `bye` command to terminate the session with `rs.internic.net` and also the current FTP session.

19. Display the contents of your current local working directory. You should see the file that you transferred.

## Key Terms

Review the following list of key terms:

- File Transfer Protocol (FTP)—A client server utility and protocol used to transfer files between two computers. In addition to transferring files, the FTP utility can create and remove directories and display the contents of directories.

- Network File System (NFS)—The NFS protocol uses RPC calls between the offering systems of two computers to transparently allow the user on an NFS client computer to access files located on a remote NFS server computer.

- Remote Copy (RCP)—This UNIX-based utility allows you to copy files between computers using syntax that is similar to the UNIX `cp` command. It provides a simple syntax to copy files and does not require the user to log in prior to initiating the file copy process.

- Trivial File Transfer Protocol (TFTP)—A client server utility and protocol used to transfer files between two computers.

# Hour 13

# Remote Access Utilities

*By Joe Casad*

Networks are for sharing resources remotely, so almost anything you do on a network could fall within the definition of remote access. Still, by tradition, a few TCP/IP utilities are classified as remote access utilities. These remote access utilities grew up around UNIX but many have been imported to other operating systems. The purpose of these utilities is to give a remote user some of the powers a local user might have. In this hour, you'll learn about the popular Telnet application, and you'll learn about the Berkeley R* utilities—a collection of utilities designed to support remote access.

## Goals for this Hour

At the completion of this hour, you'll be able to

- Explain the purpose of Telnet
- List some of the Berkeley R* utilities
- Describe trusted access security

# Telnet

Telnet is a set of components that provide terminal-like access to a remote computer. A Telnet session requires a Telnet client that will serve as the remote terminal and a Telnet server, which receives the connection request and allows the connection. This relationship is depicted in Figure 13.1. On UNIX systems, the telnetd daemon acts as the server. (In the UNIX world, *daemons* are programs that execute in the background and perform services when needed.)

**FIGURE 13.1**

*A Telnet server and client.*

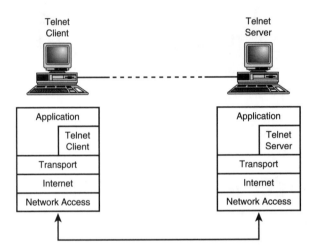

Telnet is also a protocol—a system of rules defining the interactions between Telnet servers and clients. The Telnet protocol is defined in a series of RFCs. Because Telnet is based on a well-defined open protocol, it can be and has been implemented on a wide range of hardware and software systems. The basic purpose of Telnet is to provide a means by which keyboard commands typed by a remote user can cross the network and become input for a different computer. Screen output related to the session then crosses the network from that different computer (the server) to the client system (see Figure 13.2). The effect is that the remote user can interact with the server as though he or she were logged in locally.

On UNIX systems, the telnet command is entered at the command prompt, as follows:

```
telnet hostname
```

where *hostname* is the name of the computer to which you'd like to connect. (You can also enter an IP address instead of a host name.)

**FIGURE 13.2**

*Network input and output with Telnet.*

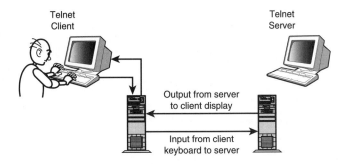

- The preceding command launches the Telnet application. After Telnet is running, the commands you enter are executed on the remote computer. Telnet also provides some special commands that you can use during a Telnet session, as follows:
  - close—Use this command to close the connection
  - display—Use this command to display connection settings, such as the port or terminal emulation.
  - environ—Use this command to set environment variables. Environment variables are used by the operating system to provide machine-specific or user-specific information.
  - logout—Use this command to log out the remote user and close the connection.
  - mode—Use this command to toggle between ASCII or binary file transfer mode (see Hour 12, "TCP/IP File Transfer and Access Utilities," for an explanation of the file transfer mode).
  - open—Use this command to connect to a remote computer.
  - quit—Use this command to exit Telnet.
  - send—Use this command to send special Telnet protocol sequences to the remote computer, such as an abort sequence, a break sequence, or an end-of-file sequence.
  - set—Use this command to set connection settings.
  - unset—Use this command to unset connection parameters.
  - ?—Use this command to print Help information.

On graphics-based platforms such as Microsoft Windows, a Telnet application might have its own icon and run in a window, but the underlying commands and processes are the same as with a text-based system. Consult your vendor documentation.

**13**

# Berkeley Remote Utilities

The Berkeley Systems Design (BSD) UNIX implementation, known as BSD UNIX, was a major step in UNIX's development. Many innovations that began with BSD UNIX are now standard on other UNIX systems and have been incorporated into other operating systems in the world of TCP/IP and the Internet.

One of the innovations of BSD UNIX was a small set of command-line utilities designed to provide remote access to UNIX systems. This set of utilities became known as the Berkeley R* utilities, because the name of each utility begins with an *R* for *remote*. The Berkeley R* utilities are still available on UNIX systems, and versions of the R* utilities are distributed with VMS, Windows NT, and other operating systems. However, even though TCP/IP is becoming more popular and more universal, these TCP/IP utilities have received comparatively less attention.

Some of the Berkeley R* utilities are as follows:

- Rlogin—This utility allows users to log in remotely.
- Rcp—This utility provides remote file transfer.
- Rsh—This utility executes a remote command through the rshd daemon.
- Rexec—This utility executes a remote command through the rexecd daemon.
- Ruptime—This utility displays system information on uptime and the number of connected users.
- Rwho—This utility displays information on currently-connected users.

The R* utilities were designed in an earlier and simpler time for TCP/IP networking. The creators of these utilities expected that only trusted users would access these utilities. And the intention was that the R* utilities would run transparently on the host to which the user is connecting. Though many consider these utilities risky on today's open and interconnected networks, the R* utilities have a security system that, if implemented properly, offers a measure of protection.

The R* utilities use a concept called *trusted access*. Trusted access allows one computer to trust another computer's authentication. In Figure 13.3, if computer A designates Computer B as a *trusted host*, users who log in to Computer B can use the R* utilities to access Computer A without supplying a password. Computer A can also designate specific users who will be *trusted users*. Trusted hosts and users are identified in the /etc/hosts.equiv file of the remote machine to which the user is attempting to gain access. The .rhosts file in each user's home directory can also be used to grant trusted access to the user's account.

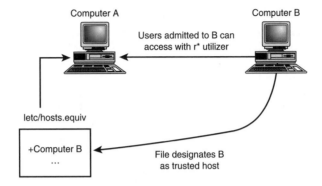

**FIGURE 13.3**

*UNIX trusted access.*

The following sections discuss some of the Berkeley R* utilities.

## Rlogin

Rlogin is a remote login utility. You can use Rlogin to connect with a UNIX host that is running the server daemon Rlogind (d stands for daemon). Rlogin serves the same purpose as Telnet, but Rlogin is considerably less versatile. Rlogin is designed specifically to provide access to UNIX systems, whereas Telnet, which is covered under a TCP/IP standard, can have a broader application. Also, Rlogin does not provide some of the configuration negotiation features available with Telnet.

A significant feature of Rlogin is that, because it uses the R* utilities security model, it supports remote login without a password. Password-less access is a property of all R* utilities, but some users consider a password-less terminal session a little more unsettling than some of the other password-less functions achievable through the R* utilities. Nevertheless, the R* utilities' security model does limit access to trusted users. Also, it is important to keep in mind that network operating systems such NetWare and Windows NT also provide methods for password-less access to network resources after the user has achieved some form of initial authentication.

The syntax for the `rlogin` command is as follows:

`rlogin hostname`

where *hostname* is the host name of the computer to which you'd like to gain access. If no username is specified, the username defaults to the user's username on the local computer. Otherwise, you can specify a username as follows:

`rlogin hostname -1 username`

where *username* is the username you want to use for the login.

**13**

The server daemon rlogind, which must be running on the server machine, then checks host.equiv and .rhosts files to verify host and user information. If this authentication is successful, the remote session begins.

## Rcp

Rcp provides remote file access to UNIX systems. Rcp is not as versatile or as widely used as FTP, but it is still sometimes used for file transfer in the UNIX world. See Hour 12 for more on rcp.

## Rsh

Rsh lets you execute a single command on a remote computer without logging in to the remote computer. Rsh is short for *remote shell.* (A *shell* is a command interface to the operating system.) The rshd daemon, running on the remote computer, accepts the rsh command, verifies the username and host name information and executes the command.

Rsh is useful when you want to enter one command and don't need or want to establish a terminal session with the remote computer.

The format for the rsh command is:

```
rsh -l username hostname command
```

where *hostname* is the host name of the remote computer, *username* is the name to use when accessing the remote computer, and *command* is the command you would like to execute.

The username (preceded by the -l) is optional. If you do not include a username, the username will default to the username on the local host as follows:

```
rsh hostname command
```

## Rexec

Rexec is like Rsh in that it instructs the remote computer to execute a command. Rexec uses the rexecd daemon.

The syntax for the rexec command is as follows:

```
rexec hostname -l username command
```

where *hostname* is the name of the host, *username* is the user account name on the remote computer, and *command* is the command you want to execute. If you omit *-l username,* the username will default to the username on the local computer.

## Ruptime

Ruptime prints a summary showing how many users are logged in to each computer on the network. Ruptime also lists how long each computer has been "up"—hence the name *r-up-time*—and displays some additional system information.

To generate a `ruptime` report, you need only type

```
ruptime
```

Both Ruptime and Rwho (see the next section) use the `rwhod` daemon. Actually, each computer on the network has an `rwhod` daemon that broadcasts regular reports of user activity. Each `rwhod` daemon receives and stores the reports from other `rwhod` daemons for a network-wide view of user activity.

## Rwho

Rwho reports on all users who are currently logged on to network computers. Rwho lists usernames, the computer each user is logged in to, the time of login, and the time elapsed since login.

The syntax of the `rwho` command is simply:

```
rwho
```

The default report excludes users whose terminals have been inactive more than an hour. For a report on all users, use the `-a` option:

```
rwho -a
```

Rwho, like Ruptime, uses the `rwhod` daemon.

# Summary

This hour covered some of the TCP/IP remote access utilities that have evolved around TCP/IP. You learned about Telnet, and the R* utilities. You can use these utilities to execute commands and access information on a remote computer.

**13**

# Q&A

**Q Is Telnet a server application, a client application, or a protocol?**

**A** The term Telnet could refer to either the server or the client Telnet application, or it could refer to the Telnet protocol.

**Q** **Which file should you use if you want to designate a host as a trusted host?**

**A** Use the /etc/hosts.equiv file to designate a trusted host.

**Q** **Which utility would tell me if the user Ethelred is currently logged in to the network?**

**A** The Rwho utility display information of current users.

# Workshop

## Key Terms

Review the following list of key terms:

- Rcp—A remote file transfer utility.
- Rexec—A remote command-execution utility.
- Rlogin—A remote login utility.
- Rsh—A remote command-execution utility.
- Ruptime—A utility that displays system information on uptime and the number of connected users.
- Rwho—A utility that displays information on currently connected users.
- Telnet—A remote terminal utility.
- Trusted access—A security system in which a system administrator designates remote hosts and users who are trusted to access the local system.

# Hour 14

# TCP/IP Internet Utilities

*By Bob Willsey and Walter Glenn*

In this hour you will be introduced to three utilities that are currently in wide use on the Internet: Web browsers, email, and newsreaders. You will also be introduced to four older utilities: Archie, Gopher, Pine, and Whois. Although these older services are not as widely used today, they still provide useful and functional access to resources on the Internet and often appear on older systems.

Keep in mind that while these are typically called Internet utilities, the Internet is really just one big TCP/IP network. The utilities described in this chapter can be, and often are, used on local TCP/IP networks. More and more companies today are providing intranets on their local networks to help streamline and simplify employee transactions. An *intranet* is just a system for using these Internet utilities on a local network. For example, a company might put scheduling information, employee manuals, and even electronic forms on an internal Web server. This would allow employees to browse and use this information using a common Web browser.

## Goals for this Hour

At the completion of this hour you will be able to

- Describe the usefulness of a Web browser, a mail reader, and a newsreader
- Discuss the SMTP, POP3, LDAP, and IMAP4 protocols
- Locate filenames within anonymous FTP servers anywhere in the world
- Navigate the Internet to view contents located in FTP servers
- Explain what Archie, Gopher, Pine, and Whois are used for

## Web Browsers

The World Wide Web has caught the attention of the American public and, over the last two to three years, its presence has become more and more pervasive. The number of Web servers has skyrocketed; nowadays hosting a Web server is easily within the means of both small businesses and even individual users.

A *Web browser* is used to display Web pages, which are also known as *HTML documents*. Web browsers are arguably the most commonly used Internet utility. Netscape Navigator is the most widely used Web browser today; however, Netscape's market lead is under pressure from Microsoft's Internet Explorer. The feature war that has ensued between these two Web browsers has brought many new features and enhancements to market. Fortunately for the average consumer, both these excellent Web browsers are available for free and can be downloaded from the Web.

Web browsers provide rich content by displaying colorful text and graphics and in some cases accompanying music or other sounds. Early Web browsers provided rather static Web content, which included hyperlinks that allow the user to easily navigate to other Web pages. However, today Web browsers are much more interactive as Web pages often include small programs that execute either inside the Web browser on the client computer or within the Web server, which is used to send Web content to the Web browser.

After a Web browser is installed, you can use it to display Web information from virtually any place in the world. Web browsers work by using uniform resource locators (URLs); an URL is a combination of a protocol domain name and filename that uniquely identifies one document somewhere in the world. Armed with the URL, your Web browser can locate the Web server that contains the document and request a copy to be sent. For example the URL `http://home.netscape.com/computing/download/index.html` (shown in the Netsite box in Figure 14.1) is a combination of the protocol `http://`, the domain `home.netscape.com`, and the directory structure and filename `/computing/download/index.html`. The URL in Figure 14.1 was used to retrieve the Web page that is displayed in the body of the Web browser. Sometimes an URL does not include the directory and specific filename. This type of URL is used as a starting point, which is the root of a Web site; it causes the display of the default document located in the Web site.

FIGURE **14.1**

*A Web browser displaying a Web page.*

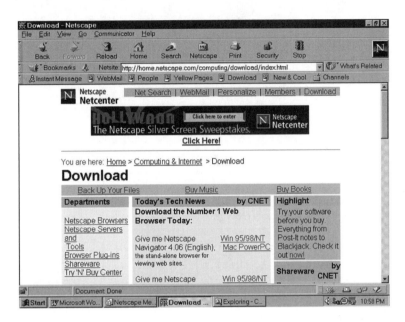

# Newsreaders

In addition to Web documents, there is a tremendous amount of information available in the form of news postings. Unlike Web servers, which typically do not allow the user to change Web content, news servers are provided specifically for end-users to be able to post messages. News servers contain what are called newsgroups, and each newsgroup is targeted at a specific topic, interest, or concern. Users use software known as a newsreader to view the list of available newsgroups and can then subscribe to newsgroups for which they have an interest. After users subscribe to a newsgroup(s) they can display messages posted by others and if desired can post messages to the newsgroup.

Some newsgroups are moderated to ensure that posted messages that are inappropriate or non-topical are discarded and not available for public viewing. However, be aware that many newsgroups are not moderated and therefore they can, and often do, contain postings that are objectionable or non-topical.

A newsreader requires some initial setup before you can view news messages. First the newsreader must download the names of available newsgroups. Then the user can select

**14**

the newsgroup(s) that she is interested in joining. Finally, news messages are downloaded from the selected newsgroup(s) for viewing, as shown in Figure 14.2.

**FIGURE 14.2**

*View the content of individual news messages.*

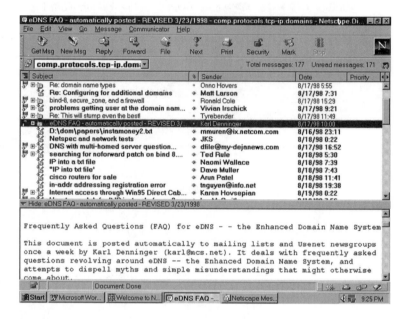

# Email Readers

An email reader allows the user to display the content of email messages that have been sent to the user or to compose and send new email messages to other people. There are several protocols involved with sending and receiving email over TCP/IP networks. These are covered in the next few sections.

## Simple Message Transfer Protocol (SMTP)

Simple Message Transfer Protocol (SMTP) is a protocol used for sending email messages between two hosts on a TCP/IP network. Most email applications send messages to Internet mail servers using SMTP. Those servers also transfer the messages to other Internet mail servers using SMTP. Messages are typically retrieved from servers by clients using either the Post Office Protocol (POP) or the Internet Messaging Access Protocol (IMAP).

## POP3

Post Office Protocol version 3 (POP3) is a message retrieval protocol that provides the capability to receive messages from a server-based inbox. If you are using Internet-based email now, the chances are good that you are using a POP3-compliant email client.

When you log on to a POP3 server, your email client copies any new messages on that server to your local computer and optionally, deletes messages from the server itself. When you read your messages, you are doing so from your local copy. As POP3 is only used for retrieving server-based messages; POP3 clients typically use SMTP to send messages.

## IMAP4

Internet Message Access Protocol version 4 (IMAP4) is a message retrieval protocol that is similar to POP3. IMAP4 is also used for retrieving messages from a server and relies on SMTP for sending messages. However, IMAP4 improves on the POP3 technology in several ways. With IMAP4, you can actually browse server-based folders and move, delete, and view messages without first copying them to your local computer. IMAP4 also allows you to save certain settings such as client window appearance on the server. This makes IMAP4 particularly useful if you tend to access your email from different locations or computers.

## LDAP

Lightweight Directory Access Protocol (LDAP) is a protocol used to retrieve directory information from LDAP-enabled email servers. A client using LDAP can retrieve a listing of information such as names, email addresses, locations, and public security keys. Many of the newer POP and IMAP clients feature support for LDAP.

# Older Utilities

In addition to the three Internet utilities previously covered in this chapter there are a number of other Internet utilities that had prominence during the formative stages of the Internet. Some of these utilities are still viable today, whereas others have effectively been replaced by more modern, easier-to-use utilities. However, knowing about these utilities is useful, as many are still used on older systems throughout the world.

## Archie

The Archie service provides a means to locate files on *anonymous* FTP servers located anywhere on the Internet. Anonymous FTP servers are FTP servers that allow anonymous logins. However, today the World Wide Web often provides similar capabilities. For instance it is easy for a user to download software files such as driver updates from a manufacturer's Web site. Even if the user does not know which Web site to download the file from, search engines can provide a list of Web sites containing the file.

14

Archie servers work by periodically, usually once per month, searching every known anonymous FTP server on the Internet for the filenames located on that computer. These file names are then sorted into alphabetical order and placed into a database that comprises the data a client can query from Archie. Accompanying each name in this database is the location of the FTP server(s) where the listed filename can be found.

Archie can be queried from a client through a number of means—the easiest is through an Archie client specifically designed to talk to the Archie service. You can also contact Archie via Telnet or even via email.

Every Archie server should contain the same information because every Archie server has access to the same anonymous FTP servers. Therefore, it really doesn't matter which Archie server you connect to in order to locate the desired files. What is important however is to try to minimize the amount of network traffic that you generate while issuing Archie requests. The user should attempt to locate an Archie server that is only a few router hops away; it makes no sense for a user in the United States to contact an Archie server in Australia.

To locate a specific file, for instance a driver for a specific sound card, the user must determine which FTP server or servers (if any) contain the file. When the user enters the filename, or even a portion of the filename, the Archie client passes the request to an Archie server. The Archie server in turn queries its catalog in order to locate the filename(s) that match the request entered by the Archie client. The response to the query includes the names of those FTP servers that contain the filename or partial file name. The list of matching filenames and their location is returned to the Archie client. The user can then use an FTP client to contact the FTP servers and download the desired file.

Figure 14.3 displays results of an Archie request to locate files that contain the characters P9000.

## Gopher

The Gopher service has, in many respects, effectively been surpassed by the World Wide Web service. The Gopher service was originally developed at the University of Minnesota to provide students and staff with an easy-to-use, menu driven means to locate and display content on the Internet. The Gopher service also allows people who are familiar with content to develop catalogs on Gopher servers that other people can use to access information.

Many Gopher servers are no longer available and when contacted display a message indicating the name of a World Wide Web server that the user should contact in order to display current information. However, Gopher does still exist and provides the user with very quick responses because it is totally character-based and is not burdened with downloading graphics as is the case with the World Wide Web. Typically a Gopher client program is installed on an end user's computer along with a number of other client utilities, such as an FTP or Telnet client.

**FIGURE 14.3**

*Archie results from a search for files that contain the characters P9000.*

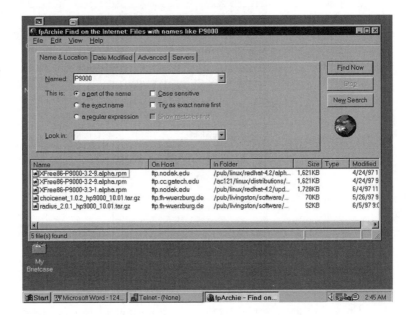

A Gopher client works by contacting Gopher servers that contain catalogs of information available on the Internet. These catalogs are listed by subject in a manner akin to a subject catalog in a library. The information that the Gopher client presents to the user appears in the form of menus. The user can choose a menu item, which displays another menu or, if the menu item is associated with the actual content, Gopher retrieves the content using the appropriate utility. For instance, if the content was contained within an FTP file, Gopher initiates retrieval of the file by using FTP.

In Figure 14.4 a Gopher client displays information available from the Library of Congress. The Gopher site information displayed in Figure 14.4 is located at the University of Iowa.

## Pine

Pine is an email system that was developed by the University of Washington. It allows a user to compose and read email using simple terminal interfaces such as Telnet. The Pine service is hosted on UNIX boxes and the user instructs Pine using simple one-character commands in conjunction with a Ctrl key. For instance, to initiate the composition of a new message a user would enter Ctrl C. Typically UNIX boxes are case-sensitive and the

14

user needs to be careful when entering uppercase or lowercase characters. However, Pine accepts and responds appropriately to either uppercase or lowercase characters.

**FIGURE 14.4**

*Gopher client listing of documents available from the Library of Congress.*

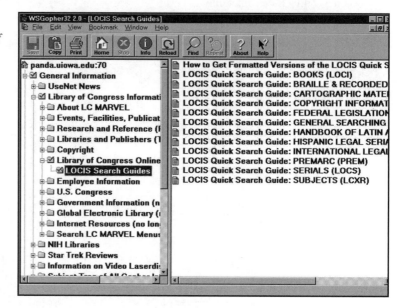

Using Pine and a simple terminal or terminal emulator, the user can compose and read email messages, maintain address books, create and manage folders, add attachments to email messages, perform spell-check functions, and reply or forward email messages to others.

Nowadays, these functions are typically handled by more sophisticated email applications; however, where users are limited to character-based terminal environments, Pine is still a viable form of communicating via email.

## Whois

The Whois utility is used to find names of companies or individuals that match criteria that is submitted to a Whois server. In the past a Whois client provided the interface for the submission of the query name and the display of the returned matching names. Today, the service is readily accessible via the World Wide Web. If you navigate to www.internic.net, the Web page displays a box where you can enter the name that you want to submit to the Whois server, and then initiate the search. Figure 14.5 shows the response returned to a query for Gopher.

**FIGURE 14.5**

*A response from a Whois server following a request for the name "gopher."*

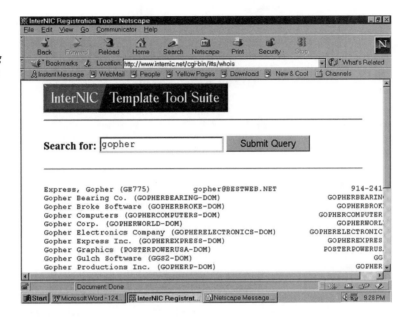

## Summary

In this hour, you learned that the Internet provides a wide variety of services to users throughout the world. However, utilizing those services requires the use of both client and server programs. In today's environment, the World Wide Web service is the most popular and widely used Internet service. Of course email services are also of vital importance, and users have the capability to send and receive email with other people virtually anywhere in the world. The use of mail reader programs makes it easy for a user to send and receive mail. Newsgroups and their associated client program newsreaders allow a user to view and post messages on forums of interest.

In addition to the Internet utilities mentioned in the previous paragraph, a host of other utilities provide specific services that can make the Internet even more useful and functional. The four older utilities addressed in this hour (Archie, Gopher, Pine, and Whois) provide functionality that is still useful in today's environment.

## Q&A

**Q  What is an URL, and what Internet service is it associated with?**

**A  URL stands for uniform resource locator; it is used to uniquely identify documents on the World Wide Web.**

14

**Q  Before you can view news messages what process must you perform?**

**A**  You must join a newsgroup.

**Q  What Internet service allows you to locate anonymous FTP servers that contain the file that you are looking for?**

**A**  Archie.

**Q  Assuming you have only Telnet access, how could you send an email message?**

**A**  You can use Pine to send and receive email messages.

# Workshop

## Key Terms

Review the following list of key terms:

- Archie—A client/server utility that is used to locate files on anonymous FTP servers.

- Gopher—A client/server utility used to navigate and display content from throughout the Internet.

- Pine—A terminal-based email reader program that runs on a UNIX box; it allows you to read, write, and exchange email messages with others.

- Uniform resource locator (URL)—An URL is composed of two or three parts that are used to locate a specific Web page on a specific Web server. The URL is composed of a protocol name such as http://, a domain name, and optionally a path and filename of the file or document to be displayed.

# PART IV
# Name Resolution

## Hour

# HOUR 15

# Host and Domain Name Resolution

*By Bob Willsey and Art Hammond*

The name resolution process accepts a name for a computer from a user and attempts to resolve the name to the corresponding IP address for that computer. As you read through this hour you will learn about host names, domain names, and fully qualified domain names (FQDN). You will also learn that there are a number of different processes for resolving these names to the correct IP address. Some of these processes are dynamic, whereas others require manual configuration to remain current.

## Goals for this Hour

At the completion of this hour, you will be able to

- Explain how name resolution works
- Explain the differences between host names, domain names, and FQDNs.
- Describe the usage of the following name resolution processes: Hosts files and the domain name system (DNS)

# Methods for Host and Domain Name Resolution

For humans, names are much more meaningful and easier to remember than numbers. However, computers are much faster at recalling, comparing, and manipulating numbers than people could ever hope to be. Because computers use 32-bit numbers, that is, IP addresses, to talk with each other, you need a way to help people resolve these numbers to easily remember names.

There are several commonly used conventions for naming computers: host names, DNS names, and NetBIOS names. NetBIOS names evolved primarily with Windows operating systems in the LAN environment. NetBIOS names are covered in Hour 17, "NetBIOS Name Resolution." This hour concentrates on host names and domain names.

## Host Names

The use of host names is a convention that has been around since the early days of the ARPAnet. In this convention a unique name is assigned to each computer. Host names are said to occupy a *flat* namespace, which means there is no hierarchy or vertical structure associated with the name. To get an idea of a flat name space, imagine if everybody you have ever known had only a first name. There is a very good chance that at some point in your life you will meet two or more people with the same name, or people would have to have very inventive names in order to be unique.

In the early days of ARPAnet, the host names for all computers were maintained in a single file named Hosts.txt. This file was centrally administered and required each computer to have a unique name. As the number of computers (and names) grew, the names assigned became rather meaningless and contrived in their attempt to be unique. The net effect of flat name spaces is they don't scale well and become unmanageable when large numbers of names are concerned.

# Domain Name System (DNS) Names

The DNS is a name resolution mechanism that was created to address the problems inherent with host names and the Hosts.txt file. Unlike the flat namespace used with host names, DNS is a hierarchical distributed database.

By hierarchical, I mean that the DNS system is comprised of multiple layers and appears as a tree (or root) structure. If you have surfed the Web then you have used DNS. A domain name is a two-tier name that is administered by a central authority such as InterNIC to ensure its uniqueness. The first part of the name identifies or is related to a specific company or organization. The second portion of a domain name is a suffix such as com, gov, or edu that provides a means of classification. These are also referred to as the top-level domains (TLD). The domain name is registered and belongs to the company or organization. The name whitehouse.gov is an example of a domain name.

Figure 15.1 shows the hierarchical structure of the DNS. The * at the top represents the root of the DNS tree. The next level is comprised of the TLDs, and below each of those is the individual domains registered by companies or organizations.

**FIGURE 15.1**

*DNS hierarchical structure.*

```
                                          *
         -----------------------------------------------------------------
              EDU              GOV              NET              COM
         -----------------------------------------------------------------
           CMU    MIT       WHITEHOUSE       INTERNIC        MICROSOFT
         -----------------------------------------------------------------
           WWW    WWW          WWW              WWW          WWW FTP HOME
```

The DNS system is actually quite amazing in how it functions and is quite literally comprised of thousands of servers running the DNS service. Although DNS is considered to be one database, it is not all stored in one place, which means it is a distributed database. It is spread out across thousands of computers called DNS servers, or name servers, each with its own part of the database. (DNS and name servers are covered in the Hour 16, "The Domain Name System.") Every company, organization, educational institution, and so on that has a DNS server is responsible for making their part of DNS accessible to the rest of the system.

To fully understand the structure of the DNS you must also understand FQDNs. A DNS server uses FQDNs to locate individual computers in domains other than its own and is derived from the combining of the host name and domain name. For example, a machine with the host name *bobscomputer* and the domain *lastingimpressions.com*, would have the FQDN of *bobscomputer.lastingimpressions.com*.

DNS allows for local control of names within the assigned domain name. DNS servers throughout the world work together to form a database where detailed information is located on DNS servers that are local to the company or organization which owns the domain name. DNS allows users to retrieve files and documents from computers that might be located virtually anywhere in the world.

 DNS servers are also known as *name servers*, and in the discussions in this and the following hour the two terms are interchangeable. If a server takes a request to resolve a name to an IP address and returns the answer to the client, it is a name server.

# Using Hosts Files and DNS

Although the InterNIC's centrally administered Hosts.txt file is no longer maintained, Hosts files are still in use on individual networks today. The use of DNS does not preclude the use of Hosts files, and the reverse is similarly true.

Whether or not you use a Hosts file depends on what type of network environment you have. On small, stable networks where the computers keep the same names and IP addresses for long periods of time and where computers are not added or removed very often, a Hosts file might be a good choice. It is simple to edit and configure and requires attention only when a change is made.

Also, if a network uses an Internet service provider (ISP), it might use the ISP's DNS servers for resolving names on the Internet and a Hosts file for resolving names on the private network.

A network needs to use a DNS server if it is particularly large and changes with any degree of frequency. Configuring and managing a DNS server can require many resources in both hours and hardware. However, running a DNS server instead of Hosts files can have its advantages (see Hour 16).

## Hosts Files

The purpose of a Hosts file is to resolve host names and optionally FQDNs to IP addresses; it is necessary when a computer does not have access to a DNS server. The Hosts file is often named Hosts, although some implementations use the filename Hosts.txt.

The Hosts file contains entries for hosts that a computer needs to communicate with, allowing you to *statically* enter an IP address with a corresponding host name, an FQDN, or other aliases. Also, the file usually contains an entry for the *loopback* address, 127.0.0.1. The loopback address is used for TCP/IP diagnostics and represents "this computer."

**15**

**NEW TERM** To *statically* enter an IP address means that after it is entered the address must be changed manually.

The following is an example of what a Hosts file might look like (the IP address of the system is on the left, followed by the host name and an optional comment about the entry):

```
127.0.0.1              localhost            #this machine

198.1.14.2             bobscomputer         #Bob's workstation

198.1.14.128           r4downtown           #gateway
```

When an application on a computer needs to resolve a name to an IP address, the system first compares its own name to the name being requested. If there is no match, the system then looks in the Hosts file (if one is present) to see if the computer name is listed.

If a match is found, the IP address is returned to the local computer and, as you learned in earlier hours, is used with ARP to obtain the hardware address of the other system. Now communication between the two can take place.

If the name doesn't match any Hosts file entry, or if there is no Hosts file present then the names are sent to the DNS servers for resolution, assuming the system is configured to use DNS servers. (See Hour 16 for more about DNS.)

> The Hosts file is often found in a directory named etc. For example, on Windows NT the file is typically found at C:\Winnt\System32\drivers\etc\Hosts. Windows 95 and 98 don't follow the \etc directory convention. The Hosts file on Windows 9.x resides in the Windows directory.

## Editing Hosts Files

To implement a change using hosts files requires manually editing or replacing the Hosts files on every computer. The reason many companies now use DNS servers in place of Hosts files is because a change made to a DNS server is quickly recognized by many machines. However, virtually every implementation of TCP/IP allows for the use of Hosts files.

You can use a number of editors to edit the Hosts file. On UNIX either the vi or Pico editor is used. On Windows, Notepad is the editor of choice, and on DOS-based computers Edit can be used.

When you create or edit the Hosts file be sure to keep the following points in mind:

- The IP address must be left-justified and separated from the name by one or more spaces.
- Names must be separated by at least one space.
- Additional names on a single line become aliases for the first name.
- The file is *parsed* (that is, read by the computer) from top to bottom. The IP address associated with the first match is used. When the match is made, parsing stops.
- Because it is parsed from top to bottom, you should put the most commonly used names at the top of the list. This can help speed up the process.
- Comments might be placed to the right of a # symbol.
- Remember the Hosts file is static; you must manually change it when IP addresses change.
- Incorrectly configured Hosts files (that is, typographic errors within Hosts files) can cause problems with name resolution. If the wrong address is returned to the requesting application during the resolution process, the application might not function properly.
- Although FQDNs are allowed and work in Hosts files, their use in Hosts files is discouraged and can lead to difficult bugs for an administrator to diagnose. For instance if a server is assigned a new IP address and the local FQDN is not updated, it continues to point to the old IP address.

# Using Utilities to Test Host and Domain Name Resolution

Because ping, Web browsers, the FTP client, and Telnet all use either a Hosts file or DNS to resolve names to IP addresses, they can be used to ensure name resolution is working as expected. If you make changes to either the Hosts file or to DNS you should run a few checks at the end to determine if your changes are error-free.

Keep in mind that you need to exclude the Hosts file when you test changes to DNS. This is because your machine checks in the Hosts file (if it is present on the machine) for the name you are testing. To exclude the Hosts file you can temporarily rename it. The opposite is true when testing new Hosts file entries; in this case you should temporarily remove the DNS server entries. Both of these methods pose small problems to single user systems, but be aware that both methods are problematic on multi-user systems such as UNIX.

To check for errors you can use some of the utilities that are covered in earlier hours. You can use FTP or Telnet to attempt to access the machine in question, using its host name or FQDN; if all the entries are correct, you should be successful (Refer to Hour 12, "TCP/IP File Transfer and Access Utilities," and Hour 13, "Remote Access Utilities," for more information).

You can also use the `ping` command (which is covered in Hour 11, "TCP/IP Connectivity Utilities") followed by the host name or FQDN; for example, the command:

```
Ping bobscomputer.lastingimpressions.com.
```

Should return a response similar to this:

```
Pinging bobscomputer.lastingimpressions.com [198.1.14.2]with 32 bytes of
➥data
Reply from 198.1.14.2 : bytes=32 time<10ms TTL=128
Reply from 198.1.14.2 : bytes=32 time<10ms TTL=128
Reply from 198.1.14.2 : bytes=32 time<10ms TTL=128
Reply from 198.1.14.2 : bytes=32 time<10ms TTL=128
```

Ping is often used to verify that a computer is active, which is what the replies here show. But notice the line before the replies. This line shows the IP address associated with *bobscomputer.lastingimpressions.com*, even though the command used only the host name. If this is the IP address you expected then name resolution was successful and is working properly. However, note that ping does not require a user ID or password, which might cause problems when testing with other utilities if you don't have the correct account information. Also note that some commercial Web sites and private networks have disabled the ICMP port, which is what Ping uses to prevent hackers from mounting attacks through this port. In these cases Ping will not work and you might need to resort to other utilities.

# Summary

Name resolution enables people to use meaningful, easy-to-remember names of computers instead of the IP address assigned to a computer. Computers often include a host name, a domain name, and therefore, an FQDN. These names can use name resolution processes such as Hosts files and DNS to translate names to IP addresses.

# Q&A

**Q What is a domain name?**

**A** It is a two-tier name that is administered by a central authority such as InterNIC to ensure the name's uniqueness. The first part of the name identifies or is related to a company or organization. The second portion of a domain name is a suffix such as com, gov, or edu that provides a means of classification.

**Q What is a host name?**

**A** It is a single name that is assigned to a particular computer. Usually the host name has some meaning such as location, usage, or ownership.

**Q What is an FQDN?**

**A** A combination of a host name concatenated to a domain name by the addition of a dot character. For example a host name of *bigserver* and a domain name of *mycompany.com* when combined becomes the FQDN *bigserver.mycompany.com*.

# Workshop

- At the command line of your computer enter the command ping localhost, and write down the IP address that you see.
- At the command line of your computer enter the command hostname and write down the host name that is returned. On Windows 95/98 the host name does not work, however, the host name is visible from WinIPCfg.
- Enter a ping command followed by the host name for your computer.
- If your computer has a domain name, ping your FQDN.
- Add a line to the bottom of your Hosts file similar to the following line. Substitute your IP address for the 10.59.66.200 address.
- 10.59.66.200 - router - gateway - exit ramp
- Enter the commands: ping router, ping gateway, ping exit ramp
- Determine if IP is configured to use a DNS server. If so try the following pings.

  ping www.internic.net

  ping www.whitehouse.gov

## Key Terms

Review the following list of key terms:

- DNS—A hierarchical distributed database that allows centralized control of domain names and local control of resources.
- Domain name—A name registered with InterNIC to ensure uniqueness.
- FQDN—The name generated by concatenating a host name with a domain name.
- Host name—A single name used to identify a computer (host).

# Hour **16**

# The Domain Name System (DNS)

*By Bob Willsey and Art Hammond*

The purpose of the domain name system (DNS) is to accept a domain name such as www.whitehouse.gov or rs.internic.net from a client application such as a Web browser and return to the application of the corresponding IP address. In essence DNS resolves domain names to IP addresses.

The dictionary defines *domain* using words such as dominion, ownership, possession, and sphere of influence. These words all aptly describe attributes of a domain name or the DNS. The right to use or own a domain name is assigned to a specific country, company, institution, organization, or entity. After a domain is assigned the owner (organization) is considered authoritative over that name and other names derived from it.

In this hour you will learn how DNS actually works as a worldwide distributed database that contains services running on thousands of servers. You will also learn the basic concepts required to implement a basic DNS server.

Finally you will learn to use the features of the NSLookup utility to examine configuration settings of other DNS servers.

## Goals for this Hour

At the completion of this hour, you will be able to

- Describe what DNS is
- Describe how DNS works
- Describe what zone files and resource records are
- Use NSLookup to view information from virtually any DNS server

## What Is DNS?

DNS is a distributed hierarchical database that includes listings for literally thousands of computers and entries for some of the services that run on them. As mentioned in Hour 15, "Host and Domain Name Resolution," DNS grew out of a pure need for a better system of resolving IP addresses to host names. In the early days of networking, a text file known as Hosts.txt was manually maintained by SRI-NIC (the Stanford Research Institute Network Information Center, an ARPAnet site). This file contained the IP address and host name for every computer on ARPAnet. It was updated and distributed to systems administrators on a regular basis, but the system for host name to IP address resolution had a number of shortcomings:

- Every name had to be unique; as more and more names were added it became increasingly difficult to invent names that were both unique and descriptive.
- SRI-NIC was saddled with the increasingly difficult burden of maintaining the Hosts.txt file.
- Local administrators had to continually replace the existing Hosts.txt file with newer versions.
- The Hosts.txt file, being sequential, took increasingly longer amounts of time to scan for a matching name, which put a burden on the servers that held them.

DNS was developed to address these shortcomings. It enables local administrators to handle the configuration and maintenance of their part of the DNS system, thereby reducing the workload at the central authority. It is the responsibility of every company, organization, educational institution, and so on that has a domain name to make their part of the DNS accessible to the rest of the system. DNS doesn't need to be stored in a huge centrally maintained file; instead, individually managed DNS servers hold the information and have the capability to query other DNS servers to quickly locate the IP address that corresponds to a domain name.

# How DNS Works

We'll start with the domain name itself. As we learned in the previous hour, DNS uses a hierarchical or multiple layered name space (as opposed to the flat name space used by host files). In the domain name system a dot (.) character is used as a separator between levels. The names farthest to the right—for example, com, edu, gov, and so on—are known as top-level domains (TLDs) and are used for broad classification purposes. Because TLDs always appear to the right they are also known as suffixes. For instance, commercial companies have a com suffix, four-year universities have an edu suffix for education, and the federal government has a gov suffix. These suffix names appear near the top of the hierarchy. A single asterisk represents the very top of the hierarchy, which is known as the *root* of the DNS name space.

The name to the left of the suffix is registered with a centralized authority to ensure that no duplicates exist. For instance, `internic.net`, `whitehouse.gov`, and `samspublishing.com` are all registered domain names.

After an organization registers a domain name, the domain can then be subdivided any way the organization sees fit, and any names that precede the domain name, such as www, ftp, home, bobscomputer and so on are under the control of the entity that owns the domain name. For instance, if an administrator who works for Sams wants to create a new Web site with the name *home.samspublishing.com*, he or she only needs to add a couple of entries known as *resource records* (more on these later in this chapter) to the DNS servers responsible for the `samspublishing.com` domain. After these entries have been entered to the local DNS servers, anyone in the world with access to the Internet can connect to `home.samspublishing.com`.

A handful of DNS servers are maintained centrally by the InterNIC in the U.S. and by a few other entities in other countries. The DNS servers located at the top of the hierarchy are known as root-level servers and each is identified by a letter of the alphabet.

Root level DNS servers contain the IP addresses of the suffix DNS servers that are located the next level down the DNS hierarchy. The suffix DNS servers in turn contain the IP addresses for the DNS servers that are maintained by each registered company or organization, again one additional level down the hierarchy. Local DNS servers contain the IP addresses of servers in that organization which provide Web, mail, FTP, Gopher, and other services. The local DNS servers could also point to additional DNS servers farther down the hierarchy within the company or organization.

As an example, let's suppose you own a gift basket company named Lasting Impressions, and you want to set up a Web server and email server with your own domain name. You contact InterNIC and verify that no one has registered

16

*lastingimpressions* as a domain name and register it. Because you are a commercial entity you request your domain name be given a com suffix. InterNIC adds an entry for the
DNS server that is responsible for your new domain to the servers that handle requests
for all domains with a com suffix.

Then you put in entries in your DNS servers' *zone files* for the computers and services
you want to make accessible to the outside world. (Zone files tell the DNS service how
to respond to queries from local clients and from other DNS servers and are covered later
in this hour.) After these entries are added, and provided your local DNS servers are
properly configured, people from around the world will able to use DNS to locate your
Web, FTP, Gopher, and mail servers.

So now that you're registered, how does it all work? Let's say someone surfing the Web
enters a Web site address such as `www.home.lastingimpressions.com/default.htm`
into a Web browser. The www denotes that this file is on a Web site, home is the name of
the Web server in the *lastingimpressions* domain, and default.htm is the name of the file
the user is requesting. In order for the browser to display the Web page, `default.htm`, it
needs to obtain the IP address of the Web server on which the page is stored, and then
contact that server and request the page.

The following is an example of the activity that takes place when an application uses
DNS to resolve a name:

1. The browser extracts the domain name *lastingimpressions* from the Web page
   address: `www.home.lastingimpressions.com/default.htm`.

2. The browser contacts the local DNS server that the user's machine is configured to
   use and requests the IP address for `home.lastingimpressions.com`.

3. This DNS server first looks at its own files for the name in question. If no match is
   found, it queries the root server responsible for the TLD com, which keeps track of
   all domains with the com extension.

4. The root server does not have an entry for `home.lastingimpressions.com`. But it
   does have an entry for `lastingimpressions.com`. So instead of answering "no,"
   the com domain responds with the IP address of the DNS server responsible for the
   `lastingimpressions.com` domain.

5. The local DNS server contacts the `lastingimpressions.com` DNS server and asks
   for the IP address of the computer `home.lastingimpressions.com`, which has the
   Web page the browser is looking for.

6. After the local DNS server has the IP address of
   `www.home.lastingimpressions.com`, it returns that IP address to the Web browser.
   Armed with the IP address, the browser can contact the Web server to retrieve the
   Web document.

There are three types of queries involved in the DNS process, and the preceding example has two of them. The client is making a *recursive* query to its local name server. With this type of query, the client wants either the requested information or an answer stating the domain in question does not exist.

The other query, an *iterative* query, is what takes place between the local DNS server and the other name servers. If the queried server does not know the IP address of the host in question, it does its best to refer the requestor to a server that is authoritative for that domain. Step 4 in the preceding example shows this process occurring.

The third type of query, an *inverse* query, is when a client provides an IP address and requests the corresponding host name from what are called *reverse lookup files*, which are covered a bit later in this hour.

**16**

# DNS Management

The organization responsible for adding new TLDs such as com, edu, and such, is the Internet Assigned Numbers Authority (IANA). Their Web site is located at www.iana.org. Registration services for a number of commonly used TLDs are listed here.

- com, edu, org, and net—InterNIC handles registration services for these four TLDs. The edu domain is reserved for four-year higher education institutions. Registration services are located at www.internic.net.

- gov—The gov domain is reserved for the U.S. federal government. State and local government names branch from the U.S. TLD. Registration services for the gov domain are located at www.registration.fed.gov.

- mil—The mil domain is reserved for the United States military. Registration services are located at www.nic.mil.

- us—The us domain registration services are handled by the Information Services Institute (ISI). The us domain registration services are located at www.isi.edu/in-notes/usdnr.

In addition to the commonly used three-character domain suffixes, every country in the world has been assigned a two-letter country code suffix. For example, the United States' domain is listed as us, Italy is it, and Spain is es (for Espana). Each country typically designates an authority to control domain name registrations under their country code. For example, the us domain name designated registration authority is the ISI.

# Implementing DNS

This section describes some of the concepts involved in setting up a DNS server and DNS client. To set up a DNS server you need to choose the type of DNS server you want to use, create zone files and resource records, and then test your implementation. Setting up the DNS client, which uses the server to resolve names to IP addresses, is a simple process described later in this chapter.

## Types of DNS Servers

When implementing DNS on your network, you need to choose at least one server to be responsible for maintaining your domain. This is referred to as your *primary name server*, and it gets all the information about the zones it is responsible for from local files. Any changes you make to your domain are made on this server.

Many networks also have at least one more server as a backup or *secondary name server*. If something happens to your primary server, this machine can continue to service requests. The secondary server gets its information from the primary server's zone file. When this exchange of information takes place, it is referred to as a *zone transfer*.

A third type of server is called a *caching-only* server. A *cache* is part of a computer's memory that keeps frequently requested data ready to be accessed. As a caching-only server, it responds to queries from clients on the local network for name resolution requests. It queries other DNS servers for information about domains and computers that offer services such as Web and FTP. When it receives information from other DNS servers it stores that information in its cache in case a request for that information is made again.

Caching-only servers are used by client computers on the local network to resolve names. They are not registered with InterNIC as DNS servers are, so other DNS servers will not know about them, and therefore will not query them. This is desirable if you want to distribute the load your servers are put under. A caching-only server is also simple to maintain, if for instance you have a remote site where client computers need name resolution services and nothing more.

The cache is preconfigured with the IP addresses of nine root-level DNS servers. If this computer has access to the Internet via a router it is ready to work. Client computers could include the IP address of this DNS server in their search order list and this DNS server would begin to service requests by contacting other DNS servers and automatically adding entries to its cache.

On Windows NT, DNS is implemented as the DNS service. On most UNIX boxes the DNS process is called *named,* which stands for the name daemon. *Daemons* are processes that provide a service to other users or other computers. Computers that handle DNS can and often do perform other functions on a network.

## Zone Files

As mentioned earlier, zone files contain the information that tells the DNS service how to respond to queries from local clients and other DNS servers. You use the zone file to define the server's *zone of authority* or as mentioned earlier in relation to the domains, its *sphere of influence.* A zone file is a text file with a standardized structure that contains records for all the computers and services that server is responsible for. You also use this file to add entries in order to make new computers available to the DNS.

In a domain with a small number of computers, the zone file probably contains all the entries for the domain. This is often the case, so it can be easy to confuse a zone and a domain for the same thing. However, the computers in a domain could be separated into two zones with each zone residing on a different DNS server.

For example, say Lasting Impressions is successful and is now a large company with an office in New York and another in Los Angeles. The computers in both cities would be in the lastingimpressions.com domain, but their DNS entries need to be managed locally. The solution would be a zone file managed by a DNS server in New York with records for all the computers in that office and a zone file on a DNS server in L.A. with entries for that office's computers. Each DNS server would then respond only to requests for computers within its zone.

### Resource Records

The entries contained in a zone file are known as resource records. Different resource records are used to identify which type of computer or service the entry represents. Each resource record type has a specific purpose. For example, an A type resource record indicates the IP address associated with the host name. A *CNAME* record is an alias. (CNAME stands for canonical name). If a user entered Web server.lastingimpressions.com, your DNS server would supply the correct IP address. However, you don't want users to have to know the names of your servers, so aliases are often used that point to the actual server. In this case you want users to enter www.lastingimpressions.com but to be directed to Web server.lastingimpressions.com. Other important resource record types include those associated with name server (NS), email exchange (MX records), and the responsible person (RP record) for this DNS server.

One resource record that every DNS server contains is a *Start of Authority (SOA)* record. This record, which is always first in a zone file, defines which entity is responsible from this point in the hierarchy downward. Figure 16.1 shows three resource records as created on a Windows NT DNS server. The NS resource record identifies the computer located at *dnsserver*.lastingimpressions.com as a DNS server. The SOA resource record identifies your name server to be authoritative for the lastingimpressions.com domain. The A resource record supplies the IP address for the hostname dnsserver.

**FIGURE 16.1**

*Resource records created during zone creation.*

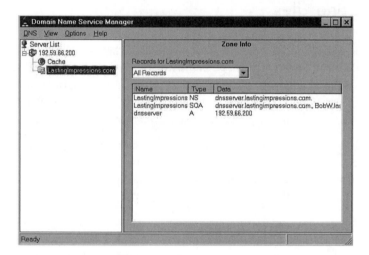

## The Reverse Lookup Zone File

One type of zone file used on DNS servers is the reverse lookup file. This file is used when a client provides an IP address and requests the corresponding host name. In IP addresses the leftmost portion is general and the rightmost portion is specific. However, in domain names the opposite is true, the left portion is specific and the right portion, such as com or edu, is general. To create a reverse lookup zone file you must reverse the order of the network address so the general and specific portions follow the same pattern used within domain names. For example, the zone for the 192.59.66.0 network would have the name 66.59.192.in-addr.arpa.

Every resource record in this file always has the host ID followed by .in-addr.arpa. The in-addr portion stands for inverse address, and the arpa portion is another top-level domain and is a holdover from the original ARPAnet that preceded the Internet.

Class A and B networks have shorter reverse lookup zone names due to the fact that they contain fewer network bits. Here are two examples; the first is for a Class A network address. Assuming the Class A network 43.0.0.0 the reverse lookup zone must have the exact name of 43.in-addr.arpa. Assuming the Class B network 172.58.0.0 the reverse lookup zone must have the exact name of 58.172.in-addr.arpa.

**16**

## Testing the Server Implementation

Once you have configured the DNS server, you should test to see that the DNS server, the zone files, and the resource records are set up properly. To do so, you can use the ping command (see Hour 11, "TCP/IP Connectivity Utilities," for more information). At the command prompt, enter

```
ping hostname.domain name
```

If everything is configured properly, the command returns the IP address.

## Configuring the Client

Another important aspect of DNS is the process of enabling a client computer to use it.

When a user enters a name in an application such as a Web browser or an FTP client, the name needs to be resolved to an IP address before the application can continue. By default this name is first compared to the local host name to determine if the destination requested is the local computer. If there is no match, the Hosts file (if present) is then scanned for a match on the name entered by the user. If the name doesn't match any Hosts file entry then the names are sent to the DNS servers for resolution but only if TCP/IP on the client computer has been configured to use DNS.

When a client is configured to use DNS to resolve names, it becomes a *resolver*. A resolver passes name resolution requests between applications on a system and DNS servers.

Configuring TCP/IP on a client computer to use DNS is simply the process of adding the IP addresses of one or more DNS servers in the proper location. Here is an example of how to configure a computer to use a DNS server. The example here is on a computer running Windows NT.

1. Choose the Network icon from Control Panel. From the Networks dialog box choose the Protocols tab then the TCP/IP Protocol, and then Properties. Finally choose the DNS property sheet from the Microsoft TCP/IP Properties dialog box.

2. The DNS property sheet appears as shown in Figure 16.2. If you have not already done so, you should enter the host name and domain name in the two fields provided for that purpose.

**FIGURE 16.2**

*The DNS property sheet on Windows NT.*

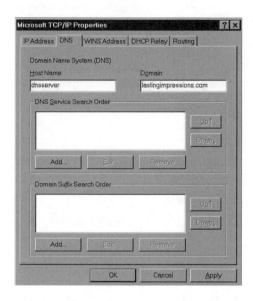

3. To add the IP addresses for one or more DNS servers choose the Add button in the DNS Service Search Order frame.

   A dialog box, as shown in Figure 16.3, is presented where you can type an IP address and add it to the existing list of DNS servers. When two or more DNS servers are referenced you can arrange their order.

   When a client uses DNS to resolve a name to an address, the top DNS server is searched first then the second DNS server is searched, and so on until either a match is found or all DNS servers have been searched.

**FIGURE 16.3**

*The DNS Server Search Order dialog box.*

# The NSLookup Utility

The NSLookup utility enables you to query DNS servers and view information such as their resource records, and it is useful when troubleshooting DNS problems. The NSLookup utility operates in two modes.

- Batch mode—In Batch mode you start NSLookup and provide input parameters. NSLookup performs the functions requested by the input parameters, displays the results, and then terminates.

- Interactive mode—In Interactive mode you start NSLookup without supplying input parameters. NSLookup then prompts you for parameters. When you enter the parameters, NSLookup performs the requested actions, displays the results, and returns to a prompt waiting for the next set of parameters. Most administrators use Interactive mode because it is more convenient when performing a series of actions.

NSLookup is a utility with an extensive list of options. A few basic options covered here give you a feel for how NSLookup works.

To run NSLookup in Interactive mode enter the name `nslookup` from a command prompt.

As shown in Figure 16.4, each NSLookup response starts with the name and IP address of the DNS server that NSLookup is currently using, for example:

```
Default Server:    dnsserver.Lastingimpressions.com
Address:    192.59.66.200
>
The chevron character ">" is  nslookup's prompt.
```

NSLookup has about 15 settings that you can change to affect how NSLookup operates. A few of the most commonly used settings are listed here:

- `?; help`—These commands are used to view a list of all nslookup commands.

- `server`—This command specifies which DNS server to query.

- `ls`—This command is used to list the names in a domain, as shown near the middle of Figure 16.4.

- `ls -a`—This command lists canonical names and aliases in a domain, as shown in Figure 16.4.

- `ls -d`—This command lists all resource records, as shown near the bottom of Figure 16.4.

- `set all`—This command displays the current value of all settings.

**FIGURE 16.4**

*NSLookup responses.*

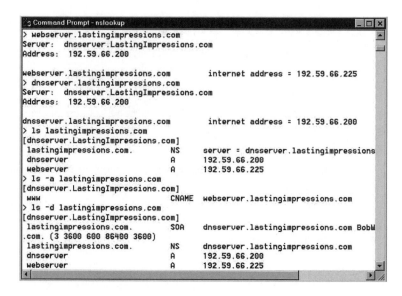

The NSLookup is not restricted to viewing information from your DNS server; you can view information from virtually any DNS server. If you have an ISP, you should have IP addresses for at least two DNS servers. NSLookup can use either IP addresses or domain names. You can switch NSLookup to another DNS server by entering the `server` command followed by either the IP address or the FQDN. For instance, to connect NSLookup to the E root server you can enter server 192.203.230.10. Then you can enter virtually any domain name such as `samspublishing.com` and see the IP addresses registered for that domain name. Be aware that most commercial DNS servers and root servers will refuse `ls` commands as they can generate a tremendous amount of traffic and may pose a security leak.

# Summary

In this hour, you learned that DNS is a hierarchical distributed database that allows for local control and distributed configuration. The registration of domain names is handled by a few authoritative agencies to ensure that duplicates do not exist.

Every domain name requires at least one primary DNS server, but at least two are recommended. The second server is used as a backup in case the first one fails. There are name servers responsible for each domain at each level of the hierarchy.

The information on DNS servers is kept in what are called zone files. The entries in the zone files are called resource records. When this information is passed from a primary DNS server to a secondary it is called a zone transfer.

NSLookup is a utility that allows you to connect to a DNS server and query its resource records.

# Q&A

**16**

**Q  Who manages domain name registrations for the com domain?**

**A**  InterNIC.

**Q  What are the three types of queries that can be used during the name resolution process?**

**A**  Recursive, Iterative, and Inverse.

**Q  What are resource records?**

**A**  Resource records are the entries contained in a zone file. Different resource records are used to identify different types of computers or services.

**Q  What type of resource record is used for an alias? And why are aliases used?**

**A**  CNAME; it is used to mask the real names of computers on a network from the rest of the world.

**Q  What is a caching-only server?**

**A**  A caching-only server responds to queries from clients on the local network for name resolution requests and stores that information in its cache in case a request for that information is made again. Caching-only servers are not registered with InterNIC as DNS servers, so other DNS servers don't know about it, and therefore won't query it.

**Q  What is the role of a resolver?**

**A**  A resolver passes name resolution requests between the applications on a system and DNS servers.

# Workshop

1. Use NSLookup to connect to one of your ISP's DNS servers.
2. Locate the A records for your ISP's WWW, FTP, and mail sites.

## Key Terms

Review the following list of key terms:

- Resource record—An entry added to zone files. There are a number of resource record types and each type has a specific purpose.

- Zone file—The configuration files used by DNS servers. These textual files are used to configure DNS servers. One zone file is created for each domain name. A single DNS server can support multiple domains and therefore multiple zone files simultaneously.

# Hour 17

# NetBIOS Name Resolution

*By Bob Willsey and Art Hammond*

The NetBIOS name resolution process accepts a name request for a computer from a user and attempts to resolve the name to the corresponding IP address. These days a discussion of NetBIOS nearly always focuses on computers running Windows operating systems, because Microsoft chose early on to base much of its network connectivity technologies on it. With Microsoft operating systems on the vast majority of desktop computers, and with the fast-growing popularity of Windows NT, a discussion of this technology and its relationship to TCP/IP is extremely relevant to the scope of this book.

As you read through this hour you will learn about NetBIOS names and that there are a number of different processes for resolving these names into the correct IP address. Some of these processes are dynamic, whereas others require manual configuration to remain current.

## Goals for this Hour

At the completion of this hour, you will be able to

- Define NetBIOS
- Describe the following NetBIOS name resolution processes: broadcast-based, LMHosts, and WINS name resolution
- Test NetBIOS name resolution
- Disable LMHosts and WINS

## What Is NetBIOS?

A bit of history is in order to help you understand NetBIOS and its importance in relation to TCP/IP. Network Basic Input/Output Operating System, NetBIOS, is a Session layer that resides in the Application layer of the TCP/IP model application programming interface (API) developed by IBM in the early 1980s. An API is a set of common rules used by applications to interface with each other. NetBIOS has its own method of addressing for computers on a network. It uses NetBIOS names (that is, names based on the NetBIOS API) instead of IP addresses to identify and locate other computers. NetBIOS soon gave rise to NetBEUI (NetBIOS Extended User Interface), a very efficient network protocol for moving NetBIOS traffic across networks. Microsoft applications used NetBIOS to connect between computers across a network with NetBEUI as its standard protocol.

However, the predominance of other protocols such as TCP/IP forced Microsoft to change its networking strategy. Nearly all applications that had been written for Windows machines had been written to use NetBIOS. Also, NetBEUI had one major flaw: It was not routable, and so it was confined to use on small networks.

In order for Windows machines to continue using these applications on larger networks, Microsoft developed NetBIOS over TCP/IP (NetBT), a method of running NetBIOS applications using TCP/IP as a transport. Just as host and domain name resolution is vital to communication over TCP/IP, so NetBIOS name resolution is also vital to the communication of many of the applications running on networks today.

 UNIX computers and other operating systems can be integrated into a NetBIOS environment, but it requires extra efforts that would likely go beyond the duties of the TCP/IP novice, and won't be covered here.

# Methods for NetBIOS Name Resolution

NetBIOS name resolution operates in much the same way as host and domain name resolution does (see Hour 15, "Host and Domain Name Resolution," and Hour 16, "The Domain Name System"). The ultimate goal of NetBIOS name resolution is to provide an IP address when given a NetBIOS name.

NetBIOS also has its own naming conventions used for assigning names to computers on a network. NetBIOS names are single names up to 15 characters in length; names such as Workstation1, HRServer, and CorpServer are examples of acceptable NetBIOS names. NetBIOS does not allow for duplicate computer names on a network.

Technically there are 16 characters in a NetBIOS name. However, the sixteenth character is used by the underlying application and in general is not directly configurable by the user. These characters are discussed later in this hour.

**17**

Typically on a LAN there are not too many computers so assigning unique names is not a difficult process. Problems begin to occur when using NetBIOS names on a large network. As the number of networked computers grows it becomes increasingly difficult to think up computer names that are both unique and meaningful. NetBIOS names, like host names, are said to be in a flat name space, as there is no hierarchy or capability to qualify the names. In the following sections you examine several ways to resolve NetBIOS names to their corresponding IP addresses:

- Broadcast-based name resolution
- LMHosts file name resolution
- WINS name resolution

## Broadcast-based Name Resolution

One way for name resolution to take place is through *broadcasts*. A broadcast occurs when a computer announces to all the other machines on its network segment that it needs the address of a particular computer so it can deliver data to it. All the computers on the segment hear the broadcast, but only the machine specified in the broadcast responds to the request.

This method of name resolution, also known as B-Node name resolution, works well in a LAN environment but does not work in networks that extend beyond the LAN due to the fact that routers, by design, block broadcasts. Broadcasts can produce a great deal of net-

work traffic, which can be disruptive to the network. Routers limit disruption by not forwarding broadcasts to the rest of the network.

The broadcast name resolution process is simple and requires no extra configuration to
set up or use. Simply installing a network card and TCP/IP networking software onto a
Windows for Workgroups, Windows 95/98, or Windows NT operating systems enables
these systems to use broadcasts to locate other computers on the local network.

## LMHosts Files Name Resolution

LMHosts files are similar to Hosts files in that they resolve names to IP addresses and
have similar formats. The IP address is listed in the left column of the file with the corresponding computer name to the right separated by at least one space; comments can be
put in the file by placing them after a # character.

The LMHosts file is included with TCP/IP protocol implementations from Microsoft
Corporation and is located in the same directory as the Hosts file (Windows 95/98 and
NT machines). When networking components are installed, there is a sample LMHosts
file named LMHosts.sam placed in this location. You can edit the LMHosts.sam file, but
you must drop the sam extension before the file is usable. The LM in LMHosts is a
holdover from Microsoft's LAN Manager, a networking product that predated
Windows NT.

The following is an example of what a basic LMHosts file looks like:

```
192.59.66.205    marketserv    #file server for marketing department
192.59.66.206    marketapp     #application server for marketing
192.59.66.207    bobscomputer   #bob's workstation
```

LMHosts files, like Hosts files, are an older technology that requires manual editing in
order to maintain the file. The newer technology often used to replace or augment
LMHosts files is known as Windows Internet Name Service (WINS), which is discussed
later in this hour. Both LMHosts and WINS enable you to locate computers on remote
networks, something that the broadcast-based method of resolution cannot perform.

On Windows NT the capability to use the LMHosts file can be turned on and off; it is on
by default. To control this either select or deselect the Enable LMHOSTS Lookup check
box on the WINS Address property page shown in Figure 17.1.

Recently resolved NetBIOS names are stored in the NetBIOS name cache. As you
learned in Hour 16, a cache is part of a computer's memory that keeps frequently
requested data in memory and ready to be accessed. Whenever a user attempts to locate a
specific computer the system always consults the NetBIOS name cache before searching
the LMHosts file. If no match is found, the entries within the LMHosts file can then be
scanned for the requested name. This can be a time-consuming process if there are many

entries in the LMHosts file, so to speed up the process you can designate certain high-use entries to be preloaded into the NetBIOS name cache by including the #PRE keyword (see Figure 17.2). The LMHosts file is scanned once in its entirety when networking starts, so, for efficiency the lines that include #PRE keywords are usually placed toward the bottom of the LMHosts file. These lines only need to be read once, and by placing them later in the file it lessens the chance that they will be re-read.

**FIGURE 17.1**

*Enabled LMHOSTS Lookup check box in the WINS Address property tab.*

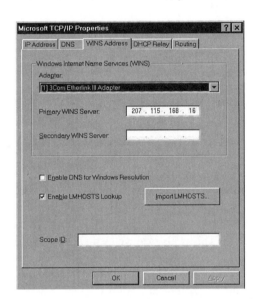

**17**

You can use the NBTStat utility discussed in Hour 11, "TCP/IP Connectivity Utilities," to view and manipulate the NetBIOS name cache. To view the contents of the cache, type nbtstat -c at the command prompt.

Maintaining static files such as Hosts and LMHosts is difficult because these files are located on each individual computer and therefore are not centralized. The LMHosts file addresses this problem by using the keyword #INCLUDE followed by an entry for the path to LMHOSTS files on other machines. With this keyword the local LMHosts file can include the location of a server-based LMHosts file for use by the local machine. The location of the file is entered in the form of its UNC name (UNC names are covered in Hour 11.) This allows edits to be performed on the server-based LMHosts file but the changes are accessible from the user's computer.

If there is more than one #INCLUDE entry, they need to be placed between the keywords #BEGIN ALTERNATE and #END ALTERNATE, as shown in Figure 17.2.

FIGURE **17.2**

*Contents of an*
*LMHosts file.*

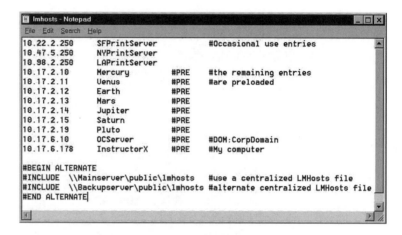

```
lmhosts - Notepad                                                    _□X
File  Edit  Search  Help
10.22.2.250      SFPrintServer              #Occasional use entries
10.47.5.250      NYPrintServer
10.98.2.250      LAPrintServer
10.17.2.10       Mercury          #PRE     #the remaining entries
10.17.2.11       Venus            #PRE     #are preloaded
10.17.2.12       Earth            #PRE
10.17.2.13       Mars             #PRE
10.17.2.14       Jupiter          #PRE
10.17.2.15       Saturn           #PRE
10.17.2.19       Pluto            #PRE
10.17.6.10       OCServer         #PRE     #DOM:CorpDomain
10.17.6.178      InstructorX      #PRE     #My computer

#BEGIN ALTERNATE
#INCLUDE  \\Mainserver\public\lmhosts   #use a centralized LMHosts file
#INCLUDE  \\Backupserver\public\lmhosts #alternate centralized LMHosts file
#END ALTERNATE
```

# Windows Internet Name Service (WINS) Name Resolution

WINS, which can be installed on Windows NT servers, was created to address the same types of shortcomings in LMHOSTS that DNS was created to address regarding Hosts files. When a client needs to get the IP address for a computer, it can query the WINS server for the information. This is also known as p-node resolution.

 WINS is the name assigned to Microsoft's implementation of what is generically known as a NetBIOS name server or NBNS. NetBIOS name servers are described in RFCs 1001 and 1002.

The other two other resolution modes are m-node and h-node. M-node computers first use broadcasts to try to resolve the name and if unsuccessful then use WINS servers. H-node computers query WINS first, and then fall back to broadcasts if unsuccessful. When Windows clients are configured to use a WINS server, that client, by default, becomes an h-node client.

WINS maintains a database of registered NetBIOS names for a variety of objects including users, computers, services running on those computers, and workgroups. However, instead of the entries in this database coming from manually edited text files, as in DNS, the client computers register their names and IP addresses with the WINS server dynamically when they start up. This can make it much less time-consuming to maintain than a DNS server.

To configure a computer to use WINS you enter the IP address of one (or two) WINS servers in the WINS Address property tab (as shown in Figure 17.1). After this is finished and the computer has rebooted, it is now considered a WINS client.

When a WINS client computer boots after being configured to use WINS, the following process occurs:

1. Service start up. As the computer boots various services are started, some of which need to be made known to other computers. Examples of some of the services are the NT server and messenger services.

2. Registration request. To be known to other computers on the network the service must register itself. A WINS client computer packages the NetBIOS name and the computer's IP address inside a name registration request, and the registration request is sent to the WINS server. Upon receiving the registration request, WINS checks its database to see if the name is already registered.

   If the name does not exist, WINS adds the NetBIOS name and IP address pair to its database and sends a name registration response indicating the name was successfully registered. If the requested NetBIOS name already exists in the WINS database, WINS challenges the computer currently registered by sending a message to the registered IP address. If the currently registered computer responds, a negative acknowledgement is sent to the other computer attempting to register the name. If the computer being challenged doesn't respond, WINS allows the registration to occur and overwrite the previous registration.

3. Lease. Assuming the computer is successful in registering its NetBIOS names and services with WINS, these names are considered leased. In essence the computer is allowed to use the NetBIOS name for a specified period of time, for instance six days, but the client can renew the lease before it expires. The client typically renews the lease at 50 percent of the total lease time or in this case every three days.

Earlier I noted that the sixteenth character of a NetBIOS name is not configurable by the user. During the WINS registration process, the sixteenth character is appended to the name by the WINS server based on what type of service the computer is trying to register before it is placed in the database. Between computer names, workgroup names, and a number of services, it is not unusual for a single computer to have 5 to 10 registration entries in the WINS database.

As another example of the WINS name resolution process, suppose a user on a computer uses a utility such as Network Neighborhood to connect to another computer on the network, or the net command with a computer name (you learned how to use the net command in Hour 11). A name query request, which includes the desired NetBIOS name, is

**17**

constructed by the application and sent to the WINS server. When WINS receives the request it queries its database for a matching registration. If the requested name is found, WINS returns the corresponding IP address in the response packet. After the client computer has the IP address for the requested computer, the client can then communicate directly.

One nice feature of WINS is that it works well in both local and remote networks and can be integrated with DNS. However that discussion is beyond the scope of this book. What I have done here is given you a basic overview of WINS as it relates to name resolution.

# Testing NetBIOS Name Resolution

You can test NetBIOS name resolution using NetBIOS-based utilities. Some of these applications are covered in Hour 11, including Net View, which I will briefly touch on again. Other examples of NetBIOS-based applications are Network Neighborhood and Windows Explorer.

One typical test of name resolution is using the `net view` command, which enables you to view the share point names on a server. (Remember that a share point is a directory where client computers can connect with another computer to view or exchange files.) To perform this test, choose a computer that has one or more share points. At a command prompt, type

```
net view \\computername
```

(where *computername* is the name of the computer you selected). If `net view` is capable of resolving the computer name to an IP address you should see the names of share points listed in the first command and response, as shown in Figure 17.3. If `net view` is unable to resolve the computer name to an IP address you should see a response that resembles the second command and response shown in Figure 17.3.

# Disabling LMHosts or WINS

Sometimes you need to disable the use of the LMHosts file and WINS to isolate a name resolution process. For example, you suspect that your WINS server has an erroneous entry in it and want to test it. You would need to disable the LMHosts file before your test to make sure it is not the LMHosts file causing the error. When you have finished testing the system be sure to undo your changes by reversing the process.

**FIGURE 17.3**

net view *commands and responses.*

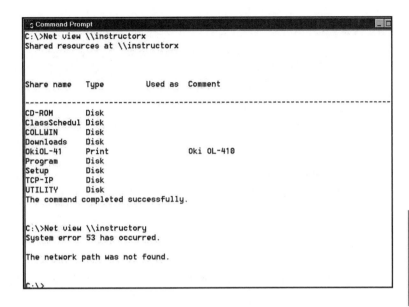

```
  Command Prompt                                                      _ □ □
C:\>Net view \\instructorx
Shared resources at \\instructorx


Share name   Type          Used as   Comment

-----------------------------------------------------------------------
CD-ROM       Disk
ClassSchedul Disk
COLLWIN      Disk
Downloads    Disk
OkiOL-41     Print                   Oki OL-410
Program      Disk
Setup        Disk
TCP-IP       Disk
UTILITY      Disk
The command completed successfully.


C:\>Net view \\instructory
System error 53 has occurred.

The network path was not found.


C:\>
```

**17**

To remove the LMHosts file from use, follow these steps:

1. Temporarily rename LMHosts to something such as `LMHosts.sav`.

2. At the command line, enter `nbtstat -R`. The `nbtstat -R` command causes the NetBIOS name cache to be purged and reloaded (note that the `R` is case-sensitive). This is normally done to load recently added entries to the LMHosts file. Because you have renamed the LMHosts file, it is nonexistent for all practical purposes, so the command will only cause preloaded entries in the NetBIOS name cache to be flushed.

To disable WINS on computers with manually configured IP addresses and subnet masks, remove the IP addresses from the WINS entries in your WINS Address property page. You can then use the `nbtstat -R` command to purge the cache.

> Because Dynamic Host Configuration Protocol (DHCP) clients have the capability to be automatically configured with WINS information, you have to mislead the NetBIOS name resolution process in order to disable WINS on DHCP clients. To do so, you leverage the fact that manually configured entries for WINS override dynamic WINS entries. Enter two IP addresses of computers that are *not* WINS servers in the Primary and Secondary WINS Server fields of the WINS Address property tab (as shown in Figure 17.1). See Hour 21, "Dynamic Host Configuration Protocol," for more information about DHCP.

# Summary

There are a number of names that can be assigned to computers. Often a computer might have a NetBIOS name, a host name, a domain name, and an FQDN. These names use several different name resolution processes to register the name of the computer and also to resolve the names of other computers.

The broadcast-based name resolution process is simple and is inherent to TCP/IP protocol stacks installed onto computers that use NetBIOS names.

Microsoft-based computers include the capability to resolve NetBIOS names using techniques such as the LMHosts file or services provided by a NetBIOS name server such as WINS.

# Q&A

**Q  How do you centrally administer entries in an LMHosts file?**

**A**  You can implement centralized administration by adding several lines to the LMHosts files found on each local computer. A line that starts with #INCLUDE and contains a UNC name of a LMHosts file located on a server provides a link to the central file.

**Q  How can you create static NetBIOS entries in the NetBIOS name cache?**

**A**  By using the keyword #PRE on the line of the desired entry in a LMHosts file.

# Workshop

Determine your computer's NetBIOS name and write down the name. To find the name, open the Network applet in the Control Panel, and look on the Identification tab.

- Is the NetBIOS name the same as the host name?
- If your NetBIOS name is different than the host name, enter ping followed by the NetBIOS name.
- If you have a NetBIOS name, enter the command net view followed by the NetBIOS name.

## Key Terms

Review the following list of key terms:

- API, application programming interface—A set of rules used by applications to interface with each other.

- NBNS—A NetBIOS name server is a server that provides a NetBIOS name to IP address mapping.
- NetBIOS name—A 16-character name that allows the user-assigned name for a computer to be up to 15 characters in length.
- WINS, Windows Internet Naming Service—A WINS server is a Microsoft implementation of a NetBIOS name server.

17

# PART V

## TCP/IP in Network Environments

### Hour

# HOUR 18

# Using TCP/IP in UNIX and Linux

*By Joe Casad*

UNIX is one of the most powerful and popular operating systems in the world, and TCP/IP is an integral part of UNIX networking. This hour introduces you to TCP/IP configuration in UNIX. You will also learn about TCP/IP in the UNIX-like operating system Linux.

## Goals for this Hour

At the completion of this hour, you'll be able to

- Describe how to install the TCP/IP package in UNIX SVR4
- List some of the files UNIX uses to store TCP/IP information
- Describe what a daemon is
- Describe how UNIX invokes TCP/IP services
- Describe the steps for installing TCP/IP with Red Hat Linux
- Use the Linux Network Configurator utility

# TCP/IP in UNIX

TCP/IP and UNIX have always been closely intertwined—much of TCP/IP's early development occurred in UNIX environments. On an operating system such as Windows 95, TCP/IP is one of several protocol options, but in UNIX networking *is* TCP/IP networking.

The other hours of this book show you much about TCP/IP in UNIX. The TCP/IP utilities, for instance (see Hours 11–14), mostly are or were originally UNIX utilities. And domain name resolution (see Hour 15, "Host and Domain Name Resolution," and Hour 16, "The Domain Name System") is an important topic for understanding TCP/IP on UNIX systems.

In general, UNIX is more text-oriented and requires more manual configuration than recent versions of Windows, Macintosh, or NetWare systems. UNIX, however, is gradually becoming more automated as hardware and software vendors adopt the powerful UNIX environment for smoother installation and configuration.

The recent popularity of the X Window user interface (discussed later in this hour) also provides opportunities for simplifying network configuration.

Many different versions of UNIX exist, and although all are similar, no two are exactly alike. The following sections take a quick look at how to install and configure TCP/IP in UNIX. The discussion is based around the UNIX SVR4 system. Later in this hour you'll learn about TCP/IP configuration in Linux, a popular computer-based UNIX-like operating system. The purpose of this hour is to provide a quick view of how TCP/IP operates on UNIX and UNIX-like systems. For a more detailed discussion see specific texts and documentation from your own UNIX flavor.

## What Is UNIX?

UNIX began with a small group of programmers at Bell Labs in the late 1960s. Originally UNIX was something of a curiosity, a toy for the computer science research group as they pursued their official duties working with an older operating system known as Multics. It soon became clear, however, that this new operating system was superior to the slow and expensive Multics system. UNIX began to gain popularity within Bell Labs.

For certain legal reasons, Bells Labs, which was part of AT&T, was not able to market UNIX, so Bell willingly made UNIX available to universities and research institutions for a nominal fee. By that time, UNIX was written in the C programming language—a fast and elegant language that was becoming popular with computer professionals. The universities that used UNIX began to add their own features and share those features with others in the UNIX community. The easily extendable UNIX soon evolved into the powerful operating system you know today.

Because UNIX is written in the platform-independent programming language C, it is easily portable to different hardware systems. UNIX can run on Intel-based computers (the same computers that run Windows 95), on large mainframe systems, and on everything in between.

Many versions of UNIX are now available for many different systems. For legal reasons most cannot officially call themselves UNIX. The Open Group now officially controls the UNIX trademark.

## Configuring TCP/IP

UNIX configuration takes place within configuration files. UNIX includes several configuration files that control different aspects of UNIX configuration.

Present-day UNIX and UNIX-like operating systems often provide automated assistance with TCP/IP configuration. You do not have to manually create and configure all the files. Nevertheless, it is important to know what information is stored in each of the files so you can use the files to change settings and troubleshoot network problems. You'll learn about some of the files that define the TCP/IP configuration later in this chapter.

> Before you install TCP/IP, make sure a network access device, such as a network adapter, is properly installed and configured in your system.

18

In UNIX SVR4 certain software components are installed separately in special installable packages. One of these packages is the TCP/IP package. To install the TCP/IP package, enter

```
pkgadd ñd device_name tcpset
```

where *device_name* is the alias of the device where the installation files are located. During installation you'll be prompted to enter configuration information such as the IP address and subnet mask.

Another installation package contains network support utilities (such as `ifconfig`, discussed later in this hour) that you can use to manage and troubleshoot TCP/IP components:

```
pkgadd -d device_name nsu
```

The TCP/IP installation process creates or modifies a few important configuration files in the /etc directory. You can open and alter these files using a text editor. Some of the TCP/IP configuration files are described in the following sections.

Some differences exist in the TCP/IP configuration file formats among the various flavors of UNIX.

## /etc/ethers

On Ethernet networks, the /etc/ethers file maps network adapter physical addresses to host names. This file is used by RARP and BOOTP services.

Format of the /etc/ethers file:

```
#
# ether_mac_addr.      hostname
#
00:55:ac:b2:32:17     mattie
32:4C:19:31:A6:10     bridget
```

## /etc/hosts

The hosts file is used for name resolution. It maps IP addresses to host names. In UNIX, the hosts file is stored as /etc/hosts. See Hour 15 for more on the hosts file.

Format for /etc/hosts file:

```
#
#IP Address hostname aliases
#
127.0.0.1                       localhost
111.121.131.141     mattie                      pentium 1
111.121.131.146     bridget
```

## /etc/hosts.equiv

The /etc/hosts.equiv file provides the names of trusted hosts and trusted users. Hour 13, "Remote Access Utilities," discussed the hosts.equiv file and trusted access.

Format of the /etc/hosts.equiv file:

```
#
#Trusted hosts
#
+bridget
+barbie     user1
-monica
```

In the preceding example, users on host bridget are granted trusted access if they have identically named user accounts on the local host. User1 on host barbie is similarly granted trusted access. Trusted access is disabled for host monica.

Recall from Hour 13 that user-specific trusted access information can reside in the .rhosts file in the user's home directory.

## /etc/netmasks

The /etc/netmasks file associates subnet masks with network numbers. See Hour 4, "The Internet Layer," and Hour 5, "Internet Layer: Subnetting," for more on network numbers and subnet masking.

A format of the /etc/netmasks file:

```
#
#Network subnet masks
#
#Network            subnet mask
133.15.0.0            255.255.255.0
195.42.0            255.255.224.0
```

## /etc/protocols

The /etc/protocols file lists protocols used with the TCP/IP configuration. UNIX uses this file to associate the numeric protocol field of the IP datagram with an actual protocol.

Format for the /etc/protocols file:

```
#-
#Internet (IP) protocols
#
ip      0   IP      #internet protocol, pseudo protocol number
icmp    1   ICMP    #internet control message protocol
igmp    2   IGMP    #internet group multicast protocol
ggp     3   GGP     #gateway to gateway protocol
tcp     6   TCP     #transmission control protocol
```

## /etc/services

The /etc/services file maps services to TCP or UDP port numbers. See Hour 6, "The Transport Layer," and Hour 7, "TCP and UDP," for more on TCP and UDP ports.

Format for the /etc/services file:

```
# service       port/protocol
ftp             21/tcp
telnet          23/tcp
time            37/udp
finger          79/tcp
```

## Starting TCP/IP Services

Typically, UNIX starts TCP/IP as part of the boot process. As the system starts, UNIX executes the following scripts:

- /etc/init.d/inetinit—This script configures protocol stacks and drivers. (Actually, this script is linked to /etc/rc2.d/s69init, and then executed.)

- /etc/confnet.d/inet/config.boot.sh—This script configures network interfaces. (Network interface information is stored in the file /etc/confnet.d./inet/interface.)

After the drivers and interfaces are configured, UNIX must start the daemons to provide network services. The script rc.inet invokes the daemons that supply basic services such as DNS, PPP, and routing.

Another daemon called *inetd* also starts at boot time. inetd is known as the *Internet supervisor daemon*. inetd listens for requests for other TCP/IP services, such as ftp, and invokes those services if they are needed.

**NEW TERM** In the UNIX world, the term *daemon* (pronounced *demon*) is a program that executes in the background and performs services when needed. You can think of a daemon as a program that *listens* for certain types of requests and invokes the necessary processes to fulfill those requests.

## Checking Your TCP/IP Configuration

UNIX includes several utilities for configuring, checking, and troubleshooting TCP/IP. Some of those utilities are discussed in Hour 11, "TCP/IP Connectivity Utilities."

The IFConfig utility lets you view and modify TCP/IP parameters. Type

ifconfig

for a listing of TCP/IP settings.

You can also use ifconfig to make temporary changes to the current configuration, as follows:

ifconfig interfaceID ipaddress netmask broadcast baddress

where *interfaceID* is the name of the adapter interface (defined when the adapter is configured—the interface name appears in a typical *ifconfig* listing), *ipaddress* is the IP address, *netmask* is the network mask, and *baddress* is a broadcast address for the network.

*ifconfig* makes temporary changes to the TCP/IP configuration and does not alter the boot configuration. For permanent changes to the TCP/IP configuration, use the Configure utility. See the documentation for your UNIX version for more information.

# TCP/IP in Linux

Linux is a UNIX-like operating system that has become immensely popular in recent years. Linux is not the only UNIX derivative designed for Intel-based systems, but it has received much attention recently, in part because it supports a wide range of devices and file systems. Linux, like the original UNIX, is the result of a worldwide cooperation among the community of programmers. Linux benefits from a very open design and from the desire of the community to incorporate all the best of UNIX.

Like UNIX, Linux is a multi-user system with an easily extendable user interface. Over the years many of the important free components of UNIX have found their way into Linux. Linux has the same close relationship with TCP/IP that UNIX has, and many of the files discussed in earlier sections (such as /etc/hosts, /etc/services, and /etc/protocols) are also present in Linux.

Because Linux began as a freeware do-it-yourself system and was mostly developed by programmers, early versions paid little attention to creating a user-friendly interface for configuring networking. Some Linux implementations, in keeping with the free-wheeling traditions of non-commercial UNIX, even call for the user to obtain networking source code and recompile the *kernel* in order to install networking. These versions also called for the user to edit the configuration files discussed earlier in this hour.

**NEW TERM**  The *kernel* is the core of an operating system responsible for tasks such as launching applications, allocating resources, and managing memory.

In recent years however some private companies have taken the Linux code and attempted to add value to it by making it easier to use. Also, freeware Linux becomes increasingly sophisticated with each passing year. The X Window graphic interface system, which is compatible with many UNIX systems in addition to Linux, has also added friendliness to the once treacherous Linux interface.

One popular Linux implementation is Red Hat Linux. Red Hat Linux offers the usual gallery of Linux/UNIX networking features along with easy installation and configuration.

In Red Hat Linux 5.1, the installation program prompts you for TCP/IP networking parameters. The installation steps relating to networking are as follows (other installation steps are omitted):

18

After you choose an installation method and select an installation device

1. The installation program tries to locate and identify your network adapter. If the installation program can't find your network adapter, you must choose an adapter driver and provide any related information before you continue to step 2.

2. In the Boot Protocol dialog box, select whether you want to supply a static IP address or whether the computer will be assigned an address through BOOTP or DHCP.

3. If you chose Static IP address in step 2, enter IP address information in the Configure TCP/IP dialog box. Enter the IP address, the subnet mask, default gateway, and primary nameserver.

4. In the Configure Network dialog box, enter a domain name, hostname, secondary nameserver, and tertiary nameserver.

Red Hat v5.1 offers some useful network configuration options through the X Window graphics interface and the Network Configurator utility. Network Configurator acts as a menu-driven interface to the TCP/IP configuration files.

> To start X Window, enter
>
> startX
>
> at the command prompt. You'll see the screen shown in Figure 18.1.

To change the TCP/IP configuration using Network Configurator

1. Click the Network Configuration button in Control Panel (fourth button from the top in Figure 18.1) to invoke the Network Configurator utility shown in Figure 18.2.

    The Network Configurator utility provides information on network names, hosts, interfaces, and routing. (See Figure 18.2.) Network Configurator serves as a combined interface to the Linux TCP/IP configuration files, which are similar to the UNIX configuration files discussed earlier in this hour. For instance, the Hosts button reveals a view of the contents of the /etc/hosts file (see Figure 18.3).

**FIGURE 18.1**

*Linux through
X Window.*

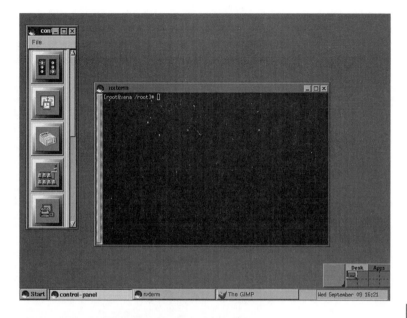

**FIGURE 18.2**

*Network Configurator.*

18

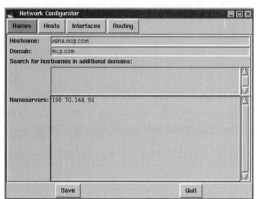

2.  To add a new host to the /etc/hosts file, click Add, and then add a new host entry in
    the Edit/etc/hosts dialog box, as shown in Figure 18.4. Click Done and then click
    Save on the Hosts page to save the new host information.

**FIGURE 18.3**

*The Network Configurator Hosts page.*

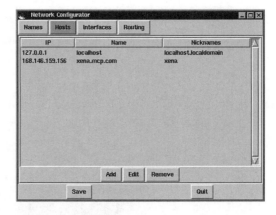

**FIGURE 18.4**

*The Edit /etc/hosts dialog box.*

The other pages of the Network Configurator utility offer a similar view of other configuration parameters.

# Summary

This hour described how to configure TCP/IP in UNIX and Linux systems. There are, of course, many different kinds of UNIX and Linux systems, and this hour is intended only as an introduction. Consult system documentation for additional details.

# Q&A

**Q  What is one reason UNIX runs on so many different systems?**

**A**  UNIX is written in the hardware-independent C language and can therefore be easily ported to different systems.

**Q  What daemon starts the Telnet service?**

**A**  The inetd daemon listens for requests and invokes services as needed.

**Q  Information on TCP and UDP port assignments is in what file?**

**A**  Information on TCP and UDP port assignments is stored in the /etc/services file.

# Workshop

## Key Terms

Review the following list of key terms:

- Daemon —A program that executes in the background and performs services when needed.
- Kernel —The core of the operating system responsible for tasks such as launching applications, allocating resources, and managing memory.
- Network Configurator—A TCP/IP configuration utility found in Red Hat Linux.
- X Window—A graphics-based user interface often associated with UNIX and Linux.

18

# HOUR 19

# Using TCP/IP in Windows Operating Systems

*By Bob Willsey and Art Hammond*

The Windows operating system includes support for several networking protocols. In Windows NT version 3.5 the default protocol was NetBEUI; in version 3.51 the default protocol changed to NWLink, which is compatible with IPX/SPX. In version 4.0 Windows NT has changed yet again; this time TCP/IP is the default protocol. Windows 98 also automatically installs TCP/IP as its default protocol.

This shift to TCP/IP is indicative of growing popularity of the Internet and therefore TCP/IP, which is in essence the protocol of the Internet. TCP/IP has become the de-facto standard protocol of choice in business and around the world. This hour focuses on installing, setting, or changing TCP/IP configuration parameters on computers running Windows.

# Goals for this Hour

At the completion of this hour you will be able to

- Install the TCP/IP protocol on Windows NT 4.0
- Change TCP/IP configuration parameters on Windows NT 4.0
- Install TCP/IP on Windows 95/98
- Change configuration settings on Windows 95/98

# When to Use TCP/IP

You should use TCP/IP when you want to use applications or provide services that traditionally use the TCP/IP protocol. A few examples of TCP/IP-based applications include Web browsers, Web servers, FTP for copying files, and SMTP or POP for sending and receiving email. Examples of applications that were not originally written for TCP/IP include Explorer, File Manager, and Server Manager. While these and other common applications were not written specifically for TCP/IP, they usually work seamlessly with TCP/IP.

Installing TCP/IP with Windows is actually easy. Typically if a network card is detected the TCP/IP protocol is installed automatically during installation of the Windows NT and Windows 98 operating systems. The person installing usually makes a few choices, the first being whether or not this machine will receive its IP address from a Dynamic Host Configuration Protocol (DHCP) server. A DHCP server is a computer that can automatically configure other computers with TCP/IP configuration information. See Hour 21, "Dynamic Host Configuration Protocol (DHCP)," for more information.

If the installer chooses to receive IP configuration parameters from a DHCP server, the configuration choices are complete and TCP/IP installation continues. If the user chooses to manually configure TCP/IP, the user is presented with a screen where the IP address, the subnet mask, and optionally the default gateway parameters are entered. Following these few entries TCP/IP installation continues. Installation and configuration are covered in greater detail later in this hour.

Assuming TCP/IP is installed, configured correctly, and operational, you use TCP/IP indirectly. A user uses application programs such as Web browsers or email packages. These applications in turn use TCP/IP to communicate with a second program, the server. For example a client application such as Internet Explorer, which is a Web browser, communicates with a Web server such as Internet Information Server. The fact that

TCP/IP is used to perform the communication is incidental. Many users don't know, care, or understand that their Web browser or any other application for that matter uses TCP/IP.

# Manually Installing TCP/IP on Windows NT

As mentioned, TCP/IP is usually installed automatically during the installation of Windows NT 4.0. However, it is possible that TCP/IP was not installed for reasons such as your computer did not contain a network card during Windows NT installation or you have upgraded an older version of Windows NT, which had different default protocols. In any case if you need to install TCP/IP manually you can follow the steps listed here. (These steps assume you have a network card or modem installed with the appropriate driver.)

The installation steps described and depicted in this chapter are relative to Windows NT 4.0. If you have an older version, you should refer to your documentation for equivalent steps.

1. From the Control Panel, double-click the Network icon.

   The Network property pages appear. Single-click the Protocols tab shown in Figure 19.1.

**FIGURE 19.1**

*The Protocols property sheet.*

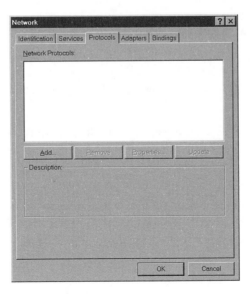

**19**

2. Click Add if the TCP/IP Protocol is not listed in the Network Protocols list box. The Select Network Protocol dialog box appears, as shown in Figure 19.2

**FIGURE 19.2**

*The Select Network Protocol dialog box.*

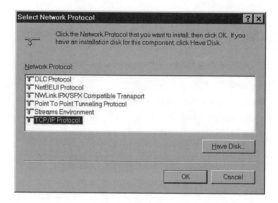

3. Single-click the TCP/IP Protocol item from the list of protocols then choose OK.

   You are prompted with a dialog box asking whether there is a DHCP server on your network, and whether you want to use DHCP, as shown in Figure 19.3.

4. You can choose by clicking either Yes or No. If you choose Yes, the DHCP server on the network should configure all your IP addressing information for you. If you choose no, you will need to provide some of this configuration information yourself. This procedure assumes you chose No. Addressing information will be configured later in the procedure.

**FIGURE 19.3**

*Choosing DHCP or manual configuration.*

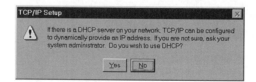

5. At this point you might be prompted to insert your Windows NT CD-ROM so the installation files can be read. If so, enter the path to the installation files, for example the D:\I386 directory then choose Continue. You will not be prompted if Windows NT is capable of locating the installation files automatically.

6 If the setup detects a modem in addition to a network card you will be asked whether you want to configure the Remote Access Service (RAS) to also support TCP/IP. You can answer by choosing either OK or Cancel.

If you choose OK to set up RAS you are presented with the Remote Access Setup dialog box where you can choose the modem to configure with RAS, as shown in Figure 19.4

**FIGURE 19.4**

*The Remote Access Setup dialog box.*

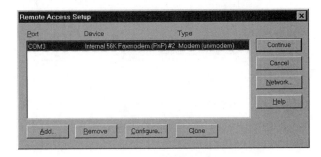

7. Use the Add… or Remove buttons to add or delete modems.

8. Use the Configure… button to select whether you want to Dial out only, Receive only, or both Dial out and Receive.

9. Use the Network… button to select which protocol(s) to use with RAS; typically you select TCP/IP.

10. Finally, choose Continue to proceed with installation of TCP/IP.

11. You are returned to the Protocols property page and can now click Close.

This loads needed files and configures the TCP/IP protocol, as shown in Figure 19.5

**19**

**FIGURE 19.5**

*Adding files and reviewing bindings.*

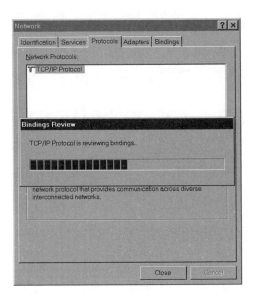

12. If you did not choose to use DHCP you will need to enter several parameters on the IP Address property sheet, as shown in Figure 19.6. Enter the correct IP address for this computer in the field provided. You might need to change the Subnet Mask field to the correct value for your network. If you have a router on your network segment, enter its IP address into the Default Gateway field.

**FIGURE 19.6**

*The IP Address property sheet.*

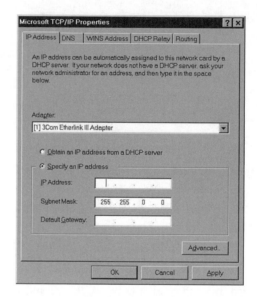

13. You can enter other configuration information at this time on the other property sheets. However, if there's nothing else you want to configure, click OK to continue with TCP/IP installation.

14. Finally, choose Yes to allow Windows NT to reboot. Following the reboot, TCP/IP should be configured and operational.

# Changing Configuration Settings on Windows NT

In addition to the basic installation, there are a number of other options you can configure from the Properties window such as advanced IP addressing, DNS, WINS address, DHCP relay, and routing. These options can either be configured during installation, or you can change these options at some later date. Running the Network applet from the Control Panel accesses all of these options.

The following sections discuss advanced IP addressing, DNS, and WINS. DHCP relay and routing are beyond the scope of this book, but here is a brief explanation of them. The DHCP Relay property sheet allows computers configured with the DHCP relay agent to forward DHCP broadcasts to DHCP servers located on other network segments. The Routing property sheet allows you to have your NT machine act as a router if it has two or more network cards installed.

> If you enable IP routing on your computer, it only enables static routing. You will need to install additional software if you want your Windows NT computer to perform as a dynamic router. See Hour 9, "Routers, Brouters, and Bridges," for more information on routing.

## Advanced IP Addressing Property Sheet

Some complex installations might require more than just the one IP address, subnet mask, and default gateway that is specified on most machines. To implement other addressing options, choose the Advanced... button on the IP Address property sheet to bring up the Advanced IP Addressing dialog box, shown in Figure 19.7.

**FIGURE 19.7**

*The Advanced IP Address property sheet.*

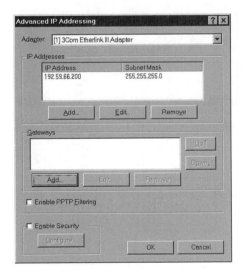

19

These options are described in the following list:

- IP Addresses—The Add... button in the IP addresses frame allows you to add a second, third, fourth, or fifth IP address and subnet mask combinations to the selected network card. Multiple IP addresses are often used by an ISP to host Web sites for multiple customers on a single machine with a single network card.

- Gateways—If your network segment has multiple routers, you can add IP addresses for additional routers by choosing Add... in the Gateways section.
- Enable PPTP Filtering—This check box tells TCP/IP to only allow packets arriving through the Point-to-Point Tunneling Protocol. All packets that arrive from any other protocol will be discarded.
- Enable Security—Checking this box and clicking the Configure button allows you to restrict the use of specific ports on TCP or UDP and to restrict certain IP protocols.

## The DNS Property Sheet

You use the DNS property sheet, shown in Figure 19.8, to configure Domain Name System (DNS) related parameters. DNS is covered in Hour 16, "The Domain Name System."

**FIGURE 19.8**

*The DNS property sheet.*

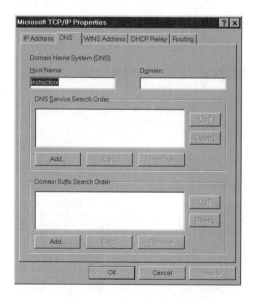

The DNS property sheet parameters are described in the following list:

- Host Name—This field is pre-filled by default with the same NetBIOS name assigned to your computer. You can change the host name although this is generally not done as it can cause confusion.

- Domain—You type your domain name in this field. A domain name might be something such as *mycompany*.com.

- DNS Service Search Order—This is where you can add the IP addresses of one or more DNS servers. Place the first DNS server to contact at the top of the list followed by others in descending order.

- Domain Suffix Search Order—This frame allows you to enter the suffix order to search. This is usually used when non-standard suffixes are used. Standard suffixes are com, edu, org, gov, mil and so on.

## The WINS Address Property Sheet

The WINS Address property sheet, shown in Figure 19.9, is used to register your computer with a WINS or a NetBIOS name server (NBNS). WINS and NBNS were covered in more detail in Hour 17, "NetBIOS Name Resolution." You can choose to register with one or two WINS servers. Enter the IP address(es) of the WINS server(s) in the Primary WINS Server and Secondary WINS Server fields respectively.

**FIGURE 19.9**

*The WINS Address property sheet.*

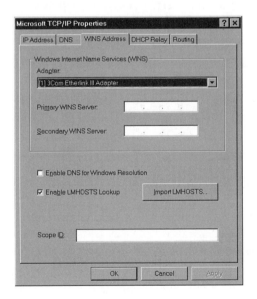

**19**

The WINS Address property sheet options are described in the following list:

- Enable DNS for Windows Resolution—If you are using Microsoft DNS, you can allow DNS to resolve NetBIOS name searches by selecting this box.

- Enable LMHOSTS Lookup—Uncheck this box if you don't want to use the LMHOSTS file for NetBIOS name resolution.

- Scope ID—The scope is appended to the NetBIOS name and effectively hides all computers that do not have an identical entry.

Don't enter anything in the Scope ID field unless you fully understand the ramifications of doing so.

Only computers with identical Scope IDs can communicate with each other.

# Adding TCP/IP Services to Windows NT Server

Windows NT 4.0 includes several services that work with computers that use the TCP/IP protocol. All of these services can be added by choosing Add on the Services property page of the Network Control Panel applet.

The following three services, DHCP, DNS, and WINS, are commonly installed on NT servers.

- The DHCP server service allows a Windows NT server to automatically assign IP configuration parameters to DHCP client computers. At a minimum the DHCP server can assign an IP address and a subnet mask. Many other IP configuration parameters can also be assigned. For example, commonly configured parameters such as the default gateway and WINS and DNS server IP addresses can all be centrally configured and assigned.

  The DHCP server is configured with a range of addresses for each network segment. The range of addresses is known as a *scope*. From a scope or pool of addresses, DHCP assigns addresses to computers configured as DHCP clients.

- The Microsoft DNS server service was totally rewritten for Windows NT 4.0. The DNS server maintains a database of host names and IP addresses, and thus provides host name resolution on a network. If a DNS client wants to locate another computer by host name, the DNS server matches that host name to the computer's IP address. The DNS service works well and is extremely easy to configure when compared to most other non-Microsoft DNS servers. DNS configuration is performed through a GUI.

Even though the Microsoft DNS service is easier to configure than its counterparts, it still is quite complicated and is beyond the scope of this book.

- The Windows Internet Name Service (WINS) is Microsoft's implementation of a NetBIOS name server. Client computers configured with the address of a WINS server register the IP address and NetBIOS names of computers, workgroups, NT domains, users, and several services with the WINS server. The WINS server maintains the registered names in a database. If a WINS client wants to locate the name of another computer, the name request is sent to the WINS server that queries its database for the name. If the name is found, the WINS server returns the associated IP address to the WINS client computer that initiated the request. After the client computer has the IP address it can communicate directly with the desired machine.

# Manually Installing TCP/IP on Windows 95/98

Windows 9.x has much less in the way of options and services to configure than Windows NT, which Microsoft has tried to position as the operating system of choice for use on networks. A Windows 9.x computer cannot function as a WINS, DNS, or DHCP server; it can only be a client to one of those servers.

TCP/IP is installed by default on Windows 98. However, if TCP/IP has been removed for some reason you need to manually reinstall it before you can use it again.

This section presents steps for installing the TCP/IP protocol on Windows 9.x. It assumes that a network adapter has already been successfully installed and configured. The installation processes for Windows 95 and Windows 98 are very similar. However where differences occur, they are noted.

**19**

To install the TCP/IP protocol, follow these steps:

1. Choose the Network icon in the Control Panel. The Network Configuration dialog box appears, as shown if Figure 19.10.
2. Choose the Add... button.

    The Select Network Component Type dialog box appears.
3. Choose Protocol from the list of four items then choose the Add... button.

    The Select Network Protocol dialog box appears.
4. From the Manufacturers list, choose Microsoft. From the Network Protocols list, choose TCP/IP. Then choose OK.

**FIGURE 19.10**

*The Network Configuration dialog box for Windows 95/98 before TCP/IP is installed.*

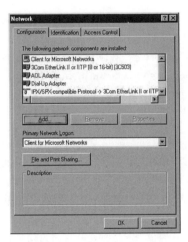

You are returned to the Network Configuration dialog box, only now there are entries for the TCP/IP protocol, as shown in Figure 19.11.

5. Choose OK and Windows will read files from the release CD-ROM. After all the required files are read, the Systems Settings Change dialog box is displayed. This dialog box indicates that you must restart the computer before your setting takes effect.

6. Choose Yes to allow the computer to restart.

**FIGURE 19.11**

*The Network Configuration dialog box for Windows 95/98.*

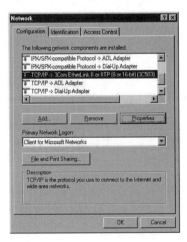

# Changing Configuration Settings on Windows 95/98

This section presents instructions for changing TCP/IP configuration and assumes that the TCP/IP software and a network adapter have already been successfully installed.

To change TCP/IP configuration settings, follow these steps:

1. Choose the Network icon in the Control Panel. The Network Configuration dialog box appears. Under The following network components are installed: choose the TCP/IP protocol for the network adapter that you want to configure.

2. You might have several entries for TCP/IP if you have for instance both a modem and a network adapter installed. After you have selected the TCP/IP and adapter that you want to configure, choose the Properties button. The TCP/IP properties dialog box contains six property sheets for Windows 95 and seven for Windows 98. The IP Address, Bindings, Advanced, DNS Configuration, Gateway, and WINS Configuration property sheets are common to both operating systems. The NetBIOS property sheet is found only in Windows 98. These property sheets are discussed in the following sections.

## IP Address Property Sheet

On the IP Address property sheet you can choose to either receive an IP address automatically from a DHCP server or manually enter the IP address and subnet mask into the IP Address and Subnet Mask fields, as shown in Figure 19.12.

On Windows 98 if this selection is set to Obtain IP address automatically, Windows 98 attempts to lease an IP address from a DHCP server. If a DHCP server cannot be found, Windows 98 automatically configures itself using a private IP address. This form of assigning IP addresses is intended for small offices of ten or fewer computers. The Internet or other remote networks cannot be accessed via this automatically configured IP address.

## Gateway Property Sheet

The Gateway property sheet allows you to add the IP address for a gateway by entering the IP address and choosing the Add button. You can enter multiple IP addresses for multiple gateways; the first IP address is considered the default gateway.

19

**FIGURE 19.12**

*The IP Address property sheet.*

## DNS Configuration Property Sheet

The DNS Configuration property sheet allows you to configure DNS. Enter a host name for your computer and the domain name to which it belongs in the Host and Domain fields respectively. (For more information on host names and domains, see Hour 15, "Host and Domain Name Resolution.")

- The DNS Server Search Order frame allows you to enter the IP addresses of up to three DNS servers; they are searched in the order displayed. For instance, in Figure 19.13 the DNS server at IP address 206.85.92.79 is searched first followed by the DNS server at IP address 206.85.92.2.

- The Domain Suffix Search Order frame is often not used. It allows you to enter additional domain names such as *corporate*.com or *intranet*.net. Assuming the host name for your computer is *mycomputer*, the DNS server will also attempt to resolve the names *mycomputer*.*corporate*.com and *mycomputer*.*intranet*.net.

## WINS Configuration Property Sheet

Use the WINS Configuration property sheet if you want your computer to be capable of registering with query names from a WINS server. (For more information on WINS, see Hour 17, "NetBIOS Name Resolution.") The WINS Configuration property sheet allows you to either enable or disable WINS resolution. If you enable WINS resolution, you can enter the IP addresses for one or two WINS servers in the Primary WINS Server and optionally Secondary WINS Server fields. (See Figure 19.14.)

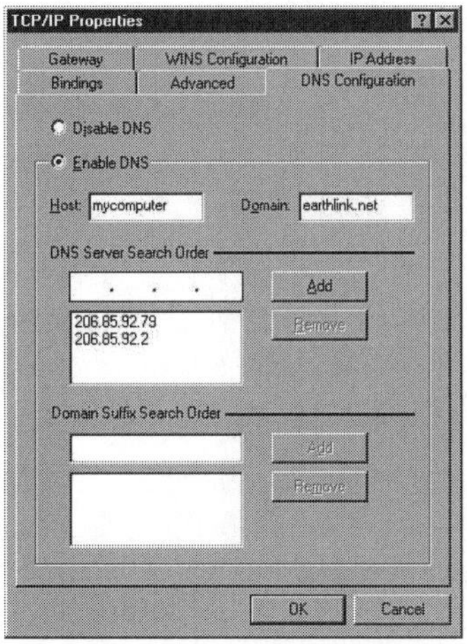

**FIGURE 19.13**

*The DNS Configuration property sheet.*

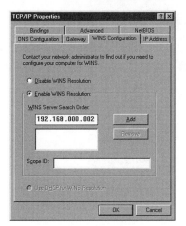

**FIGURE 19.14**

*The WINS Configuration property sheet.*

19

## Bindings Property Sheet

The Bindings property sheet, shown in Figure 19.15, allows you to enable or disable TCP/IP's capability to communicate with higher level file sharing and network printing services.

## Advanced Property Sheet

If there is an entry listed in the Advanced property sheet, shown in Figure 19.16, you can select it and change its value. In most installations there are no advanced entries listed.

**FIGURE 19.15**

*The Bindings property sheet.*

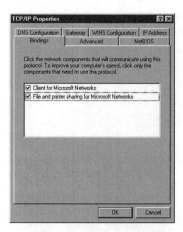

**FIGURE 19.16**

*The Advanced Property sheet.*

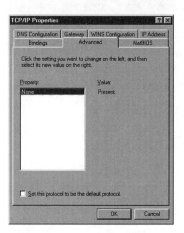

## NetBIOS Property Sheet

The NetBIOS property sheet, shown in Figure 19.17, is only found on Windows 98. (NetBIOS is covered in Hour 17.) It allows you to run NetBIOS over TCP/IP and is enabled by default. In most installations this does not change.

**FIGURE 19.17**

*The NetBIOS property sheet.*

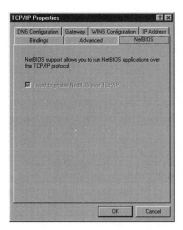

# Summary

In this hour you learned how to install TCP/IP on computers running Windows NT and Windows 9.x. On Windows NT, you learned about DNS, WINS, and DHCP services and how to configure the client settings as well. You also learned that installing and configuring TCP/IP on Windows 9.x computers is similar to NT, but has fewer options and is less complicated.

# Q&A

**Q Which version of Windows NT uses TCP/IP as its default protocol?**

**A** Windows NT 4.0.

**Q Which of the following items are required when configuring IP? IP address, subnet mask, default gateway?**

**A** IP address and subnet mask.

**Q Your company wants to host Web sites for three other companies on your Web server, which has one network card. How would you configure the IP addresses?**

**A** Using the Advanced IP Addressing dialog box you can add additional IP addresses and subnet masks.

**Q Which property sheet appears only in Windows 98?**

**A** The NetBIOS property sheet, where you can enable NetBIOS over TCP/IP. It is enabled by default.

19

# Workshop

## Key Terms

Review the following list of key terms:

- Advanced IP Address property sheet—Property sheet on a Windows NT computer where you can configure options such as multiple IP addresses and advanced security.
- DHCP server—A computer that can automatically configure other computers with TCP/IP configuration information.
- DNS Configuration property sheet—A property sheet that allows you to enter a host name for your computer and to enter the domain name to which it belongs in the Host and Domain fields respectively.

# Hour **20**

# Using TCP/IP in Macintosh and NetWare

*By Bob Willsey and Gene Steinberg*

A new Macintosh already has TCP/IP installed as part of its Open Transport networking software, but TCP/IP is not normally included in the standard setup of the NetWare operating system. However, with the increasing popularity of the Internet and the TCP/IP protocol, it is not that unusual to install TCP/IP on NetWare. This hour addresses how to configure the TCP/IP protocol on the Macintosh operating system and how to install and configure TCP/IP on a Novell NetWare client and a Novell NetWare server.

## Goals for this Hour

At the completion of this hour you will be able to

- Decide when it is appropriate or necessary to use the TCP/IP protocol on a Macintosh operating system or on a Novell client or server
- View and if necessary change existing TCP/IP configuration on a Macintosh or a Novell server
- Install the TCP/IP protocol onto a Novell server

If you have an older Macintosh computer running versions of the Mac operating system before 7.6, you might have to install TCP/IP software separately if you are not using Apple's Open Transport software (which was introduced in System 7.5.2). Rather than run updates on your existing system software, you would be best advised to upgrade to System 7.6 or later for the best possible TCP/IP performance and ease of setup.

## When to Use TCP/IP

If your Macintosh or Novell client or server needs to communicate with other computers that use TCP/IP, you might need to use TCP/IP as an additional protocol to either AppleTalk (Macintosh's network protocol) or IPX/SPX (Novell's network protocol). Examples of other computers that commonly use TCP/IP include UNIX systems, Web servers, FTP servers, email servers, and any computer that is located on the Internet.

Other examples of situations in which TCP/IP is necessary include the following

- Using client applications such as a Web browser or an FTP client.
- Printing to network printers that utilize TCP/IP as their default or only protocol.
- Allowing a client application to communicate with server applications located on UNIX computers that use TCP/IP as the default.

After TCP/IP is installed or configured (as needed), it is, for the most part, transparent. TCP/IP is typically used by the application that the user is running, so the user is unaware that TCP/IP is operating in the background. For instance, if the user is using a Web browser, the browser uses TCP/IP to retrieve Web pages from Web servers. Similarly, if the user is using other client application programs that use TCP/IP to communicate with an application server then these too would use TCP/IP.

## TCP/IP on Macintosh

As mentioned previously, TCP/IP is automatically installed on recent Macintosh computers. However if you use Dynamic Host Configuration Protocol (DHCP) the TCP/IP protocol is not initialized when the machine first boots up. The TCP/IP protocol is initiated the first time a TCP/IP-based client needs to communicate, assuming the standard option to "load only when needed" has been set in the TCP/IP Control Panel.

On a Macintosh you can see if TCP/IP is installed by doing the following

1. Click the Apple menu, then scroll down to the Control Panels menu and choose TCP/IP.

The TCP/IP Control Panel appears, as shown in Figure 20.1. If TCP/IP is properly configured for use with your network, the IP address, subnet mask, and router address are displayed in the TCP/IP Control Panel.

**FIGURE 20.1**

*The Macintosh TCP/IP Control Panel, which is part of the standard Mac operating system installation.*

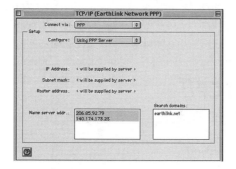

## Configuring TCP/IP on Macintosh

Even though TCP/IP is standard equipment on any recent Macintosh, you need to configure it before it can be used. You have several choices: You can manually configure the IP address, subnet mask, and default gateway; or you can choose to receive these configuration parameters from a DHCP server provided that one is available. For more on DHCP, see Hour 21, "Dynamic Host Configuration Protocol (DHCP)."

In addition to these two commonly used forms of configuring IP addresses, the Macintosh also includes configuration methods that use a BOOTP server and a RARP server. Because these two forms of configuration are rarely used they are not addressed in this section.

To manually configure TCP/IP on Macintosh, follow these steps:

1. Open the TCP/IP Control Panel by clicking the Apple menu, choose Control Panels then the TCP/IP Control Panel.

   The TCP/IP Control Panel appears, as previously shown in Figure 20.1.

2. In the Connect via drop-down list choose the network connection and media that you want to use, for example, AppleTalk (MacIP), Ethernet, or MacPPP.

3. In the Configure drop-down list choose Manually.

4. In the IP Address field, enter the IP address to be used for this computer, as shown in Figure 20.2.

5. In the Subnet mask field, enter the subnet mask to be used.

6. Optionally, in the Router Address field, enter the IP addresses for one or more routers. Note the first address listed in this field is considered the default gateway.

**20**

7. Optionally, in the Name Server addr list box enter the IP addresses of one or more DNS servers. Make sure to place the name servers in the proper order that you want them searched.

8. Optionally, in the Search domains list box, enter the domain suffixes to be used.

9. Click the Close box located in the upper-left corner of the TCP/IP Control Panel.

   A dialog box will ask whether you want to save changes to the current configuration. You can choose Save, Don't Save, or Cancel. Choose Save to make your change permanent, and your changes will be applied immediately.

**FIGURE 20.2**

*A manual configuration of TCP/IP via the TCP/IP Control Panel. In this example the Macintosh is configured for an automatic network backup.*

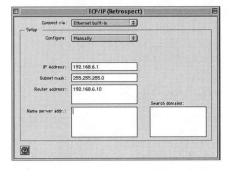

To configure TCP/IP to use a DHCP server for its configuration, follow these steps:

1. From the Control Panel choose the Connect via drop-down list, and then choose the network connection and media that you want to use, for example, AppleTalk (MacIP), Ethernet, or MacPPP.

2. In the Configure drop-down list box choose Using DHCP Server.

   The IP Address, Subnet mask, Router address, and Name Server addr fields will display: <will be supplied by the server>.

3. Optionally, in the Search Domains list box, enter the domain suffixes to be used.

4. Click the Close box located in the upper-left corner of the TCP/IP Control Panel (or type Command-W). A dialog box will ask you whether you want to save changes to the current configuration. You can choose Save, Don't Save, or Cancel. Choose Save to make your change permanent, your changes will be applied immediately.

Your Macintosh is now configured to be a DHCP client. Start an application such as Netscape Navigator to cause your Macintosh to lease an IP address from a DHCP server.

# TCP/IP on NetWare

If you own a Novell server that has two or more network adapters installed they are most likely configured to provide IPX/SPX routing automatically. If desired you can install the TCP/IP protocol onto the Novell server and have it route TCP/IP packets as well.

Before configuring NetWare, you will want to check whether or not TCP/IP is present. One way to do this is to examine the autoexec.ncf file, which is located in the SYS volume, in the system subdirectory. Look for the phrase "bind IP" in connection with its association to a networking card (Novell's version of TCP/IP is called NetWare IP or IP for short). Another way is to use the CONFIG command at the console prompt, which displays the networking cards installed and the protocols that are bound to these cards.

If neither step shows that TCP/IP is present, you need to follow the steps described in the next section to install TCP/IP.

## Installing TCP/IP on NetWare

The following steps identify how to install and configure the TCP/IP protocol onto a Novell 4.x server. The procedures listed here assume that both an existing network adapter and the Novell network operating system are currently installed and operational.

To install IP software (TCP/IP) on Novell 4.x server, follow these steps:

1. Display a command prompt at the Novell console then enter the words LOAD INSTALL. This loads the NetWare Loadable Module (NLM), a text display window that shows the setup options available to you.

2. In the Installation Options menu (the screen showing the installation choices), highlight Product options <other optional installation items> then press Enter.

   A screen with two menus appears. The lower menu is the Other Installation Actions menu.

3. In the Other Installation Actions menu, highlight Choose an item or product listed above, and then press the Tab key to place the menu selector in the upper menu, Other Installation Items/Products.

4. In the Other Installation Items/products menu, select Install NetWare IP, as shown in Figure 20.3, and then press Enter to begin installation.

   A dialog appears indicating the directory location where the install program will look for the installation files, as shown in Figure 20.4.

**20**

**FIGURE 20.3**

*Choose Install NetWare IP.*

**FIGURE 20.4**

*The File source location dialog box.*

5. If the files are available at the location indicated, press Enter to start copying files onto the NetWare volume.

   However, if the files are located on a CD-ROM or your C: drive, you might need to press the F3 key first and change the path to the drive letter where the CD-ROM or local DOS drive is located.

   See Figure 20.5 for an example of how to identify a different location. After you have identified where the files can be read, press enter to start copying files onto the NetWare volume.

If you decide to install from the CD-ROM a box appears warning you about a possible conflict between DOS and NetWare when accessing the CD-ROM. If you continue to access a CD-ROM with the conflict in effect, the keyboard will lock up and you'll need to restart the installation. To determine if there is a conflict press the F1 key.

**FIGURE 20.5**

*Specify an alternative directory path.*

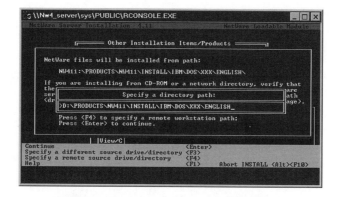

You might want to copy the following two directory structures to the C:\ drive from the CD-ROM. This can make installation easier and more efficient.

\PRODUCTS\NW411\INSTALL\IBM\DOS\XXX\ENGLISH

\PRODUCTS\NWIPSRV

## Configuring TCP/IP on NetWare

During the installation of the TCP/IP files you are presented with a dialog box indicating that a readme.txt file explains how to configure TCP/IP. You can choose to read or ignore the file by choosing Yes or No. Following the installation of the TCP/IP files, a screen appears (as shown in Figure 20.6) indicating that TCP/IP is not currently configured, and that you need to switch to the Other Installation Items/Products screen.)

**FIGURE 20.6**

*Instructions to configure TCP/IP before completing the installation.*

TCP/IP is not configured. Switch to system console using <Alt>-<Esc> keys
and configure TCP/IP. Then switch back to install screen to continue
<Press ESCAPE To Continue>

**20**

To configure TCP/IP on a NetWare server, follow these steps:

1. Press the Alt-Esc key combination to switch screens.

   The upper menu is labeled Other Installation Items/Products.

2. From this menu choose Configure Network Protocols.

   The Internetworking Configuration menu appears.

3. From this menu highlight the word Protocols then choose Enter.

   The Protocol configuration menu appears.

4. Highlight TCP/IP and choose Enter.

   The TCP/IP Protocol Configuration dialog box appears and indicates whether TCP/IP is enabled.

5. From this menu you can choose to turn the Novell server into a router by enabling the IP Packet forwarding option. If your Novell server is configured as a router, you can choose a routing protocol such as RIP or OSPF, or you can statically enter routing information, as shown in Figure 20.7. After the choices presented on this menu are configured correctly, press the Esc key to return to the Internetworking Configuration menu.

**FIGURE 20.7**

*The TCP/IP Protocol Configuration menu.*

6. Highlight Bindings then press Enter.

7. The Binding TCP/IP to a LAN Interface menu appears, as shown in Figure 20.8. In the Local IP Address field enter the IP address you want your Novell server to respond to.

**FIGURE 20.8**

*The Binding TCP/IP to a LAN Interface menu.*

The default subnet mask appears in the Subnetwork Mask of Connected Network field. The default subnet mask for the address class you entered is displayed. (The subnet mask is displayed in hexadecimal format. If desired change the default subnet mask to match your custom subnet mask.)

8. Press Esc several times until you're presented with a dialog box asking you whether you want to exit the installation program. Click Yes.

TCP/IP has been installed and configured under Novell NetWare server.

# Summary

During this hour you learned how to configure TCP/IP on a Macintosh computer and how to install and configure this protocol on a Novell NetWare server. You also learned when it is appropriate to install TCP/IP onto one of these computers.

# Q&A

**Q Is it necessary to purchase additional software to support the TCP/IP protocol on a Novell server?**

**A** No. Support for TCP/IP is included in Novell NetWare.

**Q Can a Macintosh receive its IP address from a DHCP server?**

**A** Yes. A Macintosh can be a DHCP client.

**Q When a Macintosh is configured as a DHCP client, is the TCP/IP protocol available immediately following a boot?**

**A** No. TCP/IP is not configured until a client program that requires TCP/IP is launched.

# Workshop

## Key Terms

Review the following list of key terms:

- AppleTalk—Apple's original networking protocol.
- NetWare—An operating system manufactured by Novell.
- NetWare Loadable Module (NLM)—An installation module used as part of your NetWare setup.

20

# PART VI

## Advanced Topics

### Hour

# HOUR **21**

# Dynamic Host Configuration Protocol (DHCP)

*By Bob Willsey*

The Dynamic Host Configuration Protocol (DHCP) enables computers to automatically be assigned TCP/IP configuration settings from another computer. The computer receiving configuration information is considered a DHCP client, whereas the computer that is supplying configuration information is considered a DHCP server. At a minimum, the DHCP server configures the DHCP client with an IP address and a subnet mask. It is possible to also configure the DHCP client with additional configuration settings such as IP addresses for the default gateway, DNS servers, and WINS servers.

In this hour you learn what DHCP is, how DHCP works, why it is important, and in what situations DHCP implementations are most useful. Additionally, you will learn how to install and configure DHCP services.

## Goals for this Hour

At the completion of this hour, you will be able to

- Describe what DHCP is and what benefits it provides
- Describe the process involved when a DHCP client leases an IP address
- Explain what a scope is and how it is configured
- Describe the process to install and configure a DHCP server

## What Is DHCP?

DHCP is a protocol used to automatically assign TCP/IP configuration parameters to computers. DHCP is a standard described in RFC 1531. Three other RFCs, 1534, 2131, and 2132, address enhancement and specific vendor implementations of DHCP. DHCP can configure required parameters such as IP addresses and subnet masks as well as optional parameters such as DNS and WINS server IP addresses.

The use of DHCP can make deploying a large number of computers a much simpler task. It can reduce support costs by not requiring technicians to go into the field to individually configure TCP/IP parameters on each computer.

> In installations where computers are configured at a staging center instead of in the field, it is still possible to encounter TCP/IP address problems—even when the proper TCP/IP address has been assigned to the computer. If for instance a properly configured computer were incorrectly installed on the wrong network, its IP address and default gateway parameters would not allow the computer to network properly on that network.

DHCP is especially important in today's environment where many employees carry notebook computers between offices of a large corporation. Using manually configured IP addresses on the notebook allows the computer to network using TCP/IP on only one network. Either the employee must reconfigure TCP/IP every time she travels to another office, or the user simply cannot use TCP/IP on the network. However, if DHCP is installed in every office, the employee simply attaches the notebook computer to the network, powers up the computer, and starts working as normal with full TCP/IP capabilities. (Be aware that the traveling user could cause other network problems such as a duplicate NetBIOS name if for instance, the name of the user's computer conflicts with a NetBIOS name of another computer on the local network that it is being attached to.)

# How DHCP Works

To get DHCP to work, you install the TCP/IP stack software onto a client computer but you do not configure TCP/IP with configuration parameters.

> Not all TCP/IP software stacks support DHCP. Check the documentation that accompanies your TCP/IP software to determine whether it can be configured via DHCP.

When a DHCP client computer is started, the TCP/IP software is loaded into memory and starts to operate; however, because TCP/IP has not been given an IP address yet it is incapable of sending or receiving directed datagrams. TCP/IP can however transmit and listen for broadcasts. This capability to communicate via broadcasts is the basis for how DHCP works. Another protocol known as the BOOTP protocol also operates in much the same manner, that is, by using broadcasts. In fact DHCP and BOOTP both use the same UDP ports, which are 67 for the DHCP client and 68 for the DHCP server.

The process of leasing an IP address from the DHCP server involves four steps:

1. DHCP discover—The DHCP client initiates the process by broadcasting a datagram destined for UDP port 68 (used by BOOTP and DHCP servers). This first datagram is known as a DHCP Discover, which is a request to any DHCP server that receives the datagram for configuration information. The DHCP discover datagram contains many fields but the one that is of most importance contains the physical address of the DHCP client.

2. DHCP offer—If a DHCP server receives the datagram and also contains unleased IP addresses for the network on which the DHCP client resides, the DHCP server constructs a response datagram known as a DHCP offer and sends it via broadcast to the computer that issued the DHCP Discover. This broadcast is sent to UDP port 67 and contains the physical address of the DHCP client, which is used to return the datagram to the same computer that issued the DHCP discover. Also contained in the DHCP offer are the physical and IP addresses of the DHCP server as well as the values for the IP address and subnet mask that are being offered to the DHCP client.

**21**

> At this point in time it is possible for the DHCP client to receive several DHCP offers, assuming there are multiple DHCP servers with the capability to offer the DHCP client an IP address. In most cases however the DHCP client accepts the first DHCP offer that arrives.

3. DHCP request—The client selects an offer and constructs and broadcasts a DHCP request datagram. The DHCP Request datagram contains the IP address of the server that issued the offer as well as the physical address of the DHCP client. The DHCP request basically performs two tasks. First it tells the selected DHCP server that the client requests it to assign the DHCP client an IP address (and other configuration as well). Second, it serves to notify all other DHCP servers with outstanding offers that their offer was not accepted, and that they can retract their offer and utilize the IP address somewhere else.

4. DHCP ack—When the DHCP server in which the offer was selected receives the DHCP request datagram, it constructs the final datagram of the lease process. This datagram is known as a DHCP ack (short for acknowledgement). The DHCP ack includes an IP address and subnet mask for the DHCP client. Optionally, the DHCP client is often also configured with IP addresses for the default gateway, several DNS servers, and possibly one or two WINS servers. In addition to IP addresses, the DHCP client can receive other configuration information such as a NetBIOS node type, which can change the order of NetBIOS name resolution.

Three other key fields are contained in the DHCP ack; all three fields indicate time periods. One field identifies the length of the lease. Two other time fields are known as T1 and T2 and are used when the client attempts to renew its lease. The use of these three time fields is explained later in this hour.

## Relay Agents

If both the DHCP client and the DHCP server reside on the same network segment then the process proceeds exactly as previously indicated. If however the DHCP client and DHCP server reside on different networks separated by one or more routers, the process can't work as explained. This is because routers do not forward broadcasts to other networks. To allow DHCP to work, a "middleman" must be configured to assist the DHCP process. The middleman can either be another host on the same network as the DHCP client, or often the router itself. In any case, the process that performs this middleman procedure is called either a BOOTP relay agent or a DHCP relay agent.

A relay agent is configured with a fixed IP address and also contains the IP address of the DHCP server. Because relay agents have configured IP addresses, they can always send and receive directed datagrams to the DHCP server. And because the relay agent resides on the same network as the DHCP client it can communicate with the DHCP client via broadcasts. Basically, relay agents listen for broadcasts destined for UDP port 68; when heard the datagram is retransmitted as a directed datagram to the DHCP server. When directed datagrams destined for UDP port 67 are received by the relay agent, the datagrams are rebroadcast on the local network. This explanation has eliminated a few details for brevity but conveys the essence of the function performed by a relay agent. For more detail on relay agents you can read RFC 1542.

> Not all routers are capable of providing BOOTP relay agent services. Routers that do have this capability are said to be RFC 1542 compliant.

## Time Fields

DHCP clients lease IP addresses from DHCP servers for a fixed period of time, with the actual lease length being configured on the DHCP server. The T1 and T2 time values mentioned in the DHCP ack are used during the lease renewal process. The T1 value indicates to the client when it should begin the process of renewing its lease. T1 is typically set to 50 percent of the total lease time. Assume in the following example that leases are issued for a period of eight days.

At 50 percent, or four days into the lease, the client sends a DHCP request to attempt to renew its IP address lease with the DHCP server that issued the lease. Assuming the DHCP server is online, the lease is typically renewed using a DHCP ack. Unlike the DHCP request and ack explained earlier in the four-step process, these two datagrams are not broadcast, but are sent as directed datagrams. This is possible because both computers at this time contain valid IP addresses.

If the DHCP server is not available when the DHCP client issues the first request at 50 percent (four days), the client waits and attempts to renew the lease at 75 percent of the lease period, or at six days into the lease. If this request also fails, the DHCP client tries a third time at 87.5 percent or 7/8 of the lease. Up to this point the DHCP client has attempted to renew its lease with the DHCP server that issued the lease by sending directed datagrams. If the DHCP client is incapable of renewing its lease by 87.5 percent of the total lease, the T2 time period comes into effect. The T2 time allows the DHCP client to begin broadcasting requests for any DHCP server. If the DHCP client is incapable of either renewing its lease or obtaining a new lease from another DHCP server by the time the lease expires, the client must stop using the IP address and stop using TCP/IP for normal network operations.

# Installing DHCP

**21**

DHCP server software is commonly installed on UNIX platforms as well as computer-based network operating systems such as NetWare 4.x and Windows NT server. The installation, configuration, and option examples in the following sections use Windows NT server.

The first step is to ensure the DHCP server computer is manually configured with an IP address, subnet mask, and default gateway, that is, the DHCP server itself cannot be a DHCP client. To do this, follow these steps:

1. In Windows NT server, start the software installation by choosing the Network icon from Control Panel. When the Network dialog appears, choose the Services tab, and then choose Add.

   The Select Network Service dialog box appears, as shown in Figure 21.1.

**FIGURE 21.1**

*The Select Network Service dialog box.*

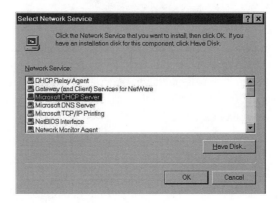

2. Select Microsoft DHCP Server from the list and then press OK; this closes the Select Network Service dialog box.

   A dialog box appears reminding you that if any adapters receive their IP address from DHCP, you must change them to statically assigned IP addresses. Press OK to dismiss the Warning dialog box. At this time, files required by the DHCP service are copied to the hard disk, and then the Network dialog appears again in the foreground.

3. Press OK to close the Network dialog box.

   Windows NT reconfigures the network settings for the DHCP server service, and then presents a Network Settings Change dialog box. This dialog box indicates that the computer must be restarted in order for the new settings to take effect. The dialog has both a Yes and No button.

4. Choose Yes to reboot the system.

   At this point in time all files required by the DHCP server service have been installed. Also the DHCP service has been configured to start automatically the next time the computer is rebooted.

# Configuring DHCP Scopes

Following the reboot, the DHCP service is operating but is incapable of leasing IP addresses. This is because the DHCP server is not yet configured with IP addresses to lease. You configure DHCP with blocks or ranges of IP addresses that it can use to satisfy lease requests. Each block of IP addresses is called a *DHCP scope*. If for instance the DHCP server supplies IP addresses to seven networks, you must configure seven DHCP scopes. Each DHCP scope contains the block of addresses that will be used to configure DHCP clients on a given network segment.

To configure the DHCP server in Windows NT, follow these steps:

1. Launch the DHCP Manager utility by choosing Start, Programs, Administrative Tools, DHCP Manager from the Start menu.

   The DHCP Manager (local) utility appears. There is a single entry labeled Local Machine; if you double-click this entry, a character at the far left representing expansion and contraction toggles between + and -. Make sure that the Local Machine entry displays the - symbol, which indicates it is currently expanded.

2. Choose Scope followed by Create from the menu.

   You are presented with the Create Scope (Local) dialog box as depicted in Figure 21.2. The Start Address and End Address fields define the two ends of the block of IP addresses you will allow the DHCP server to control. In Figure 21.2 you can see the starting address in the range is 192.59.66.10 and the ending address is 192.59.66.254. If any statically assigned IP addresses fall within this range you must exclude those addresses from the scope so that they are not assigned to other computers, which would cause networking problems. In this example the DHCP server itself is statically configured with an IP address of 192.59.66.200, therefore, you can see that this address has been excluded from the scope.

> It is not required, and probably not desired, to configure a scope with the full range of allowable IP addresses on a network or a subnetwork. If you do so be sure to exclude the IP address of any configured routers and other nodes with static IP addresses.

3. Configure the Subnet Mask field with the proper subnet mask. If you desire you can optionally alter the length of the lease and make entries into the Name and Comment fields. The text you enter in these two fields is only used for labeling purposes.

**21**

**FIGURE 21.2**

*The DHCP Manager utility.*

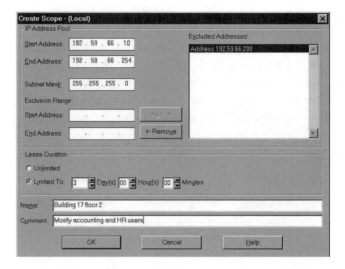

When you are finished, choose OK; this closes the Create Scope (Local) dialog box and displays the DHCP Manager dialog box. The DHCP Manager dialog box indicates that the scope has been successfully created but is not yet active. The dialog box asks you whether you want to activate the scope at this time. You can choose from either the Yes or No buttons. Typically, you would choose not to activate the scope at this time if you want to add options such as the IP addresses of the default gateway or DNS servers.

Often two (or possibly more) DHCP servers are configured with scopes to service a network. The additional DHCP server(s) provide fault tolerance and allow a DHCP client to successfully acquire a lease when a DHCP server is offline. Be aware however that each DHCP server operates independently and does not share information regarding leased IP addresses. For this reason, do not configure multiple DHCP servers with scopes that contain overlapping addresses. Otherwise it is just a matter of time until two DHCP clients are configured with the same IP address and cause network problems.

## Configuring DHCP Options

Usually you want the DHCP server to configure DHCP clients with more configuration parameters than the IP address and subnet mask. In Windows NT, the DHCP Options menu allows you to add a number of other configuration options. These options are typically configured at two levels. One configuration level establishes Scope options, which are used to configure parameters that change from scope to scope, whereas the other establishes Global options, which are used to configure parameters that do not change from scope to scope.

## Scope Options

As previously mentioned, you use Scope options to configure parameters that change from scope to scope. For instance, the default gateway parameter is different for every network and therefore for every scope. For this reason the default gateway parameter is configured as a scope option.

To configure Scope options in Windows NT, follow these steps:

1. Choose DHCP Options then Scope from the DHCP Manager menu.

   The DHCP Options Scope dialog box appears.

2. From the Unused Options list select the options that you want applied at the scope level. In this case 003 Route, which now appears in the Active Options list, is selected and added.

3. Click the Value>>> button to expand the dialog box so it appears as depicted in Figure 21.3.

**FIGURE 21.3**

*The DHCP Options Scope dialog box.*

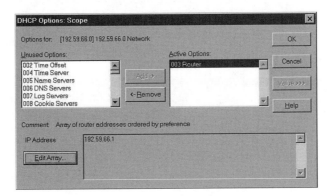

4. After it is expanded choose the Edit Array button and add the IP address for the default gateway using the dialog box provided. Once all scope level options for the currently selected scope have been entered and configured, you can choose OK to close the DHCP Options Scope dialog box.

**21**

## Global Options

You use Global options to configure parameters that remain constant from scope to scope. For instance, computers on every network segment typically use the same DNS server IP addresses. For this reason the DNS server IP addresses are typically configured using a Global option.

To configure Global options in Windows NT, follow these steps:

1. Choose DHCP Options then Global from the DHCP Manager menu.

   The DHCP Options Global dialog box appears.

2. From the Unused Options list select the options that you want applied at the scope level. In this case 006 DNS Servers is selected and added, and now appears in the Active Options list.

3. Click the Value>>> button to expand the dialog box so it appears as depicted in Figure 21.4.

**FIGURE 21.4**

*The DHCP Options Global dialog box.*

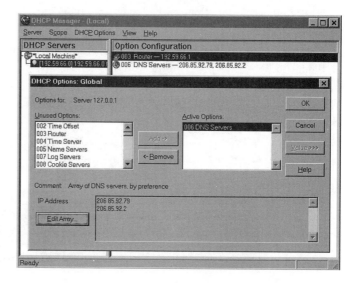

4. After it is expanded choose the Edit Array... button.

   The IP Address Array Editor dialog box appears, as shown in Figure 21.5. The IP Address Array Editor is used to enter several IP addresses, as in the case of DNS servers.

**FIGURE 21.5**

*The IP Address Array Editor dialog box.*

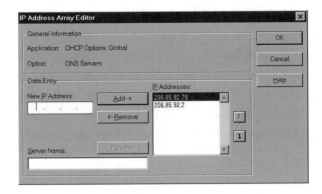

5. Add the IP addresses for the DNS servers. After all Global Level options have been entered and configured, you can choose OK to close the DHCP Options Global dialog box.

At this point you have configured one DHCP scope with options. If you have not done so previously, you must activate the scope before the DHCP server can begin leasing IP addresses to DHCP clients on that network.

To activate a scope, do the following:

1. Select the scope to be activated, choose Scope, and then choose Activate from the menu as shown in Figure 21.6.

   DHCP is configured and active and should successfully lease IP addresses to DHCP clients. This can be readily tested from DHCP client computers using the `ipconfig` or `winipcfg` commands with the Release and Renew options, as described in Hour 11, "TCP/IP Connectivity Utilities."

**FIGURE 21.6**

*The Scope menu.*

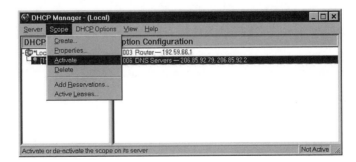

21

# Summary

DHCP provides an easy way to compose IP address configuration information onto many client computers. It is especially useful when changes occur; for instance if you change ISPs you will need to change the DNS server entries. If your company has 5,000 manually configured computers spread over 10 states, making this change can be an expensive and time-consuming process. However, with a DHCP server you can affect this change by simply changing a Global Scope option. The next time each DHCP client renews its IP address it will receive the IP addresses for the new DNS servers.

In this hour you learned how DHCP works. You also learned about configuring scopes and how to install and configure DHCP on a Windows NT server.

# Q&A

**Q** **What must you create, configure, and activate before a DHCP server can provide IP addresses to DHCP clients?**

**A** A DHCP scope.

**Q** **How does a DHCP client communicate with a DHCP server when it is first started?**

**A** By broadcasting and receiving broadcasted datagrams.

**Q** **If no Scope or Global options have been configured, what TCP/IP configuration parameters does the DHCP server supply to the DHCP client?**

**A** Only the IP address and subnet mask.

**Q** **What is required to enable a DHCP client on one network to lease an IP address from a DHCP server on another network?**

**A** A DHCP relay agent.

**Q** **Can a router be a BOOTP relay agent? Can any router be a relay agent?**

**A** Yes. A router can be a relay agent. No. Not all routers can be relay agents, only those that are RFC 1542-compliant can.

# Workshop

## Key Terms

Review the following list of key terms:

- DHCP client—A computer that contains TCP/IP software and is not manually configured with TCP/IP parameters.

- DHCP server—A computer that is capable of configuring DHCP client computers with an IP address, a subnet mask, and optionally other TCP/IP configuration parameters.
- Scope—A range of IP addresses controlled by a DHCP server. These IP addresses are intended for lease to DHCP client computers.

**21**

# Hour **22**

# Network Management Protocols

*By Bob Willsey and Art Hammond*

Corporations or other organizations with large networks often employ people whose title or job description includes the words *network manager*. A network manager is a person who is responsible for ensuring that the network remains up and operational for employee or customer use. When a network is widely distributed, for instance national or international in scope, the network manager needs to be aware of abnormal events that occur on distant network segments. Special network monitoring software utilizes network management protocols to monitor and notify the network manager automatically when unusual events occur. In addition to reporting unusual events, network management software and protocols are used to query devices such as routers, hubs, and servers that are located at distant network locations. These queries could determine for instance whether all the ports are operational or what the average and peak datagrams processed per second values happen to be.

This hour covers the different ways to monitor a network, including the use of and differences between Simple Network Management Protocol (SNMP) and Remote Monitoring (RMON).

## Goals for this Hour

At the completion of this hour you will be able to

- Explain why network monitoring is essential in large networks
- Describe the software elements involved with network monitoring
- Discuss how SNMP exchanges information between a network monitoring agent and the network monitor
- Explain what a Management Information Base (MIB) is and how it is used
- Explain what RMON is and how it differs from SNMP
- Describe the functions you can perform using a network management console

## Simple Network Management Protocol (SNMP)

The process of network management involves the exchange of information between network management software that is located on two different machines. The network management software used by the network manager at a central location is known as a *network monitor*; it can display status information about the network as a whole, or specific segments, and it can also notify the network manager when unusual events occur. Many network devices such as routers, hubs, bridges, gateways, and servers can contain network monitoring software that is known as a *network monitoring agent*. (When used with RMON, which is discussed later in this hour, this software is called a *network monitor probe*.) Often these two pieces of software are simply referred to by the terms *monitor* and *agent* (or probe).

The monitor and the agent communicate with each other by using the Simple Network Management Protocol (SNMP), which is one of the protocols within the TCP/IP suite of protocols. SNMP utilizes UDP port 161 for communication. Because SNMP uses UDP for communication, a session is not established before the transmission of data (that is, there is no three-way handshake, as used with TCP). This means that a logon with a user ID and password is not performed prior to transmission of data. This can be considered a security hole because the software that is receiving a datagram has no way to verify the identity of the software that sent the datagram.

SNMP does however provide a simple form of security by utilizing what is known as a community. During installation of the monitor and agent software the installer enters one or more community names; for example a community name could be the word *public*. The network management software is then configured to only accept datagrams from or send datagrams to specific communities. In addition to the community names, the network software can be configured to only allow the receipt of datagrams from specific IP addresses. Agents are configured with the IP addresses of network monitors to which they can send unsolicited messages.

## The SNMP Address Space

The SNMP process is predicated on both the monitor and agent software being capable of exchanging information regarding specific addressable locations within a data structure known as the Management Information Base (MIB). The MIB, shown in Figure 22.1, allows the monitor and agent to accurately and unambiguously exchange information. Both the monitor and the agent require identical MIB structures, as they must be capable of uniquely identifying a specific unit of information.

**FIGURE 22.1**

*A small portion of the MIB.*

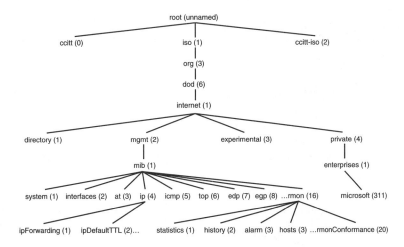

The MIB is a hierarchical address space that includes a unique address for each piece of information. In many ways, the MIB resembles DNS in that it is hierarchical, with the upper levels being centrally administered whereas specific companies can administer their assigned location within the MIB tree. The MIB also uses a dotted notation to identify each unique address within the MIB object.

The majority of the addressable locations within MIB refer to counters, which are obviously numeric. An example of a counter is ipForwarding, as shown in Figure 22.1, or ipInReceives (not shown), which counts the number of received inbound IP datagrams because either the networking software was started or the counter was last reset.

The remainder of the locations comprise configuration information for either the networking software or for SNMP itself. This information could be in any of several forms, it could be numeric, textual, IP addresses, and so on. An example of this configuration information is ipDefaultTTL; this location holds the numeric value of the TTL (Time To Live) value inserted into every IP datagram that originates on this computer.

The MIB structure is addressed by always starting at the root and progressing down through the hierarchy until you have completely identified the location that you want to read. For example, to address where ipDefaultTTL and ipInReceives are located, the SNMP monitor would send to the SNMP agent to the following MIB addresses respectively:

```
.iso.org.dod.internet.mgmt.mib.ip.ipDefaultTTL
```

```
.iso.org.dod.internet.mgmt.mib.ip.ipInReceives
```

Alternatively, these locations can also be referred to by their numerical addresses; in fact, it is this form that the network monitor uses when querying information from the agent.

```
.1.3.6.1.2.1.4.2
```

```
.1.3.6.1.2.1.4.3
```

## SNMP Commands

The network monitoring agent software responds to four commands: `get`, `getnext`, `walk`, and `set`. They perform the following functions:

- `get`—The `get` command instructs the agent to read and return one specific unit of information from the MIB.

- `getnext`—The `getnext` command instructs the agent to read and return the next sequential unit of information from the MIB.

- `walk`—The `walk` command instructs the agent to recursively read and return the contents of every address location within the MIB structure starting at a specific starting location.

- `set`—The `set` command instructs the agent to set a configurable parameter, or to reset an object such as a network interface or a specific counter.

SNMP software actually works in several different manners, depending on the needs of the network administrator. Different types of SNMP behavior are described in the following list:

- A network monitor agent always operates in a query/response type of manner where it can receive requests from and send responses to the monitor. The agent receives either a `get` or `getnext` command and returns the information from one addressable location. The `walk` command allows the agent to send multiple responses for a single command as it walks through all the addressable locations downstream for the address supplied.

- Although optional, agents are often configured to send unsolicited messages to the network monitor when unusual events occur. These unsolicited messages are known as *trap messages* or *traps*; they occur when the agent software traps some unusual occurrence.

  For example, SNMP agent software usually operates in a mode where it monitors for established thresholds to be exceeded. These thresholds are established using the `set` command. In the event that a threshold is exceeded, the agent traps the occurrence then constructs and sends an unsolicited datagram to the network monitor identifying the IP address of the machine where the trap occurred, as well as which threshold was exceeded.

- Agents can also receive requests from the monitor to perform certain actions such as to reset a specific port on a router, or to set the threshold levels that are used in trapping events. Again the `set` command is used for setting configurable parameters or resetting counter or interfaces.

The following example illustrates three query and response commands used by SNMP. This example uses a diagnostic utility called snmputil, which allows a technician to simulate being a monitor. Through the utility a technician can issue `get`, `getnext`, and `walk` commands to the agent. In this case the agent is located on a computer with an IP address of 192.59.66.200 and the agent is a member of a community named public. Notice the .0 at the end of the first two commands, this is used as a suffix when reading simple variables such as counters. Notice that many of the items in the `walk` command list the contents of counters.

```
D:\>snmputil get 192.59.66.200 public .1.3.6.1.2.1.4.2.0
Variable = ip.ipDefaultTTL.0
Value    = INTEGER - 128

D:\>snmputil getnext 192.59.66.200 public .1.3.6.1.2.1.4.2.0
Variable = ip.ipInReceives.0
Value    = Counter - 11898

D:\>snmputil walk 192.59.66.200 public .1.3.6.1.2.1.4
Variable = ip.ipForwarding.0
Value    = INTEGER - 2

Variable = ip.ipDefaultTTL.0
```

```
Value    = INTEGER - 128

Variable = ip.ipInReceives.0
Value    = Counter - 11898

Variable = ip.ipInHdrErrors.0
Value    = Counter - 0

Variable = ip.ipInAddrErrors.0
Value    = Counter - 9746

Variable = ip.ipForwDatagrams.0
Value    = Counter - 0

Variable = ip.ipInUnknownProtos.0
Value    = Counter - 0

Variable = ip.ipInDiscards.0
Value    = Counter - 0

Variable = ip.ipInDelivers.0
Value    = Counter - 11070

Variable = ip.ipOutRequests.0
Value    = Counter - 5128
```

This output for the walk command continues for pages.

SNMP is useful to network administrators but is not perfect. Some of the shortcomings of SNMP are described in the following list:

- Cannot see lower layers—SNMP resides at the Application layer above UDP, so it cannot see what is happening at the lowest layers within the protocol stack, such as what is happening at the Network Access layer.

- Requires an operational protocol stack—In order for an SNMP monitor and agent to communicate it requires a fully operational TCP/IP stack. If you're having network problems that prevent the stack from operating correctly, SNMP cannot help troubleshoot the problem.

- Generates heavy network traffic—The query response mechanism used by SNMP causes a great deal of network traffic. Although unsolicited traps are sent when significant events occur, in actuality network monitors generate a rather constant amount of network traffic as they query agents for specific information.

- Does not provide proactive notifications—SNMP traps notify the network monitor when an unusual event has occurred. There is however no provision to anticipate impending problems and notify the network monitor before a problem becomes serious.

- Provides too much data and too little information—With the literally thousands of address locations within an MIB you can retrieve many small pieces of information. However, it requires a powerful management console to analyze these minute details and to be capable of providing useful analysis of what is occurring on a specific machine.

- Provides view of the machine but not the network—With SNMP and the MIB you can see what is happening on a specific machine; you can't however see what is occurring on the network segment.

# Remote Monitoring

Remote Monitoring (RMON) is an extension to the MIB address space and was developed to allow monitoring and maintenance of remote LANs. Unlike SNMP, which provides information retrieved from a single computer, RMON captures datagrams directly from the media and, therefore, can analyze the entire datagram and provide insight to the LAN as a whole.

The RMON MIB begins at address location .1.3.6.1.2.1.16 (as shown in Figure 22.1) and is currently divided into 20 groups, for example .1.3.6.1.2.1.16.1 through .1.3.6.1.2.1.16.20. RMON was developed by the IETF to address shortcomings with SNMP and to provide greater visibility of network traffic on remote LANs.

> When used in conjunction with RMON, the agent software is typically referred to by the term *probe*.

There are two versions of RMON: RMON1 and RMON2.

- RMON1—RMON 1 includes 10 groups (numbers 1 through 10) and is oriented toward monitoring Ethernet and token-ring LANs. All groups within RMON 1 are concerned with monitoring the bottom two layers, for example the Physical and Data Link layers of the OSI reference model (corresponding to the Network Access layer in the TCP/IP model). RMON 1 is described in RFC 1757, which updates RFC 1271, which was published in November 1991.

- RMON2—RMON 2 also includes 10 groups (numbers 11 through 20). They are concerned with the upper five layers of the OSI reference model, which are the Network, Transport, Session, Presentation, and Application layers (corresponding to the Internet, Transport, and Application layers of the TCP/IP model). The specifications for RMON 2 are contained in RFCs 2021 and 2034, which were released in 1997.

Because the specifications are so new, the 10 groups of RMON 2 are not as widely used yet. This hour mostly addresses RMON 1.

RMON addresses many of the shortcomings of SNMP, and in some cases collects useful information that SNMP is incapable of gathering. RMON 1 works by looking at the Network layer of datagrams that have been retrieved from the network media. At this layer datagrams are independent of transport protocols, therefore, RMON 1 can examine datagrams from TCP/IP, IPX, NetBEUI, AppleTalk, or any other upper-level protocol.

RMON1 can examine the source and destination physical address fields of the datagram to determine where the datagram came from and where it is intended to be delivered to on the local network. RMON 1 can also detect invalid datagrams, those datagrams that are too short or too long to be processed by higher level protocols. These datagrams would normally be discarded or ignored by the protocol stack.

RMON software decodes and analyzes every datagram and then places entries in the appropriate MIB counters. After this process has been completed the datagram is usually discarded. However, if there is something unusual about a datagram, for instance if it is too short or too long, then the RMON could store the datagram for later examination by the network manager.

RMON information is gathered in the context of groups of statistics, which correlate to different kinds of information. The RMON1 group names are described in the following list:

- Statistics—The statistics group holds statistical information in the form of a table for each network segment attached to the probe. Some of the counters within this group keep track of the number of packets, the number of broadcasts, the number of collisions, the number of undersize and oversize datagrams, and so on.

- History—The history group holds statistical information that is periodically compiled and stored for later retrieval.

- Alarm—The alarm group works in conjunction with the event group (described later). Periodically the alarm group examines statistical samples from variables within the probe and compares them with configured thresholds; if these thresholds are exceeded, an event is generated that can be used to notify the network manager.

- Host—The host group maintains statistics for each host on the network segment; it learns about these hosts by examining the source and destination physical addresses within datagrams.

22

- Host Top N—The host top n group is used to generate reports based on statistics for the top defined number of hosts in a particular category. For instance, a network manager might want to know which hosts appear in the most datagrams, or which hosts are sending the most oversized or undersized datagrams.

- Matrix—The matrix group constructs a table, which includes the source and destination physical address pairs for every datagram monitored on the network. These address pairs define conversations between two addresses.

- Filter—The filter group allows the generation of a binary pattern that can be used to match, or filter, datagrams from the network.

- Capture—The capture group allows datagrams selected by the filter group to be captured for later retrieval and examination by the network manager.

- Event—The event group works in conjunction with the alarm group to generate events that notify the network manager when a threshold of a monitored object has been exceeded.

- Token ring—The token-ring group maintains collected information that is specific to this network protocol.

# Network Management Consoles

A network management console allows the network manager to manage a large distributed network from a single location. Using a network management console, the network manager can view the current status of individual hosts that contain SNMP agents and can receive and be notified of trap messages when they arrive. In addition to these functions, a network management console can be used to reset remote equipment and monitor for congestion or down network interfaces on routers.

The network management console is typically housed on a powerful workstation computer that runs the network management software; this software is both complex and processor-intensive. Usually the network management console employs a graphical interface to display status information in an easy to interpret format. As mentioned before, SNMP returns minute details of information; it is the network management console that takes these shreds of information, analyzes them and produces useful information for the network manager.

# Summary

In this hour you learned that the SNMP protocol is integral to providing centralized monitoring and maintenance of distant remote networks. You also learned that by using a network management console and a central site, a network manager can be notified when abnormal events occur, and can view network traffic status as reported by agents operating on routers, hubs, and servers. Also, by using the network management console the network manager can perform functions such as resetting ports on routers or even resetting remote equipment in the event that less drastic measures don't cure a problem.

Many newer network devices include embedded RMON features. RMON provides enhanced capabilities over simple SNMP. When both RMON 1 and the newer RMON 2 groups are employed the network manager has the capability to view what is happening at all layers within the TCP/IP stack. RMON can greatly reduced network traffic that is normally associated with SNMP and does not require a powerful network management console in order to interpret information returned by SNMP from the MIBs. However, when using RMON, a significant amount of processing occurs on the computer that is running the RMON software; much of the analysis is performed at the network segment where the datagrams are being captured.

# Q&A

**Q  What does the acronym MIB stand for?**

**A**  Management Information Base.

**Q  The SNMP protocol uses which transport protocol and which port?**

**A**  UDP port 161.

**Q  What are the four commands that an SNMP agent responds to?**

**A**  `get`, `getnext`, `walk`, and `set`.

**Q  What is the name of the message that an agent can send in an unsolicited manner when an event occurs?**

**A**  A trap message.

**Q  What layer of the TCP/IP model does RMON address?**

**A**  The Network Access layer.

**Q  What layers of the TCP/IP model does RMON 2 address?**

**A**  The Internet, Transport, and Application layers.

# Workshop

**22**

## Key Terms

Review the following list of key terms:

- Agent—The software loaded onto a host that can read the MIB and respond to a monitor with the desired results. Agents have the capability to transmit unsolicited messages to the monitor when significant abnormal events occur.

- Management Information Base (MIB)—A hierarchical address space used by monitors and agents. Specific locations within the MIB are found by using dotted notation from the top of the MIB structure down to the MIB address you want.

- Monitor—Another name for a network management console.

- Network management console—A workstation running network management software that is used to centrally monitor, maintain, and configure a large distributed network.

- Probe—Another name for an agent. The term probe is often used in situations involving RMON.

- Remote Monitoring (RMON)—An extension to MIB that provides enhanced capabilities over traditional SNMP functions. In order to store data in the RMON MIB, the agent or probe must include RMON software.

# Hour **23**

# Recent and Emerging Technologies

*By Joe Casad*

The Internet is changing every day and TCP/IP is changing with it. This hour examines some emerging technologies that could shape the networks of tomorrow. You'll learn about Point-to-Point Tunneling Protocol (PPTP) and automatic IP configuration. And you'll also learn about a new standard for IP addressing that will lead TCP/IP into the next generation: IPv6.

## Goals for this Hour

At the completion of this hour, you'll be able to

- Describe the reason for the change to IPv6's 128-bit address format
- Describe IPv6's extension headers
- Describe how IPv6 will coexist with IPv4

- Explain what a virtual private network is
- Describe how PPTP provides private networking over an Internet connection
- Describe the reasons for automatic private IP addressing (APIPA)

# IPv6

The IP addressing system described in Hour 4, "The Internet Layer," has served the Internet community for nearly a generation, and those who developed it are justifiably proud of how far TCP/IP has come. But for the past few years they've been worrying about one thing: The world is running out of addresses. This looming address crisis might seem surprising, because the 32-bit address field of the current IP format can provide over three billion possible host IDs. But it is important to remember how many of these three billion addresses are actually unusable. A network ID is typically assigned to an organization, and that organization controls the host IDs associated with their own network.

Recall from Hour 4 that IP addresses fall within address classes depending on the value of the first octet in the address field. The address classes and their associated address ranges are shown in Table 23.1. Table 23.1 also shows the number of possible networks within an address class and the number of possible hosts on each network. A Class B address can support 65,534 hosts. Many Class B organizations, however, do not have 65,534 nodes and therefore assign only a fraction of the available addresses—the rest go unused. The 127 Class A networks can support 16,777,214 addresses, many of which also go unused. It is worth noting as well that the 16,510 Class A and B networks are reportedly all taken. The Class C networks that remain face a limitation of only 254 possible addresses. (Refer to Hours 4 and 5 for more on the anatomy of IP addresses.)

**TABLE 23.1**  NUMBER OF NETWORKS AND ADDRESSES FOR IP ADDRESS CLASSSES

| Class | First Octet Range | Number of Networks | Possible Addresses per Network |
|-------|-------------------|--------------------|--------------------------------|
| A     | 0–126             | 127                | 16,777,214                     |
| B     | 128–191           | 16,383             | 65,534                         |
| C     | 192–223           | 2,097,151          | 254                            |

Internet philosophers have known for some time that a new addressing system would be necessary, and that new system eventually found its way into the standard for IP version

6 (IPv6), which is sometimes called *IPng* for *IP next generation*. The IPv6 specification is RFC 1883, which appeared in December 1995. (Several other preliminary RFCs set the stage for RFC 1883 and newer RFCs continue to discuss issues relating to IPv6.)

The IP address format in IPv6 calls for 128-bit addresses. Part of the reason for this larger address space is supposedly to support "one billion networks." As you'll learn later in this hour, this large address size is also spacious enough to accommodate some compatibility between IPv4 addresses and IPv6 addresses.

RFC 1883 lists the following goals for IPv6:

- Expanded addressing capabilities—Not only does IPv6 provide more addresses, it also provides other improvements to IP addressing. For instance, IPv6 supports more hierarchical addressing levels. IPv6 also improves address auto-configuration capabilities and provides a new kind of address called an *anycast* address, which enables you to send a datagram to any one of a group of computers.

- Simpler header format—Some of the IPv4 header fields have been eliminated. Other fields have become optional.

- Improved support for extensions and options—IPv6 allows some header information to be included in optional extension headers. This increases the amount of information the header can include without wasting space in the main header. In most cases these extension headers are not processed by routers; this further streamlines the transmission process.

- Flow labeling—IPv6 datagrams can be marked for a specific *flow level*. A flow level is a class of datagrams that require specialized handling methods. For instance, a real time service might require a different flow level than an email message.

- Improved authentication and privacy—IPv6 extensions support authentication, confidentiality, and data integrity techniques.

The following sections discuss IPv6 and some of its *next-generation* features.

## IPv6 Header Format

The IPv6 header format is shown in Figure 23.1. Note that the basic IPv6 header is actually simpler than the corresponding IPv4 header. As we just mentioned, part of the reason for the header's simplicity is that detailed information is relegated to special extension headers that follow the main header.

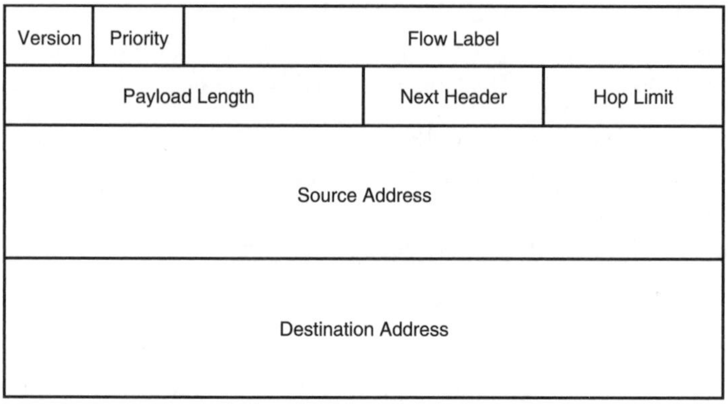

**FIGURE 23.1**

*IPv6 header.*

| Version | Priority | Flow Label | | |
|---|---|---|---|---|
| Payload Length | | | Next Header | Hop Limit |
| Source Address | | | | |
| Destination Address | | | | |

The fields of the IPv6 header are as follows:

- Version (4-bit)—Identifies the IP version number (in this case, version 6).
- Priority (4-bit)—Identifies a priority setting for the datagram.
- Flow label (16-bit)—Designates the flow level (described in the preceding section).
- Payload length (16-bit)—Determines the length of the data (the portion of the datagram after the header).
- Next header (8-bit)—Defines the type of header immediately following the current header. See the discussion of extension headers later in this section.
- Hop limit (8-bit)—Indicates how many remaining hops are allowed for this datagram. This value is decremented by one at each hop. If the hop limit reaches zero, the datagram is discarded.
- Source address (128-bit)—Identifies the IP address of the computer that sent the datagram.
- Destination address (128-bit)—Identifies the IP address of the computer that receives the datagram.

As mentioned earlier, IPv6 provides for bundles of optional information in separate *extension headers* between the main header and the data. These extension headers provide information for specific situations and at the same time allow the main header to remain small and easily manageable.

The IPv6 specification defines the following extension headers:

- Hop-by-hop options
- Destination options
- Routing

- Fragment
- Authentication
- Encrypted security payload

Each header type is associated with an 8-bit identifier. The *next header* field in the main header or in an extension header defines the identifier of the next header in the chain (see Figure 23.2).

**23**

**FIGURE 23.2**

*The next header field.*

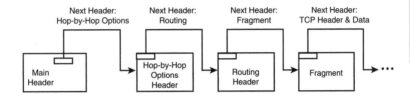

Of the extension headers described in the preceding list, only the hop-by-hop options header and the routing header are processed along the transmission path by intermediate nodes. Routers do not have to process the other extension headers; they just pass them on.

The following sections discuss each of these extension header types in greater detail.

## Hop-by-Hop Options Header

The purpose of the hop-by-hop options header is to relate optional information for routers along the transmission path.

The hop-by-hop options header, like the destination options header discussed in the next section, was included in the specification largely to provide the industry with a format and a mechanism for developing future options. Appendix A of RFC 1883 includes guidelines for designing new options.

The specification includes an option type designation and some padding options for aligning the data. One option that is defined explicitly in the specification is the *jumbo payload* option, which is used to transmit a data payload longer than 65,535 bytes.

## Destination Options Header

The purpose of the destination options header is to relate optional information to the destination node. Like the hop-by-hop options header, the destination options header is included primarily as a framework for developing future options.

## Routing Header

The routing header is used to specify one or more routers that the datagram will route through on the way to its destination.

The routing header format is shown in Figure 23.3.

**FIGURE 23.3**

*The routing header.*

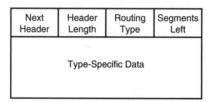

The data fields for the routing header are as follows:

- Next Header—Identifies the header type of the next header following this header.
- Header Length (8-bit)—Specifies the length of the header in bytes (excluding the next header field).
- Routing Type (8-bit)—Identifies the routing header type. Different routing header types are designed for specific situations.
- Segments Left—Indicates the number of explicitly defined router segments before the destination.
- Type-Specific Data—Identifies data fields for the specific routing type given in the Routing Type field.

## Fragment Header

Each router along a message path has a setting for the maximum transmission unit (MTU). The MTU setting indicates the largest unit of data the router can transmit. In IPv6, the source node can discover what is called the *path MTU*—the smallest MTU setting for any device along the transmission path. The path MTU represents the largest unit of data that can be sent over the path. If the size of the datagram is larger than the path MTU, the datagram must be broken into smaller pieces so that it can be delivered across the network. The Fragment header contains information necessary for reassembling fragmented datagrams.

## Authentication Header

The authentication header provides security and authentication information. The authentication field provides a means of determining whether a datagram was altered in transit.

### Encrypted Security Payload Header

The Encrypted Security Payload header (ESP) provides encryption and confidentiality. Using IPv6's ESP capabilities, some or all of the data being transmitted can be encrypted. Using tunnel-mode ESP, an entire IP datagram is encrypted and placed in an outer unencrypted datagram. In Transport node ESP, authentication data and ESP header information are encrypted.

**NEW TERM** *Encryption* is a technique for encoding data so that it passes over the network in an unreadable form.

**23**

## IPv6 Addressing

As you'll recall from Hour 4, 32-bit IPv4 addresses are commonly expressed in dotted-decimal notation, in which each byte of the address is expressed as a decimal number of up to three digits (for example, 111.121.131.142). This string of 12 decimal digits is easier to remember than the 32 binary digits of the actual binary address, and it is possible, if you try, to even remember a dotted-decimal address. This method for humanizing a 32-bit address, however, is utterly useless for remembering a 128-bit address. A dotted-decimal equivalent of an IPv6 address looks something like this:

```
111.121.35.99.114.121.97.0.0.88.250.201.211.109.130.117
```

It's too early to predict how network administrators will accommodate these long addresses. You can certainly bet that name resolution methods such as DNS (see Hour 16, "The Domain Name System (DNS)") and NetBIOS (see Hour 17, "NetBIOS Name Resolution") will have even greater importance on IPv6 networks.

Engineers typically use a hexadecimal (base 16) format to express 128-bit IPv6 addresses as eight 4-digit hexadecimal values (each signifying 16 digits). Colons separate 4-digit values. This string of eight 4-digit hexadecimal numbers is easier to remember than the dotted-decimal equivalent, but it still isn't easy to remember.

As a consequence of the address assignment scheme for IPv6, it appears that all-zero bytes will be common. Eliminating leading zeros and leaving out zero strings (with a double colon to signify missing digits) should further improve memorability.

But if you traffic in 128-bit addresses every day, think about using DNS.

## IPv6 with IPv4

The only way IPv6 will ever take hold, of course, is if it phases in gradually. A full-scale retooling of the Internet isn't going to happen, so engineers designed IPv6 so that it could coexist with IPv4 over a long-term transition.

The intention is that an IPv6 protocol stack will operate beside the IPv4 protocol stack in a multiprotocol configuration, just as IPv4 now coexists with IPX/SPX, NetBEUI, or other protocol stacks. The software components necessary for multiplexing IPv4 and IPv6 will then have to operate at the Network Access layer (refer to Figure 23.4).

**FIGURE 23.4**

*Multiplexing IPv4 and IPv6.*

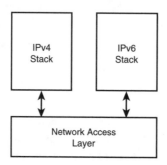

The addressing systems also provide a measure of compatibility or at least convertibility. One scheme suggests that the 32 bits of an Ipv4 address could fill the lowest 32 bits of IPv6 address. The top 96 bits could then contain a standard bit pattern.

However they decide to relate the IPv4 and IPv6 address systems, you can expect to see more on IPv6 in the coming years.

# Point-to-Point Tunneling Protocol (PPTP)

You can protect your home network all you like with access permissions, firewalls, and protocol isolation, but if you want to connect to the Internet, sooner or later your data must travel over the wires. On the open Internet your data is vulnerable to capture, corruption, alteration, or eavesdropping. Internet vandals can capture usernames, passwords, and other pertinent secrets by listening to the wires at the right place and time.

For the past several years, software designers have busily looked for ways to make transmissions more secure. One of the more promising developments in recent years is the arrival of virtual private network (VPN) technology. VPN is a technique that allows a *virtual* private connection over a public network.

One of the more popular VPN protocols is Point-to-Point Tunneling Protocol (PPTP). PPTP calls for a Point-to-Point Protocol (PPP) packet to be encapsulated in an IP datagram. Thus, the sending and receiving computers can establish a point-to-point connection (with PPP's sophisticated authentication and encryption options) and send the data directly over the Internet. The PPTP encapsulation process is depicted in Figure 23.5.

**FIGURE 23.5**

*PPTP encapsulation.*

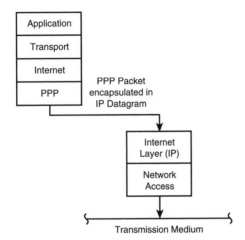

**23**

In PPTP, the details of the LAN address space are hidden from the Internet because the LAN header is enclosed in a PPP packet, which is then enclosed in an IP datagram. In addition to providing encryption for Internet data, PPTP offers other advantages.

First of all, if you use PPTP, the IP address space of your private network doesn't have to be compatible with the Internet. Private networks often use private IP addressing schemes that are not compatible with the Internet address space. Because the private network's addressing information is encapsulated in a public-network datagram, the details of the private network remain hidden from Internet components (see Figure 23.6).

**FIGURE 23.6**

*Interfacing private and public addresses with PPTP.*

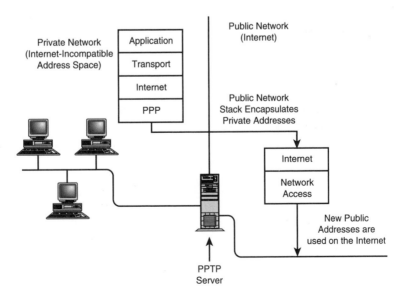

A second advantage of PPTP is that because PPP supports other protocols in addition to TCP/IP, PPTP enables those other protocols to pass over the Internet. In other words, you can use PPTP to deliver non-TCP/IP data over the Internet. For instance, you could use PPTP and the Internet to connect two NetWare LANs running IPX/SPX.

# Automatic Private IP Addressing (APIPA)

As TCP/IP becomes the standard for large and complex networks, it is also becoming a popular choice for small office LANs. The small LAN market is very different from other TCP/IP environments. Often there are no paid technical personnel, and users are not eager to undertake the arcane business of deciphering IP addresses.

Microsoft introduced a new feature with Windows 98: APIPA. APIPA configures computers automatically for TCP/IP. The configuration is very rudimentary. APIPA does not support DNS or WINS, and Microsoft recommends that it only be used for networks with fewer than 10 computers. Nevertheless, APIPA is an interesting new feature because it provides the capability for a local TCP/IP network even when no one in the organization knows anything about IP addressing. APIPA also provides a way for a computer that is supposed to receive a dynamically assigned IP address to go online even when the DHCP server is down.

With the departure of old, self-configuring proprietary protocols and the coming of IPv6 128-bit addresses, expect to see more innovation in the area of automatic TCP/IP configuration.

# Summary

This hour discussed some recent technologies that will change the way networks operate. You learned about some IPv6 innovations, including extension headers, jumbo payloads, and the formidable 128-bit IPv6 address. You also learned about VPN using PPTP, and you learned about APIPA.

# Q&A

**Q  Why do many IP addresses go unused?**

**A**  An organization that is assigned a network IP often doesn't use all the host IDs associated with that network ID.

**Q What is the advantage of placing header information in an extension header instead of in the main header?**

**A** The extension header is only included if the information in the header is necessary. Also, many extension headers are not processed by routers and therefore won't slow down router traffic.

**Q How does PPTP enable you to transmit datagrams from Internet-incompatible address spaces?**

**A** The details of the LAN address space are hidden from the Internet when the LAN header is encrypted in a PPP packet. (The outer IP header that directs the data over the Internet must have Internet-compatible addressing.)

**23**

# Workshop

## Key Terms

Review the following list of key terms:

- Automatic private IP addressing (APIPA)—A technology available in Windows 98 that enables networked computers to self-configure TCP/IP without requiring a user to enter IP addresses, subnet masks, and so forth.

- Dotted decimal—A common format for the decimal equivalent of a 32-bit IP address (for example, 111.121.131.144).

- Extension header—An optional header following the main header in an IPv6 datagram. The extension header contains additional information that may not be necessary in all cases.

- Flow level—A designation for an IPv6 datagram specifying special handling or a special level of throughput (for example, real-time).

- Hop limit—The number of remaining router hops a datagram might take before it is discarded. The hop limit is specified in the IPv6 main header and then decremented at each router stop.

- IPv6—A new standard for IP addressing that features 128-bit IP addresses. The intent of IPv6 designers is for IPv6 to phase in gradually over the next several years.

- Jumbo payload—A datagram payload with a length exceeding the conventional limit of 65,535 bytes. IPv6 enables jumbo payload datagrams to pass through the network.

- Payload length—The length of the data portion of an IPv6 header (excluding the header).

- Point to Point Tunneling Protocol (PPTP)—A virtual private networking technology that calls for network data to be encapsulated in a PPP packet, which is then encapsulated in an IP datagram for transport over the Internet.

- Virtual private network (VPN)—A private connection over a public network. In other words, a connection that achieves *virtual* privacy even though it shares the transmission medium with a greater network.

# Hour **24**

# Implementing a TCP/IP Network—Seven Days in the Life of Maurice

*By Joe Casad*

The preceding hours of this book introduce many of the important components that make up a TCP/IP network. In this hour, you'll witness many of
these components in a real, although hypothetical, situation.

## Goals for this Hour

At the completion of this hour, you'll be able to

- Describe how the tools, services, and protocols of TCP/IP interact in a
  real networking situation

## A Brief History of Hypothetical, Inc.

Hypothetical, Inc. is a large and ponderous company that began with little and has magnified it many times. It is one of the largest companies in the world—one of the $1\times10^8$ largest, to be precise—and is the largest employer in Mordechai, Kansas. Since its birth in 1987, Hypothetical, Inc. had been devoted to the production and distribution of hypotheticals. The mission statement of the company is as follows:

*To make and sell*

*the best hypotheticals*

*anytime and for any price*

*the buyer will pay.*

In keeping with trends throughout the economy, Hypothetical, Inc. has recently been in transition, and now the strategic focus of the company is to align itself so that a hypothetical is regarded not as a *product* but rather as a *service*. This seemingly innocuous change has brought forth severe and extreme measures with regard to implementation, and the tumultuous consequences of those measures have resulted in low employee morale and increased petty theft of business supplies.

A morale committee, consisting of the president, the vice president, the chief of operations, and the president's nephew (who is working in the mail room), analyzed the state of dissatisfaction and agreed the company's longstanding no-computer policy must end. The committee members, some of whom had gained their skills within the public sector, voted immediately to purchase a bulk lot of 1,000 assorted computers at a volume discount, assuming that any disparities of system or hardware would be resolved later.

They placed the 1,000 computers on desktops, counter tops, break rooms, and board rooms throughout the company and wired them together with whatever transmission media they could make fit with the assorted adapter ports. To their astonishment, the network's performance was not within a window of acceptability. In fact, the network did not perform at all, and the search began for someone to blame.

## Seven Days in the Life of Maurice

Maurice never doubted that he would find a job, but he didn't think he would find a job so soon after graduating. It didn't occur to him that he would suddenly be presented with an interview at the random corporate office where he had stopped to use the restroom. He was young enough and brash enough to accept the job of network administrator for Hypothetical, Inc., although in hindsight he should have realized that this was not a job for the upwardly mobile. When he told the interviewers that he had "no experience at all, but they didn't have to pay him much either," instead of showing him the door, they immediately placed a W-4 form in front of him and handed him a pen.

Still, he had his library of fine computer books to guide him, including his copy of *Sams Teach Yourself TCP/IP in 24 Hours,* which had provided him with an accessible and well-rounded introduction to TCP/IP.

## Day 1: Getting Started

When Maurice arrived at work the first day, he knew his first goal must be to bring all the computers onto the network. A quick inventory of the computers revealed some DOS and Windows machines, some Macintoshes, several UNIX machines, and some other computers that he didn't even recognize. Because this network was supposed to be on the Internet (several of the committee's morale-enhancing measures required visits to certain recreational Web sites), Maurice knew that the network would need to use TCP/IP. He performed a quick check to see if the computers on the network had TCP/IP running. For example, he used the IPConfig utility to output TCP/IP parameters on the Windows computers. On the UNIX machines, he used the IFCconfig utility.

In most cases he found that TCP/IP was indeed running, but much to his surprise, he found complete disorganization in assignment of IP addresses. The addresses were seemingly chosen at random. No two addresses had any similar digits that might have served as a network ID. Each computer believed it was on a separate network, and because no default gateway had been assigned to any of the computers, communication within and beyond the network was extremely limited. Maurice asked his supervisor (the nephew who worked in the mailroom) if an Internet network ID had been assigned to the network. Maurice suspected that the network must have some preassigned network ID, because the company had a permanent connection to the Internet. The nephew said he did not know of any network ID.

Maurice asked the nephew whether the value-added retailers who sold them the 1,000 computers had configured any of the computers. The nephew said that they had configured one computer before abruptly leaving the office in a dispute over the contract. The nephew took Maurice to the computer the value-added retailers had configured. It had two computer cables leading from it: one to the corporate network and one to the Internet.

"A multihomed system," Maurice said. The nephew did not seem impressed. "This can serve as a gateway," Maurice told the nephew. "This computer can route messages to the Internet."

An Ethernet cable led from the gateway computer to the rest of the network. Maurice entered a quick IPConfig for the computer (a Windows NT machine) and obtained the IP address of the Ethernet adapter. He had a hunch the value-added retailer must have configured the correct network ID into this computer before taking his leave. The IP address was:

`198.100.145.1`

Maurice could tell from the first number in the dotted-decimal address (198) that this was a Class C network. On a Class C network, the first three bytes make up the network ID. "The network ID is 198.100.145.0," he told the nephew.

It occurred to Maurice that the network would only be capable of supporting 254 computers with the available host IDs in the Class C address space. But, he concluded, that probably wouldn't matter, because many users did not want their computers anyway. He configured IP addresses for the members of the morale committee:

| | |
|---|---|
| `198.100.145.2` | (president) |
| `198.100.145.3` | (vice president) |
| `198.100.145.4` | (chief of operations) |
| `198.100.145.5` | (nephew) |

and he configured computers for all other possible host IDs. He also entered the address of the gateway computer (198.100.145.1) as the default gateway, so that messages and requests could be routed beyond the network. For each IP address, he used the standard network mask for a Class C network: 255.255.255.0.

Maurice used the Ping utility to test the network. For each computer, he typed `ping` and the address of another computer on the network. For instance, from the computer 198.100.145.155, he typed

`ping 198.100.145.5`

to ensure that the user of the computer would be able to communicate with the nephew. Also, in keeping with good practice, he always pinged the default gateway:

`ping 198.100.145.1`

For each `ping`, he received four replies from the destination machine, ensuring that the connection was working.

Maurice was thinking that the network had come far for one day, and he was feeling like this would be an easy and rewarding job, but the last computer he configured couldn't ping the other computers on the network. After a careful search he noticed that the computer appeared to be part of a token ring. Someone had attempted to connect the token ring with the rest of the network by ramming a 10Base-2 Ethernet cable into one of the ports for the token-ring hub. When the cable didn't fit, the responsible party had jumped the circuit with a nail and wrapped the whole assembly with so much duct tape that it looked like something they'd used on Apollo 13.

"Tomorrow," Maurice said.

## Day 2: Subnetting

When Maurice arrived for work the next day, he was carrying something he knew he was going to need: routers. And although he arrived early, many users were already impatient with him. "What's the matter with this network?" they said. "This is really slow!"

24

Maurice told them that he wasn't finished. The network was working, but the large number of devices competing directly for the transmission medium was slowing things down. Also, some computers that were configured for a different network architecture (such as the token ring described in the preceding section) could not communicate directly with the Ethernet machines. Maurice strategically installed some routers so that they would reduce network traffic and integrate the token ring with the rest of the network.

Maurice also knew that some subnetting was in order. He decided to divide the final eight bits after the Class C network ID so that he could use three bits for a subnet number and the other five bits for host IDs on the subnetted network.

To determine a subnet mask, he wrote out an 8-bit binary number (signifying the final octet) with 1s for the first three bits (the subnet bits) and 0s for the remaining bits (the host bits):

`11100000`

The last octet of the subnet mask was therefore 32+64+128 or 224, and the full subnet mask was 255.255.255.224.

Maurice added the new subnet mask for his new subnetted network and assigned IP addresses accordingly. He also changed default gateway values on many of the computers, because the original gateway was no longer on the subnet.

## Day 3: Dynamic Addresses

The network was now functioning splendidly, and Maurice was gaining a reputation for results. Some even suggested him as a possible candidate for the morale committee. The nephew, however, differed from this view. Maurice was *not* destined for the morale committee or for any committee, the nephew mentioned, because so far he was not meeting the objective of his employment. The committee clearly stated that the network should have 1,000 computers, and so far Maurice had only given them a network of 254. "How can we expect morale to improve if the directives of the morale committee are ignored?" he added.

But how could Maurice bring Internet access to 1,000 computers with only 254 possible host IDs? He knew the answer was that he must configure a DHCP server to lease the IP addresses to users on a temporary basis. "The theory behind DHCP," he explained, "is that *all* users won't be using their computers all at once." The DHCP server keeps a list of available IP addresses, and when a computer starts and requests an address, the DHCP server issues an address temporarily. As long as users are only occasionally accessing their computers, it is possible to support 1,000 computers with these 254 IP addresses.

Configuring the DHCP server was easy, at least for Maurice because he read the documentation carefully and wasn't afraid to look for help on the Web. (He did need to make sure the routers were configured to pass on the DHCP information.) The hard part was manually configuring each of the 1,000 computers to access the DHCP server and receive an IP address dynamically. To configure the 1,000 computers in an eight-hour day, he had to configure 125 computers per hour or a little more than two per minute. This would have been nearly impossible for anyone but Maurice. He knocked several people down, but he finished in time for the 6:00 p.m. bus.

## Day 4: Domain Name Resolution

The next day Maurice realized that his hasty reconfiguration of the network for dynamic address assignment had left some unresolved conflicts. These conflicts would not have occurred in any other company, but in Hypothetical, Inc., they were real and acute.

The president spoke to Maurice privately and informed Maurice that he expected that he, the highest ranking official in the company, would have the computer with the numerically lowest IP address. Maurice had never heard of such a request and could not find reference to it in any of his documentation, but he assured the president that this would not be a problem. He would simply configure the president's computer to use the static IP address 198.100.145.2 and would exclude the president's address from the range of addresses assigned by the DHCP server. Maurice added that he hoped the president understood the importance of not tampering with the configuration of the computer that was acting as an Internet gateway. That computer, which was configured by the value-added retailer, was the only computer that would have a lower address: 198.100.145.1. (Actually, Maurice could have changed this address to something higher, but he didn't want to.) The president stated that he did not mind if a computer had a lower IP address as long as that *computer* didn't belong to another employee. He just didn't want a *person* to have a lower IP address than his address.

The arrangement between Maurice and the president would have posed no impediment to the further development of the network had not other high managers claimed their own places on this sad ladder of vanity. It was easy enough to give the vice president and the chief of operations low IP addresses, but a bevy of middle managers, none higher or lower than the others, began to bicker about whose computer would be 198.100.145.33 and whose would be 198.100.145.34. At last, the management team was forced to adjourn to a tennis retreat where they sorted out their differences and tried to begin each match with love.

In the meantime, Maurice implemented a solution he knew they would accept. He set up a DNS server so that each computer could be identified with a name instead of an address. Each manager would have a chance to choose the host name for his or her own computer. The measure of status, then, would not be who had the *numerically lowest* computer address but who had the *wittiest* host name. Some examples of the middle managers' host names include:

**24**

- Gregor
- wempy
- righteous_babe
- Raskolnikov

The presence of a DNS server also brought the company closer to the long-term goal of full Internet access. Recently, they had been able to connect to Internet sites, but only by IP address. The DNS server, through its connection with other DNS servers, gave them full access to Internet host names, such as those used in Internet URLs.

Maurice also took a few minutes to apply for a domain name through InterNIC so that the company would someday be able to sell their hypotheticals through their own Web page on the World Wide Web.

## Day 5: NetBIOS Name Resolution

A group of Windows NT workstation users in one of the new subnets told Maurice that some of the other Windows machines they wanted to access were not present in Network Neighborhood. "It all worked fine the first day," they told him. "But on day 2, the computers in accounting stopped showing up."

Maurice knew that day 2 was the day he installed the routers and instituted subnetting. He realized suddenly that, after he subdivided the network with routers, NetBIOS names could no longer be resolved through broadcast. Maurice knew he had two choices for implementing network-wide NetBIOS name resolution:

- LMHOSTS
- A Windows Internet Name Service (WINS) server

He chose to implement NetBIOS name resolution using a WINS server. Because the computers received their TCP/IP configurations automatically from the DHCP server, he used the DHCP server to configure the client computers to access WINS.

## Day 6: Firewalls

Despite all the recent networking successes, the morale of the company was still very low. Employees were rapidly resigning and departing like moviegoers exiting a bad film. Many of these employees had intimate knowledge of the network, and managers worried that the disgruntled ones might resort to cyber-vandalism as a form of retribution. The managers asked Maurice to implement a plan by which network resources would be protected, but network users would have the fullest possible access to the local network and also the Internet. Maurice asked what the budget was, and they told him he could take some change from the jar by the coffee machine.

Maurice sold approximately 50 of the 1,000 computers and used the money to buy a commercial firewall system that would protect the network from outside attack. (The 50 computers were completely unused and were blocking the hallway to the service entrance. Janitorial personnel had tried to throw them away at least six times.) The firewall provided many security features, but one of the most important was that it allowed Maurice to block off TCP and UDP ports to keep outside users from accessing services on the network. Maurice closed off all non-essential ports. He kept open TCP port 21, which provides access to FTP, because Hypothetical, Inc. information is often dispensed in large paper documents for which FTP is an ideal form of delivery.

## Day 7: PPTP

The chief of operations called Maurice into his office to ask whether federal law prohibited the wagering of large sums of money on sporting events over the Internet. Maurice told the chief that he wasn't a lawyer and didn't know the specifics of gambling law. The chief asked whether, on an unrelated note, Maurice knew of a way by which all correspondence over the Internet would be strictly private so that no one could find out what he was saying or with whom he was communicating. Maurice told him the best technique he knew about was virtual private networking using PPTP. PPTP could provide a connection that would be nearly as private as a point-to-point connection. The gateway machine discussed in day 1, Maurice said, "was an NT server 4.0 machine that could provide PPTP virtual private networking through NT Remote Access Server (RAS)."

"You don't understand," said the chief. "NT RAS is a dial-up server. I don't want to make any phone calls. I'm talking about direct and expeditious throughput on a live Internet line."

Maurice explained to the chief that PPTP encapsulates PPP packets in an IP datagram. PPP is usually a dial-up protocol, so it is perfectly understandable that a dial-up server would play a part in PPTP, even if the interface wasn't through a dial-up line.

# Summary

This chapter takes a look at a TCP/IP network in a hypothetical company. You received an inside view of how and why network administrators implement IP addressing, subnet masking, DNS, WINS, DHCP, and other services.

**24**

In case you're wondering what happened...

Federal agents arrived at company headquarters sometime after the seven days and arrested the chief of operations. This left an open seat on the morale committee, which the president gratefully offered to Maurice.

# Q&A

**Q  Why did Maurice decide to subdivide the network?**

**A**  Subdividing the network provided two advantages. First, it reduced traffic. Second, it offered a means by which Maurice could connect the token ring with the rest of the network.

**Q  Why did Maurice use a DNS server instead of configuring Hosts files (as described in Hour 15)?**

**A**  Maurice would have had to configure each Hosts file separately, which would have taken a long time. Also, the Hosts files would have to be updated whenever a change occurred on the network.

# INDEX